Praise for Rock Monster

"Told with an aching straightforward vulnerability, peppered with massive superstars and seedy hangers-on, this addictive spiral catapults you into what life with an unpredictable rock god is really like. Hooked on each other, the booze fueled muse and her man, Joe Walsh, take 'monstering' to a harrowing level. The writing is so good it feels like spending a chatty couple of weeks with your wildest best friend, spilling oh so many scintillating secrets."

—**Pamela Des Barres**, bestselling author of *I'm With the Band*

"This ain't no fanboy account, it's the genuine lived experience of Walsh's most intimate rela⸻ ⸻while you're there check out the pictures! (Walsh may be cra⸻ ⸻itarist, The Scabs

"Kristin Casey's m⸻ ⸻s us into a world we've all dreame⸻ ⸻e with a famous rockstar, the drugs, the sex, and the romance⸻ ⸻ack the curtain to reveal what actually happens backstage."

—**Kerry Cohen**, author of *Loose Girl*

"*Rock Monster* gives an unflinchingly honest, crisply detailed look into Casey's years as a young stripper dating a famous rock star. It's everything you ever wondered about that life and more. Her writing is so intimate and revealing that you almost feel guilty, as if you're reading somebody's diary. Her spot-on descriptions of the yearnings, the urge to please, her own feelings of inadequacy as well as the insidious slide into drug addiction amidst the glamorous touring life makes this a must read."

—**Amy Dresner**, author of *My Fair Junkie*

"I knew I was gonna love this book the moment I got to the line, 'Can we please fuck normally now?' And that was within the first dozen or so pages. I mean, seriously, what more do you want from a whirlwind romance between a stripper and a rock star? You want drugs, too? Well you're in luck, fancypants. It's like they raided Hunter S. Thompson's personal stash, and then fucked like demons. If this isn't what constitutes as great literature, then I give up. If nothing else, read this book and the next time 'Life's Been Good' comes on the radio you [will] smile knowingly to everyone around you and say, 'You guys have *no* idea.'"

—**Eric Spitznagel**, author of *Old Records Never Die*

Rock Monster

Rock Monster

MY LIFE WITH JOE WALSH

Kristin Casey

Barnacle | Rare Bird
Los Angeles, Calif.

A GENUINE RARE BIRD BOOK

Rare Bird Books
6044 North Figueroa Street
Los Angeles, CA 90042
rarebirdbooks.com

2023 TRADE PAPERBACK EDITION

Set in Dante
Printed in the United States

Photos from the Personal Archive of Krisitin Casey
Cover Design by Jennifer Nelson
Interior Design by Hailie Johnson

HARDCOVER ISBN: 9781945572791
PAPERBACK ISBN: 9781644281307

10 9 8 7 6 5 4 3 2

Publisher's Cataloging-in-Publication data
Names: Casey, Kristin, author.
Title: Rock monster : my life with Joe Walsh / Kristin Casey.
Description: First Hardcover Edition | A Barnacle Book | New York, NY;
Los Angeles, CA: Rare Bird Books, 2018.
Identifiers: ISBN 9781945572791
Subjects: LCSH Casey, Kristin. | Walsh, Joe—Relations with women.
| Drug addicts—United States—Biography. | Rock musicians—United
States—Biography. | Eagles (Musical group). | BISAC BIOGRAPHY
& AUTOBIOGRAPHY / Personal Memoirs | BIOGRAPHY &
AUTOBIOGRAPHY / Music
Classification: LCC ML421 .W35 2018 | DDC 782.42166/092/2—dc23

To Bruce Hughes, my muse
Lalo my love
Chuck and Mutt

Prologue

THE FIRST TIME I heard his voice was in 1981 while spinning the radio dial in search of a good song—a suitable anthem to launch another day as an earnest, angsty high school freshman. Being too young for concerts and too broke to buy records, my intro to rock and roll took place during carpool. For twenty-five minutes, twice a day, seventies rock, pop, and new wave hits washed over me in the back seat, crammed between schoolmates watching the world fly by. One morning I got shotgun—finally, DJ privileges—and surfed FM stations before Dad's Oldsmobile cleared the driveway.

A guitar lick grabbed my attention. Like a kitten to a laser light, I was captivated by its uniquely funky groove. The vocals, however, sounded vaguely familiar. I keyed into the singer's haunting, plaintive voice and in a flash of recognition I thought, *I know him.* It made no sense at all and yet I was certain.

A story unfolded in my head and chest. *Once upon a time—a very, very long time ago—I knew this man and he knew me. We'd been together and in love, and then something happened to tear us apart…permanently.*

I was in the passenger's seat of an olive-green, four-door Cutlass sedan, heading south on the freeway in light traffic. I was wearing a Catholic school uniform: plaid skirt and white blouse, with a training bra, knee socks, and Top Siders. My bangs were feathered, a skill I'd mastered just in time for the trend to go out of style. I was skinny and freckled, a bookworm and a virgin. I had no idea what true love felt like, yet I was suddenly awash in the pain of its loss.

It seemed a mite unfair. Also, *I must be nuts*.

I cracked my window open, letting a whoosh of air drown out the rest of the song. With rapid-fire mental gymnastics, I latched onto a temporary insanity diagnosis. *Yes, that's it. Probably stress-induced like my eczema, and hadn't that disappeared on its own?* Then so would this nonsensical turmoil. Music was powerful and had strange effects on people. Also, I was in puberty, and according to Mom, even more irrational than usual. This one time, I decided to believe her.

I twisted the knob and changed the station. Reincarnation wasn't real, love didn't survive death, and I preferred new wave music, anyway.

◆◆◆

THE FIRST TIME I had a drink was in 1982 on a babysitting job for a medical intern and his nervous wife. It was their first night out since the baby, a six-month-old who slept for two hours while I scrolled through basic cable, wondering how to unscramble the adult channel.

When the couple returned, it was clear they'd been fighting. The wife marched into the baby's room and shut the door behind her. Her husband sighed and disappeared from view. I sat on the arm of the couch, unsure what to do, until the handsome doctor summoned me to the kitchen. I entered to find him pouring the two smallest drinks I'd ever seen.

"Ever had one of these?" he asked, breezy as could be.

"Uh-uh," I replied, trying to sound cool, as if my jet-setting teenage schedule were simply too packed to have sampled every exotic liquor in the world yet. "What's the lemon for?"

He grinned. "I'll show you." And he did...the whole salty, juicy ritual.

When it was my turn, I did as I was shown: lick, gulp, suck. A sharp intake of breath, then warmth spread through my belly. Suddenly the skies parted.

Revelatory.

I'd never felt anything like it, not known such pleasure existed. *I get it now. This is how other people feel. How they smile, laugh, and make friends easily. This is what it's like to be* normal.

Why hadn't anyone told me?

The dashing doctor poured two more shots. "So," he said, serious now. "Were you able to unscramble the adult channel?"

I laughed—the easiest, most alluring laugh of my life. He joined in, and my heart swelled with a fleeting sense of intimacy. I felt pretty for the first time ever. Sexy, desirable, and free of the nagging self-consciousness that had all but defined me till then. Barriers melted and walls disappeared, as the cramped galley kitchen became a red carpet passage to an award ceremony in my honor. I had never felt so deserving. I wanted the night to last forever.

"C'mon," he said. "Time to get you home."

Driving through pouring rain, the doctor fixed his eyes on the road. I pretended we were on a date, his silence a sign that he was plotting how to kiss me good night. We couldn't, of course, since he worked with my mother. It could get awkward for him. (That I'd intuited and accepted this fact served to cement my newfound sophistication.) When he dropped me off and left in a rush, I forgave him the missed opportunity. Someday, other men would want to kiss me. If I could hold onto this feeling for the rest of my life, they'd be *lining up* for me.

I shouted good night to my dad from the hallway, lest he notice my stunning transformation, and floated up the stairwell to bed. (Literally, my feet did not touch the carpet.) *How do I get more of this stuff?* I wondered. I had found my solution to life.

❋❋❋

AT AGE FOURTEEN I had two epiphanies: love hurts and alcohol heals. What's more, they seemed to complement each other. Alcohol elevated me to a place where I could be loved, and when I stumbled it would cushion my fall. I spent the next fifteen years testing that theory.

Night Moves

I WAS NOT EXACTLY thrilled about being fixed up, initially. Especially not about being tricked into it. Not until I found myself being led down the Radisson's sixth-floor hallway did I feel a twinge of excitement. Intrigue is a better word. Or openness—that's it. I was *open* to meeting a new guy and the possibility of liking him. Open to the idea of hitting it off, without getting my heart shredded in the process. In truth, I expected to exchange a few pleasantries before faking a yawn, saying good night, and driving home. I'd give this guy twenty minutes, tops.

Earlier that evening, Vicki had asked for a ride after work to meet up with the bass player she'd been dating. He was in town to play a gig that weekend. Only later, flying down the freeway at 2:30 a.m., did she casually suggest I come upstairs to hang out… *and meet his best friend.* The bassist's bandmate had recently become single, and Vicki thought I'd like him. Based on what, she didn't say.

Only twenty, my history with men was already long and convoluted. Working in a strip club for two and half years had padded that experience. But while I thrived on the fleeting intimacies inherent to the job, in the real world I wasn't lucky with men. Well, I *was*, just not the way I wanted—with a lasting, loving commitment. As a result, my approach to dating spoke more of trepidation than excitement. Maybe that's why Vicki sprang it on me like she did. Or maybe I was her only single friend available on short notice.

I trusted her, though, my closest work friend and favorite fellow stripper. A long, lean, Romanian beauty with a throaty laugh and glowing skin, the girl oozed sex appeal in everything she did. She had a tight, round ass, legs that wouldn't quit, and more worldliness than she probably should've at twenty-six. I had coarse red hair, freckled skin, a boyish frame, and my mother's chiseled calves—*fabulous gams*, customers called them. Despite the glaring differences, our DJ had taken to calling both Vicki and me *thoroughbreds*. I let the lack of originality slide, seeing as he'd been her lover first (with some degree of overlap I pretended hadn't occurred). Besides, I liked the moniker. A couple of hot-bloods, my racehorse to her show jumper—we were restless, passionate, and spirited. Vicki owned these traits unapologetically, inspiring me to do the same. I saw her as an older version of myself, which was at once comforting and unsettling because if I were still single at her age, I wasn't sure I'd want to go on living.

We hadn't hung out in months. I was back in college for the first time in two years. Vicki had been traveling with her new guy, out on tour or in Los Angeles where he lived. Austin was crawling with musicians—you couldn't swing a dead bat in that town without hitting eight or ten—so I'd yet to work up interest in this guy's credentials or the name of his band. Sugar's was loud and I drank a lot. With a steady stream of regulars, I tended to tune out dressing room chatter in pursuit of the almighty dollar. Which might explain why, earlier that night, I'd promised Vicki a ride to the hotel, then forgotten about it minutes later.

Compounding my distraction was the unexpected appearance of a guy *I'd* been dating. A rugged, handsome, super sweet soldier from nearby Fort Hood, whose open adoration triggered a guilty claustrophobia in me. Three weeks earlier, he'd come to the club for a beer and fallen for me, hard—the stripper me, that is, the sexy, sassy, seductive stuff. Not the dark moodiness that drifted underneath. I was a sucker for his shaved head and killer smile, but the boy was too unscathed, and his optimism gave me a headache. I had decided to end it that night, over scrambled eggs at Denny's, but before we could drive off Vicki caught up and yanked his two-hundred-pound frame right out of my passenger's seat. The guy was so sweet that he'd let her, helping her into the car and flashing me that smile. *Call me tomorrow*, he'd made me promise. I never saw him again.

❋❋❋

OUR DATES AT THE Radisson were rock musicians, Vicki said. At "fortyish" they'd been around awhile, but I liked older men— preferred them, actually—and though their names didn't ring a bell, that didn't mean anything. I'd been in the punk scene through my teens, exposed to rock only recently, through Sugar's DJs and Vicki's extensive record collection. I didn't buy many albums or attend rock concerts. I avoided mainstream crowds. I avoided anything mainstream. I liked my men on the edgier side, as well, and I was worried a forty-year-old rocker might be a little milquetoast for me, or worse—a shirtless, longhaired Joe Perry– type, which was more Vicki's thing. The main reason I followed her into the hotel was to expand my horizons. To escape the rut of DJs, bouncers, managers, and fellow strippers I'd been dating.

Vicki gave their door a hard, solitary knock. I whispered in a rush, "What are their names, again?"

"My guy is Rick the Bass Player," she said, stringing the words together like a title (which it was, I later discovered—spelled out like that on album credits and promotional materials). "The singer and guitar player's name is Joe Walsh."

Jowwaalshh, I repeated in my head. I liked its soft yet powerful sound, like a wave crashing.

Rick answered the door (no cheesy arena rocker, thankfully), a tidily dressed, Native American–looking guy, with long hair and a stolid face. He wore suede boots, tapered jeans, and an untucked dress shirt. He and Vicki hugged, and then she introduced us.

"Hey," Rick mumbled in greeting, tucking a loose strand of hair behind his ear.

I liked his dark eyes and gentle demeanor. "Nice to meet you," I said, though he'd already looked away. I wondered if he was shy or stoned. The guy was as low-key as Eeyore, and I thought that if his friend were equally subdued, I'd be home and in bed within the hour. Then I met Joe and wasn't sure of anything anymore.

It was a slightly off-kilter sensation, like going to the animal shelter for a fully-grown dog and being given an overgrown puppy instead. He was definitely cute—nice-looking in an offbeat way—with a bouncy kind of energy not entirely contained. He had a way of speaking that was both boozy and hyper, like Jerry Lewis mixed with Dean Martin and channeled by Jeff Spicoli. After we'd exchanged hellos, Joe cocked his head and smiled at me for no apparent reason, swaying gently side to side, like a boat on the ocean. He wasn't doing anything out of the ordinary and yet he was. He totally was. Despite all my experience sizing up customers at the club, I was at a loss.

Vicki and Rick took the couch. I sat in an armchair near the door and hung my purse off the back. Joe moved to the center of the room and proceeded to entertain us with a string of jokes, funnier for his exaggerated delivery than hit-or-miss punch lines. Meanwhile, I was transfixed by a mass of man-boy contradictions:

sinewy biceps, boyish mop, and tender green eyes that were simultaneously curious and world-weary. He had large, strong hands with smooth, nimble fingers and a big nose, nicely offset by a wide grin and animated lips.

But that shirt. Salmon-colored jeans were weird enough, but the cartoonish bicycle design was just plain dorky. Converse high-tops redeemed him, and I decided to withhold further judgment until he finished drawing on the TV. The work in progress turned out to be devil horns, eyeglasses, and a pointy beard arranged around the CNN anchor's face. As the camera cut away and back again, the mask and newscaster realigned, eliciting cheers from Vicki and the men every single time. It was a thing they did, I realized, an inner-circle private joke, so far removed from typical bad-boy behavior I couldn't help laughing. When Joe stole a glance at me, I joined in, hollering like a drunken sports fan at the clueless anchor's expense.

It was rebellion turned on its head—strippers and rockers tearing up a hotel suite at 3:00 a.m. *with Sharpie pens.* I had no idea what this guy would do next.

Joe jumped up. "Wanna see my moonwalk?"

"Sure," I said. "Wait, what?" The Michael Jackson thing? Seriously?

Rick chuckled and shook his head like he knew what was coming. I prepared myself for more eccentricity. What I got was the sorriest excuse for a moonwalk I had ever seen.

I'd been fairly quiet, taking Joe in like a foreign film minus the subtitles. Was it a mystery? Art film? Slapstick? Who knew? But his jerky, self-conscious "moonwalk" was too much. His boyish face, contorted in concentration while raking shoe rubber across the carpet, had me doubled over in giggles. I pulled myself together for fear of embarrassing him. Instead, I'd spurred him on.

"Wait, wait!" he cried. "Watch this!" He leapt onto the windowsill—a wide, smooth surface for a better glide, and one pane of glass away from a six-story plunge.

"Careful," Rick cautioned, before turning back to Vicki. At that point, it seemed clear the performance was for me.

Joe's windowsill moonwalk was as bad as the carpeted version, yet I couldn't look away. Whether a brilliantly conceived anti-seduction or authentically clumsy charm, it hooked me. I was not a playful or silly person. I'd grown up in a small house with overworked parents and rambunctious siblings. Roughhousing was a no-no. Drawing and jumping on things was a good way to get a spanking. Once, at age two or three, I'd jumped on a tall, round table to impress the babysitter with my agility. When I fell and gashed my chin, my parents rushed home, where neither the babysitter nor I could explain what I'd been thinking. I knew even then that, as far as Mom was concerned, the sooner I grew up and calmed down, the better.

Joe's brand of childlike glee had long been suppressed in me. Amidst his many attractive features I spotted one of my discarded parts, and the effect was mind-blowing. I may not have understood chemistry then, but I knew it when I felt it. Like a veil lifting, a moment of clarity came as a voice in my head, stating with complete authority that this man before me was the man I was meant to marry. And, just like that, I was in love. *I've met my soul mate,* I thought.

Joe stepped down and walked toward me. I was too nervous to make eye contact, but when he ducked behind my chair and started rubbing my shoulders, I knew he felt it, too. Maybe not the "soul mate" thing, but something. Our spark filled the room.

Vicki nudged Rick, looking over with a smirk. I blushed. Joe laughed, then moved to the couch and lit a cigarette. (I was on my third.) The court jester disappeared and we chatted idly with Rick and Vicki. When a plate of cocaine materialized, Joe offered it to me.

"No, thanks." He looked so surprised, I tried to explain. "I had a problem with speed a couple of years ago—crystal meth, I mean. Anyway, I quit all that kind of stuff."

Joe smiled. I don't think he knew what to say. It was the first thing he learned about me—I didn't do cocaine.

###

I'D BEEN OFFERED BLOW twice before. Both bumps were small, just enough to make me alert and completely nonsexual. Snorting coke killed my sex drive, an effect I did not care for (nor, coincidentally, did either of the men who'd given it to me).

Speed had been different, heightening my arousal while demolishing everything else. My spiral had started upon leaving home at seventeen, when routine drug dabbling turned into intravenous meth-bingeing for a life-threatening, eye-opening, eight-month period of insanity. I'd blown tuition grants on drugs, turned my back on friends, pissed away my future, and nearly wound up dead. I quit cold turkey around the time I got hired at Sugar's, where I was soon introduced to crack though a new fuck-buddy coworker. Our weekend binges turned into three-day runs, until my lust for Freddie's drugs overtook my lust for Freddie. Thankfully, another dancer caught his eye, ending our fling and my crack habit, both. *I'm done with drugs*, I'd thought, relieved—well, hard drugs anyway (no reason to go overboard).

Two years had passed and I hadn't touched them, though Joe didn't pry into all that. He asked standard stuff, like where was I from and what was I studying. Raised in San Diego, I'd moved to West Texas in high school, then to Austin to attend UT. Though I'd switched to community college, my goal was a film degree. I told Joe I wanted to work in cinematography, a white lie based on my inability to say *I want to be a screenwriter* without cringing for the overreach.

Joe was in town for the T-Bird Riverfest, held every Memorial Day weekend on the banks of the river near downtown. The only local music fest I'd attended was Woodshock in '85, a two-day punk thing. That was back when things were good, before the meth addiction and the mugging. I'd dropped out of the scene the following spring, after being beaten and robbed by my dealer and his posse. Since then I'd hit up a few Stevie Ray Vaughan all-age shows, but having lost my fake ID in the mugging, I'd made little effort to explore Austin's vast music scene.

The Fabulous Thunderbirds were ubiquitous, their bluesy pop all over the airwaves. I'd met (and gotten handsy with) their drummer, Fran, one night at Sugar's, but the only other name on the lineup I recognized was Carlos Santana. I figured Joe must really know his way around a guitar to share a stage with that dude.

"Please come," Joe said. "I'll leave a backstage pass at will call with Vicki's."

I had to bite my lip to keep from beaming. We had a second date—this thing had legs.

Joe pulled me onto the couch as Vicki and Rick made room. I was face-to-face with my soul mate and this time I would not look away. When he kissed me it was soft and sweet, and that's where it stayed—until I bit him. Just a nibble, really, on his upper lip, but since I disliked that move myself, I wasn't sure why I'd done it to him. Maybe I wanted to stir things up, like jumping on a table or window ledge, as if being edgy would make me seem special. I think I thought it would impress him. I must have; I kept doing it.

The third time, Joe smiled. "You like to bite…okay then."

"No! I'm sorry," I stammered. "I really don't." He laughed and I laughed with him, scolding myself in my head—*Stop being an idiot. Do not screw this up!* We kissed again and this time I followed his lead, but sharing the couch soon began to feel awkward and frustrating. I suggested going somewhere private.

Joe led me to the suite's adjoining bedroom where I kicked off my shoes, flew to the bed, and waited for him to jump me. And waited and waited, because jumping was not Joe's style.

His approach was so unrushed as to be cautious, even tame. I was way ahead of him, pulling, pressing, and grinding with multiple maneuvers that all came up empty. I didn't get it. Why was he holding back, controlling the situation instead of responding? The more wound up I got, the more he restrained himself. I was all for extended foreplay, but this wasn't it, as my every lip lock and hip grind was countered or restricted. He seemed intent on cooling my jets, which defied every instinct I had.

It was downright Sisyphean, with *me* as the boulder, raised up repeatedly only to roll downhill again. After what felt like an hour of running in place, Joe went to the bathroom, then called for me to join him. And that's when things got weird.

"Let's look at each other *only* through the mirror."

"Um, *what*?"

"It'll be sexy, trust me."

I had no idea what to say. I shrugged. *Whatever, dude…sure.*

He lit a candle—finally, a gesture I recognized—and turned out the light. Flickering shadows danced on the walls as he positioned me at one end of the long counter and himself at the other. As we held each other's reflected gaze, I wondered what he was thinking: if he thought my eyes were as uniquely beautiful as I thought his were, if he was aroused by this exercise or could tell that I wasn't. I tried to ask, but he put a finger to his lips, so I shushed and played along. Nothing he'd done thus far negated the windowsill experience. *This is the man you're meant to marry.* That hadn't changed. The rest was details.

Back in bed it was more of the same: I still wore most of my clothes, and Joe's manner was still withholding. *Did I miss a memo?* Had the rest of the world found a new way to "do it" and forgotten to tell me? Never had I had a more frustrating experience. The man had abandoned the universal, tried-and-true, baseball diamond method: kiss, pet, grope, penetrate. Score! This bathroom-mirror shit was practically un-American.

What the hell, man?

But I couldn't say it. I thought I would embarrass and lose him in one fell swoop, that I couldn't communicate my needs without automatically discounting his. I didn't know any other outcome was possible. I bit my tongue for the rest of the night, not saying what I was thinking: *Can we please fuck normally now?* I never said it, not once, for many years.

When it was time to go, he asked for my number. "I'll see you at the show later, but just in case…"

I wrote it next to my name on the legal pad he'd thrust at me—KRISTIN. Joe did a double take. "That's how you spell your name?" Vicki had introduced me as Kristi, and like most people, Joe had assumed I spelled it with a "Ch."

"Yeah, why?"

He stared deep into my eyes. "I had a daughter… She died years ago. Her name was Emma. Her middle name was Kristin." I didn't know what to say. "It's a sign," he continued, and I knew he knew. Maybe not the whole *soul mate* and *future husband* thing, but a hint, a whisper of it. A divine nudge had taken place.

I was so relieved I babbled the entire drive to Vicki's about how perfect he was, how perfect we were together. The poor girl looked more worried by the minute.

"I don't want you to get hurt," she said. "He *is* a rock star, after all. The long distance and touring…well, you know. You can't have expectations."

I refrained from announcing my plan to spend the rest of my life with him. Besides, I had worries of my own: the sexual compatibility thing, plus one other. The voice had been very clear. *This is the man you're* meant *to marry. Not* going to—*meant* to.

❖❖❖

THE NEXT DAY, I followed Vicki through the makeshift backstage area at Auditorium Shores. On our left was the river; to the right, a string of RV dressing rooms. Vicki was looking for the one with our guys inside (*our guys!*) as I took in the scene.

The day was cloudy and damp, though thankfully not too warm. Beyond the partition, thousands of fans awaited, passing joints, playing hacky sack, and chasing their kids through a maze of picnic blankets. The pleasantness didn't call to me. In the egalitarian punk scene such dividers were anathema, but damned if I didn't appreciate the extra breathing room on our side of it.

Roadies and technicians hustled this way and that. Industry insiders hovered like gnats around cocksure musicians and pretty, young women in headscarves and sundresses. I wore my usual: boots and jeans. But fashion was easy in Austin; it was their breeziness that eluded me.

Joe's trailer was at the end of the line and Vicki announced our arrival with the same lone rap from the Radisson—their secret knock, I'd since learned. Joe came to the door, making my heart swell with those eyes, that mop, and every inch of him resonating as thoroughly as the night before. Daylight hadn't broken the spell, after all...and yet something seemed amiss. A furrow in his brow caused me to hold back, just as Joe shot Vicki a tense, imploring look.

A figure appeared behind him. Was it Rick? No, it was female—petite, stylish, beautiful.

"Vicki!" she squealed. "I'm so glad you're here."

At once, all three of us—Vicki, Joe, and me—scrambled to adjust. Joe ducked inside the RV as I stepped behind Vicki and tried to blend into the scenery. Vicki rushed over to hug her friend, who I assumed to be Joe's ex.

"Lisa!" Vicki exclaimed. "I didn't know you were coming!"

I turned away and fumbled for a cigarette, pretending to look for a friend across the grass. Lisa beckoned Vicki inside, but she found an excuse to debrief me first. I'd been right—Joe's "ex" (however much that term applied, I had to wonder) had made a surprise visit. Vicki had no choice but to abandon me before Lisa realized what was up—that the befuddled figure outside the RV wasn't a casual acquaintance Vicki had run into, but Joe's invited guest *and soul mate.*

"You okay?"

I took a hard drag on my cigarette, exhaling with a nod. "I'll be fine."

As I marched backward through time, the pretty, privileged VIPs faded from my view. Only the image of Lisa remained, that one glance enough to burn her image into my brain—the petite, entitled vibrancy that put my mediocrity to shame. Lisa looked perfectly at home backstage. She was the kind of girl who belonged there and knew it.

Meanwhile, I entered the belly of the beast, winding through the crowd to secure a spot near the stage. I had no reason to stay, beyond a compulsion to see this tragedy through, to get a full picture of what I'd almost had before it slipped through my fingers. I half hoped I'd hate Joe's music. It would be a small comfort.

I don't recall a single note of the bands that played before him. Eventually it was Joe's turn and his roadies sauntered out. The drummer settled in behind his kit. Rick approached a mic. Lisa appeared at side stage, confirming what I'd seen—head-to-toe perfection. She looked like the singer for the Bangles, except prettier, and nothing like a woman going through a breakup. I'd seen sadder faces on beauty queens.

When Joe stepped out, the crowd exploded. Everyone had the piece of him they wanted—bandmates, girlfriend, and fans. I felt myself fall away like an eyelash. Then one of the first songs—maybe the first—jarred loose a faded memory. I grabbed hold and followed it to a six-year-old mental snapshot. I'd heard "Life's Been Good" on the radio many times, yet until now I hadn't connected it to that ancient carpool memory. Something about the tune, in relation to Joe, sent a shiver through me. Like a switch flipped, a light went on. It was the song I'd heard at fourteen. The one that made my heart hurt. That made me think, *I know him and he knew me.*

My head was spinning.

As if that weren't enough, I now also had a fuller picture of Joe's fame. Vicki had said "rock star" once or twice. It's just that he hadn't seemed like one—not *this* big of one. The crowd was gaga for him; this was bona fide stardom—a rarified space in which my silly fairy tale had no place. Rock stars didn't fall in love with girls like me. *I was a one-night stand and he's never going to call me.* What a slap in the face.

Blind optimism wasn't my style. I knew the score and what men saw in me. It's not that I wasn't a fun, cool chick. Quite the contrary—that was me to a T. The girl with few expectations, who didn't ask questions or make demands. Amenable to one-night stands, I was a top choice for married men requiring discretion and emotional distance. I was even popular with wives and girlfriends casting their first threesome. I fit the bill as cute and sexy yet unthreatening, not "too" captivating. Not "Susanna Hoffs" stunning. I could be trusted to divest and detach, to go home afterward without being asked.

I shouldn't have been surprised. Of course Joe had wanted a fling. This was not my first rodeo, though it had felt different. The way I felt with Joe was like nothing I'd experienced.

Thirty minutes in, I'd heard enough recognizable songs to see the writing on the wall. I went home and cried until the phone rang. A man on the other end told me Joe had reserved a separate room at his hotel for me. He would sneak away shortly to join me there.

"Who is this?"

"This is Kevin, Joe's road manager," he said. "Now get your ass to the Radisson."

Cruel Summer

KEVIN MET ME IN the lobby and led me to the fourth floor with enough scowling and sighing to assure me the task was beneath him. He followed me into the room muttering about his thankless job, and I resisted the urge to point out that he'd have one less thing to do if he would go away and leave me alone. Instead, he peppered me with inappropriate questions and comments, all of which implied that I met up with rock stars on the sly regularly. I was still scrambling for a retort when Joe arrived.

Kevin disappeared, and my tension went with him, as Joe showered me with affection beyond expectation. Gone were the previous night's games and dodges as we consummated our connection the way I'd been wanting. Afterward, Joe lay on his back with one arm around my shoulders. I rolled on my side and pressed up against him, my head resting in the soft spot between his shoulder and chest.

"I guess I should explain a few things," he said and filled me in on Lisa. She'd been his girlfriend for four or five years before having an affair with John Entwistle—the bass player for The Who, who was now her boyfriend.

"Why is she in Austin?" I asked, trying to sound offhanded.

"Some breakups are quick and clean, I guess. Others peel off slowly, like a Band-Aid."

I thought of my high school boyfriend, our two-month relationship and six-week-long breakup. I asked Joe the only question that I thought mattered. "Do you want her back?"

"It's over with Lisa," he assured me.

I slid my leg around his waist and squeezed him like a seatbelt. We talked until Kevin returned with the now-familiar "secret" knock. He informed Joe that the party upstairs was not so large that his absence had gone unnoticed. "I'm running out of lies to tell Lisa," he said.

Dressing quickly, Joe promised we would be together again soon. "Don't worry," he said, holding my chin and locking my gaze. "I'll make it happen. Know that. Trust it."

I did. Despite his lingering breakup and creepy road manager, I did—one hundred percent.

❊❊❊

I'D BEEN IN LOVE once before, in high school. At twenty-one, Brad had been five years my senior and an engineer at DuPont. Preppy and all-American, he'd been the furthest thing from my type, but an irreverent wit and progressive intellect had quickly drawn me in. He'd been attracted to my punk-rock edge and my refusal to tone it down for small-town Texas. I'd tried not to be hurt about the cheating and to be open-minded about non-monogamy, but whether it was "evolved" or not, I longed for a conventional relationship. We'd managed to reconcile briefly, right before he moved to Austin. Devastated, I sobbed in bed as my parents comforted me, saying that if Brad and I were truly meant to make it, God would not have sent him away. It was their sole comment on the most anguished moment of my young life, and when it only made me cry harder, Mom rolled her eyes and left the room. Senior year I made the honor roll and graduated early. Every moment that year I wasn't studying or binge drinking, I spent silently condemning love and questioning everything about my self-worth. The following year, I bumped into Brad on a street corner in downtown Austin. I was at the peak of my meth addiction. He was hand in hand with a new girlfriend—stylish and sophisticated, as unlike me as they come.

In the four-year span between Brad and Joe, I'd had a string of casual flings and passionate infatuations. In the mid-eighties, there was no surer path to an active and varied sex life than employment in an upscale strip club. Attractive customers (to me) were uncommon, but smokin' hot coworkers, a dime a dozen. The rampant sexual tension bouncing off Sugar's mirrored walls was regularly acted upon, and few took more advantage than the general manager, Chris Ramos. He had a young, blond, Sylvester Stallone thing going on and once had been an exotic dancer at Houston's famed La Bare. Before that, rumor had it, a Green Beret in the Special Forces. I had no reason to doubt it. The man scared the shit out of me. He also made me weak in the knees, and I'd been one of dozens of strippers rotating in and out of his bedroom for years.

My real crush was on a bouncer named Weasel. Just as sexy as Chris, if in a less conventional way, he had long, frizzy hair, a Fu Manchu mustache, and a booming voice to match his larger-than-life personality. Weasel liked to gamble, drink, and fight but was genuinely good-natured, barring any disrespect toward the women in his life. One night a customer made the twofold mistake of insulting a dancer and following it with a flippant "yo mama" remark in Weasel's direction. The guy was pinned to the floor before he could blink, and his drinking buddy one second later—

an innocent bystander who'd done nothing wrong (aside from befriending a loudmouthed buffoon). I'd watched it all from the stage, blood flying everywhere (and none of it Weasel's). It was hard not to fall for a guy like that. Alas, Weasel himself could not be pinned, and our dalliance was short-lived.

I'd made lovers of DJs, one club owner, and a fellow stripper or three, but the only one I'd loved was Eileen, a cat-like beauty so far out of my league I sabotaged our relationship six weeks in—before she left on her own and shattered me. I rebounded with Wren, an earthy brunette who came as a package deal with her husband, Lucky. Our polyamorous adventure ran its course in a month, at which point I washed my hands of one-night stands, fuck buddies, and third-wheel situations. Fun as they were (ridiculously, at times), a trail of crumbs only left me hungrier.

I'd never found it easy to get close to people. Like the boy in a plastic bubble, I both feared and craved intimacy as a vital force that made life worth living and would also surely kill me. At nineteen, I had found a caring therapist right before he moved out of state. The colleague he referred me to seemed annoyed, more than anything, by my ill-defined ennui. I couldn't help but agree with him and promptly quit therapy.

Outwardly, my life appeared smooth sailing. In truth, I was rudderless and adrift. Depression crept in, and in a scramble to escape it I enrolled at Austin Community College. Halfway through spring semester, I started dating Charles Trois, a forty-four-year-old artist, musician, explorer, and builder who'd been profiled in *National Geographic* and *Architectural Digest*. A sexy, charismatic, green-eyed Italian, Charles was further out of my league than Eileen. Over dinner once a week, we'd talk about life and creativity. He'd encourage me to write stories, read philosophy, and project the kind of self-respect others could reflect back to me. Dating Charles boosted my self-esteem and made me think I could accomplish things. Eight weeks later, I met the soldier, a man who'd truly cherished me (despite the lack of mutuality). Three weeks later, I did one better—I landed my soul mate.

❀❀❀

AFTER JOE LEFT TOWN, I did what any woman in love would do: research. In the pre-Internet era, that entailed raiding a record store and interrogating our sole mutual friend. According to Vicki, Joe was sweet, shy, humble, and a little nuts. Though not the typical playboy, neither did he lack for female companionship. I was not the only woman attuned to his unique charms, and Vicki's message was clear: *Joe's a good man, but not boyfriend material.* I appreciated her honesty, which didn't scare me off so much as prepare me for a challenge.

Joe called as promised, and we had a few lighthearted conversations. Between times, I played all his records, scouring their artwork and lyrics for the nature of his soul and its compatibility with mine. What I found was profound awe at the scope and quality of his work, as the man I'd met became overshadowed by the genius on my turntable.

By week two, our rapport was off. Where I'd been engaging and authentic, I was suddenly artless and self-conscious. Joe shared witty stories from the road. I told stilted club anecdotes that sounded funnier in my head. One day he called when my friend Christine was over. She landed a joke just as I picked up, causing me to guffaw into the receiver. Christine cracked up, triggering a fit of nervous giggles so strong I couldn't manage a proper hello. At first, Joe was amused. He quickly grew frustrated.

"Sorry, sorry... I'm okay," I said, regaining my composure. "I can talk now, I swear."

"It's cool. You girls have fun. I'll call back another time," he said and hung up.

Weeks passed without a word. When I realized he'd moved on, the shock sent me reeling. I withered and withdrew, at home with my cat, with loud bouts of sobbing that his feline brain couldn't grasp. Seven days later, I pulled myself together and threw out every reminder of Joe—records, cassettes, doodles of his name inside bubbly hearts on my phone pad. When I was done, I went back to work—my number one, fail-safe haven.

###

WHEN I'D JOINED THE Sugar's family, I was a highly sexual, insecure teen whose tough-chick image was falling apart at the seams. In a mad dash to earn an entire month's rent, I'd stumbled into the unlikeliest redemption. Stripping not only saved me financially, it provided a much-needed space to explore my identity and the power of female sexuality.

If the mid-eighties phenomenon of "upscale gentlemen's clubs" was a newly discovered universe, then Sugar's was the mother ship calling me home. At its forefront were my three favorite things: dancing, men, and money. *What wasn't to like?* I was paid to dress up and show off to generous men in a rarefied era of decorous hedonism. Eighties customers kept their hands at their sides, relinquishing control to a teenager who'd never been in control of anything in her life. To my mind, in celebrating my sexuality they celebrated *me*. It was an intoxicating environment that, right or wrong, largely defined me.

###

BACK AT THE CLUB, I threatened the life of any DJ who dared play "Rocky Mountain Way," then went about my business. I drank and danced and talked and laughed; for eight hours a day I managed. The remaining sixteen were tougher. I wasn't any more alone than I'd been two months earlier, and yet I felt the void much more strongly.

I needed a change of scenery. I went to Houston for a stint at Rick's Cabaret, known as the classiest club in the country. The weekly commute was a drag, Rick's customers were a bore, and Houston humidity was nothing short of Dante's *Inferno*. I told myself it was worth it. Rick's dancers were the cream of the crop and I liked the prestige, if not the stress of measuring up. Among actual Penthouse Pets and professional bikini models, I strived to stand out. Instead, I became my own worst nightmare—*average*—and quit one month later.

With a renewed appreciation for Austin, I decided it was time to check out local venues. I'd been on a blues kick all summer and was enamored with a swinging East Coast band with a world-class saxophonist. They happened to be scheduled that week at Antone's, Austin's legendary blues bar. I invited an older couple to join me—my customer Chet and his open-minded wife, Nina—whose dowdy, white-haired company got me past the bouncer, as planned.

The band played on a low stage to a smattering of patrons and empty tables. I zeroed in on the sharply dressed singer. Having barely glanced at their cassette insert, I'd pictured him a stereotypical bluesman—aging, weathered, and either bony or fat—yet that was not the case by a long shot. The man behind the mic was devastatingly sexy and it stopped me in my tracks. I'd caught his attention too, judging by the ripple in his otherwise-smooth performance. Our eyes met with a spark that rooted me in place and made him flub the lyrics, almost imperceptibly—only by one word—and yet there it was: a surge of chemistry so strong it knocked the breath out of me.

I didn't feel like we were destined to marry, but we were damn sure meant to do something.

As I pulled up a chair, Chet informed me that he had to get Nina home early, so after a round of beer he'd drive her home, then return for me.

I waved him off. "I have another ride lined up." Chet looked confused—*Are you sure?* I glanced at the singer and smothered a grin. "I've never been more sure of anything in my life."

When my companions left, I took a seat at the bar. On a break, the singer came and sat two stools over. He turned to me at the same time I swiveled in his direction, and without a word, we broke out laughing. A nod—as I saw it—affirming our connection, a sign we were in sync on this chemistry thing. In his laughter I heard, *I feel it, too... I'm in, let's do this.* If I were wrong, it hardly mattered. It was happening regardless, I knew.

We spent his break getting to know each other. Abe was affable and suave, with a gift for easy banter. He had mobster good looks, killer cheekbones, and a voice so slick it made my back arch. He was playful, mischievous, and downright cool, sipping on plain soda water. He was enjoying the tour and Antone's low turnout didn't faze him. It was all about the music, he said. The band was his full-time gig. They'd have to hit the road come morning, in town for one night only. By the time he retook the stage, I was squirming in my seat. I had never wanted a man so badly.

When the show was over and the equipment loaded, Abe sat at my table where I moved onto his lap like I owned it. "I came here with friends and don't have my car. Do you have one or shall I call us a cab?"

He laughed, caught off guard by my boldness. To be honest, I was too, but there was a preordained union to arrange and no time to waste. Abe finagled a ride from Kim Wilson, The Fabulous Thunderbirds' singer. Ten minutes later, we were in my apartment ripping each other's clothes off. We had the kind of sex I'd only glimpsed before: primal and mindless, fueled by something bigger than us, bigger than humanity, the cosmos, and all of outer space.

This was dawn-of-time sex. We were gods; we were animals. We were fucking mythological.

With daylight came the cruel honk of Kim's VW bug, but Abe and I were still at it, separating long enough to reach the front door, then attaching again like magnets. One last desperate connection before the final, agonizing split. I slumped in the doorframe, watching him fly down the stairs, tucking and buttoning as he went. Kim looked on from the driver's seat, wide-eyed and chuckling. Abe reached the car and turned to wave goodbye. I tightened my robe and ducked inside, still quivering.

I knew chemistry well. Like a wayward friend, it appeared at my door without notice in varying degrees of promise. The thing with Abe was off the charts, and I saw it as a karmic gift. Love was a lie and I'd lost faith in it, but I had this—the consolation prize of raw, wild, passionate sex.

✦✦✦

By SEPTEMBER, I'D FILED Joe away as one of life's many inevitable disappointments. When Vicki mentioned her plans to meet Rick out on tour, my wound reopened. I tried to hide it, but she saw through me and jumped into action, calling Joe to personally sweet-talk him into flying me out with her. It worked. I was ecstatic but on Vicki's advice would wait to talk to him in person. The next thing I knew, we were on a plane to St. Louis, then traversing the terminal to meet the boys at their gate.

When Joe emerged from the jet bridge, a calm came over me, just to be near him again. Five seconds later, I was back to square one when two pretty young blondes appeared, sandwiching him in their arms. Vicki and I exchanged a look as Rick hurried over. I steeled myself. The girls couldn't have been sixteen years old, which meant there was either a simple explanation or a really, really bad one.

It was a little of both.

Apparently, Joe had been drinking when Vicki talked him into inviting me. He'd had Kevin arrange my flight, then forgotten all about it (the really, really bad part). At the previous night's gig, he'd impulsively invited two young fans to St. Louis (the simple part, from a rock star's perspective). With the promise of a separate hotel room and enthusiastic permission of their parents (who were even bigger fans), the trio had set out for St. Louis.

The girls' adventure began and ended with a tense limo ride to the hotel, where they went straight to their room and booked a flight home. Rick confided that they'd felt awful for me. If Joe did, he kept it to himself, pretending he'd assumed I'd be cool with the girls' company. I wasn't upset about the girls as much as I was embarrassed to have fallen off of Joe's radar. I played it cool to save face, partly for Vicki's sake, without whom I wouldn't be there in the first place. I couldn't bring myself to ruin her trip, and when Joe realized he wasn't in the doghouse, all awkwardness disappeared. *Poof.*

I wasn't a control freak. I prided myself on that fact. If a meaningless good time was what Joe had in mind, who was I to force things? Twenty-four hours in a presidential suite with a fun, sexy rock star? *Let's do this.*

The penthouse encompassed the entire top floor, and I *oohed* and *aahed* over the luxury. The boys snorted lines at the massive dining table. I helped myself to the minibar, and Vicki took pictures of us all with her Nikon. Joe staged silly poses with Rick and romantic poses with me. He ordered room service, but I was too excited to eat. I didn't realize how drunk I was getting.

The boys left for sound check while Vicki and I dressed. We arrived later at will call to find our backstage passes missing, but the staff refused to send a message backstage, and my drunken snark did nothing to persuade them. Vicki pulled me outside, taking charge in her usual way, until we found a rear entry through the alley. Incredibly, it led directly into Joe and Rick's dressing room. We burst upon them moments before showtime and were greeted with cheers and hugs. Those guys really loved cheering for shit. It was weirdly contagious.

Back at the hotel, in our separate bedroom, Joe walked me through another offbeat scenario. I was happy just to be with him, even blindfolded and tied, naked, to a chair.

I'd been wondering all day what to expect that night. More mirror weirdness? Tenderness? Passionate sex? Instead, I had my first bondage lesson.

Alrighty then.

I was nothing if not open-minded, especially about sex. I'd had twosomes, threesomes, lesbians, gay men, one-night stands, and bought-and-paid-for sex. One of my lovers had been a crack-smoking cross-dresser who'd introduced me to the joys of the Anal Intruder Kit, but that's as "alternative" as I'd been. Ignorant of BDSM, I was intrigued...in theory. Because, again, things never really seemed to *get going.*

To me, sex was about touching. Not so damn much talking, teasing, and taunting.

Say please, he instructed. When I did, I'd be pinched, caressed, or presented with things to kiss and lick. It was like a party game, if somewhat befuddling. (I just really didn't get the tease-and-denial thing.)

When Joe left the room, promising to return, I tried to find the uncertainty erotic, but mostly it was boring. At one point, I thought I heard the door open, but when nothing happened, I assumed I'd imagined it. (Months later, I found out Joe had sneaked Rick in for a peek, but by the time Vicki told me, it was too late to get mad at him.)

Late that night, I was hit with an excruciating urinary tract infection. Joe, frantic, turned to Vicki for help, who saved the day again, ordering me into the tub with a cup of room-service vinegar.

Soon I was symptom free and able to sleep. When I awoke, Joe ordered breakfast, but I couldn't eat a thing, only sip on a "hair of the dog" Bloody Mary.

I had such fun being part of our little group, lounging in the spacious living room, joking around, and climbing over furniture to freshen drinks or retrieve food from the dining room table. It felt privileged and intimate, like a double-date destination vacation. Vicki read aloud from the newspaper a positive review of Joe's show. Joe wandered off, and when he was out of earshot I asked why the review had called him self-deprecating.

"He is," Vicki said. "He's known for it—publicly, anyway."

I still knew very little about his public image but felt the puzzle expanding. My feelings for Joe were pretty straightforward, but nothing about him was. He had an abiding sweetness and childlike innocence packed in layers of outrageous baggage. From underage fans to bondage games, cocaine binges, and memory lapses, it was a lot to take in...not that it mattered. I didn't expect to hear from him again.

Mirror in the Bathroom

JOE DIDN'T WASTE ANY time asking to visit me in Austin. "It's short notice, but is tomorrow okay?" He actually sounded worried.

"Are you kidding? You can come *today*."

At the airport our vibe was off, but that didn't faze me. Off was the new normal, apparently. Thus far, Joe had been silly, romantic, scattered, and dominant. So now he was sullen, so what? I'd been navigating sullen all my life. I didn't take it personally—from Joe, anyway—and to prove it, I kept up a mindless chatter the whole way home. Joe sat slumped in the passenger's seat, silent except for one mumbled request, which I addressed with no questions asked. No sooner had I parked in front of a neighborhood record store than his mournful gaze alerted me to my mistake. "Oh!" I half gasped, half laughed, embarrassed to have misheard him, and sped to the *liquor* store he'd requested.

At my apartment, Joe restored his "dangerously low blood alcohol level," chugging a double vodka screwdriver, and then pouring another to sip from as I showed him my apartment. In my bedroom he asked to lie down, and I found myself apologizing again, this time for my flimsy mini-blinds that let so much daylight in.

"Honey, please," he scoffed. "If I had to, I could sleep on the sun." As if to prove it, he returned to the much brighter living room, lay on the couch with his back to me, and fell asleep.

He stayed there for three days.

At first, I chalked it up to fatigue, probably the result of his usual rock star shenanigans. As the days passed, I wondered if there were more to it, but Joe remained tight-lipped and I dropped it. It was enough that he wanted to be with me. I had to respect his privacy.

Not three years earlier, I'd spent a week curled up on a vinyl-upholstered rocking chair, eating and sleeping off a meth habit with nothing but Doritos, Snickers, and a childhood blanket. Joe's demons were his business. I recognized the need for space when I saw it, and I went about my routine. Each day, I returned from work or shopping to find him burrowed deeper in the same spot. One afternoon, after a string of errands, in heavy traffic on an empty stomach, I spilled my takeout dinner outside the front door. Hearing my screams, Joe was alert and upright when I burst inside, kicking the door shut behind me. I froze—my dry cleaning in one hand, his chicken sandwich in the other—wondering how to gloss over my childish tantrum. On the bright side, I still had a side dish.

"That's a good album title," Joe said thoughtfully. "Maybe I'll use it: *My Coleslaw Survived*, by Joe Walsh."

I laughed and he laughed with me. I practically skipped to the kitchen to heat myself a can of soup, but by the time I returned with drinks and napkins, Joe was done eating and back asleep.

I missed the silly, playful Joe, but there was something about this wounded fellow, too. I liked doting on him, stopping short of a sponge bath (only because he refused). I was the type driven nuts by an askew accent pillow, and yet this sullen, smelly sofa slug was all right with me. I liked having someone to come home to.

The next night, he asked me to pick up a whole frozen fish, with its head attached and everything. I left without asking whom he planned to send it to and returned with the biggest one I could find. His surprised delight was all the reward I needed. I put the fish in the freezer, as instructed. The next morning, he told me to throw it out, then smiled as if a spell were broken.

❅❅❅

I'D BEEN MISUNDERSTOOD ALL my life. As a middle-class, Catholic girl and honor student turned punk rock–addict/dropout/stripper, my choices were illogical to everyone I knew. I couldn't always explain myself from moment to moment. Life was complicated, more for some of us than others. Joe was in that group, too. He didn't have to tell me—I could see it all over his face. I could smell it from the kitchen.

I tried to close the gap a few times, approaching him with sex in mind, but he refused to even cuddle. Later he confessed to taking a whiff of my panties from the dirty-clothes hamper while I'd been at work. *Why?* I asked. *I missed you,* he said, which was so weirdly romantic I forgave him everything. Our first long weekend together and the extent of our intimacy was inhaling each other's personal scents from a distance. *Whatever.* Chaos and uncertainty were fine by me. It was boredom I couldn't stand.

❅❅❅

JOE RETURNED A FEW weeks later, back to his normal (for him) self. I brought him to Sugar's, where he was given free rein yet chose to hole up in the DJ booth—a high perch with a view of the main floor. That's when I decided to work. I wanted my man to see what I could do.

My grand plan fell apart when extra tequila shots, meant to calm my nerves, backfired. Though the effect was probably minimal (I had danced drunk often enough, after all), no compliment from Joe was forthcoming. I could only assume he'd been unimpressed, oblivious to his ambivalence watching me be sexual with other men—a simple misunderstanding (not straightened out for years) that absolutely hit me where I lived. My sexy stripper image was integral to my identity, and I never worked in his presence again.

One night, two friends from the club came by my apartment with a gift. Joe had never heard of MDMA and, though hesitant, eventually gave in. For the rest of the night, he kept me and my friends, Stephanie and Bear, in stitches. By the time they left, I was dying for sex and about to jump him when Joe made a request. "You have to find me a guitar. I feel so good right now, I'll go insane if I can't play." I'd seen meth addicts less desperate for a fix.

I called an old punk friend, a soft-spoken boy I'd tripped with on acid many times. Gordon was no stranger to sudden drug-induced yearnings, and within minutes he had procured the item from under his own roof. His roommate—the instrument's owner—was slightly less enthused about a supposed "rock star" with a 4:00 a.m. equipment crisis. It did sound like a prank. Even Gordon became suspicious.

"For real...*the* Joe Walsh?"

"I can have him there in fifteen minutes."

The boys took a chance. There was just one problem. "It only has five strings," I relayed to Joe. "Is that okay?"

He looked at me like I'd lost my mind, eyebrows shooting up so hard and fast I thought they might fly off his face. "No!" he exclaimed, staring at me in disbelief. I succumbed to a giggle fit as he shook his head—*tsk, tsk*—mocking me. "I need *six*, Kristi. Jeez."

We arrived at Gordon's, where the missing string had been found. After quick introductions, Joe played for a captive three-person audience, sitting cross-legged on a stranger's floor, more centered and content than I'd seen him before.

###

I INTRODUCED HIM TO my best friend, Christine. Like me, she'd recently dropped out of the punk scene, though unlike me she worked a straight job in retail, fully clothed and absent fuck-buddy coworkers and tequila shooters. Christine was the type of person who found humor in every situation and accepted my moods and quirks as fully as I did everyone else's. Other punk "friends" had beaten and robbed me. Christine made me laugh on a daily basis. Christine had given me a kitten.

We christened her and Joe's friendship by dropping acid and ransacking the Walgreens across the street, like spastic toddlers on a toy-shopping spree, carting home everything we could carry: fluorescent poster boards, watercolors, magazines, Polaroid film, rubber balls, hairy trolls, glow sticks, and all manner of bouncy, lighted, fuzzy things. Joe had a way of immersing himself in wonderment in the simplest things, a trait all but alien to me. LSD put us on the same page, and it was euphoric and bonding.

I'd taken hallucinogens many times over three years, with some bad trips along the way. The worst was at eighteen years old, upon ingesting four grams of high-grade, lab-grown mushrooms. The evening had begun in a hot tub with a new friend: a young male grad student I'd met at the club. It ended in a mad, terrifying dash into the street, chased by a pack of demons from the corners of his bedroom. Bad trips were a risk I was willing to take. But with Joe, I felt protected somehow, as if evil spirits lost my scent in his presence.

Most nights, I went to bed at 2:00 or 3:00 a.m. while Joe stayed up in the living room. I'd find him on the couch in the morning, scribbling on legal pads, the coffee table littered with evidence of his activities: cigarette packs (empty and full), overflowing ashtrays, Zippos, Zippo fluid, dead and dying glow sticks, corks and corkscrews, wine glasses, beer bottles, and two to three screwdrivers in varying degrees of drainage. There would be rolled-up dollar bills, an empty ballpoint pen tube, and a small plate with traces of cocaine on it.

Sometimes Joe brought his scribbles to bed. Then he would fall asleep sitting up, fingers curled around a pen poised over a legal pad. When I found him like that—too many times to count— I'd set aside his glasses and writing tools, then pull him around me like a cloak, to spoon me in his sleep all night.

I introduced him to Don King, manager of the Yellow Rose, Sugar's main competitor. DK, as he was known, convinced Joe to do an acoustic set at his club to benefit the American Transplant Association. Joe agreed as a favor to me, and because DK could talk anyone into anything. He was charming and gregarious, yet also down to earth, and treated Joe like one of the guys. One night at Mezzaluna, our favorite restaurant, a customer from a nearby table offered to analyze our body language. DK was in the kitchen chatting with the chef. Joe wasn't interested in the matronly woman's offer, but I was, and I thought the first thing out of her mouth hit the nail on the head: *The way he tucks his thumbs inside his other fingers is a sign of self-protection.*

I'd begun to see Joe's jester act as something he did less to attract attention than to deflect it. Other times, he'd pull into himself entirely. I saw no reason he shouldn't feel safe with me, but now and then he'd act cold and distant for no apparent reason. I knew two ways to handle that—sugary sweetness and confrontational bitching, and I'd rather die than be labeled a bitch. Joe had just played a free gig on short notice to make me happy.

If he wanted to sit across the table, staring at his fork instead of talking to me, well…okay then.

Besides, other times I couldn't peel him off of me. He got me to go hot-air ballooning, claiming he couldn't bear to leave me behind, seducing me with his pleas until I faced my fear of heights. The best part had been witnessing the mix of serenity and excitement on his face. I preferred my feet on the ground, but head-in-the-cloud moments were where Joe thrived. And so that's what I prioritized.

❀❀❀

DESPITE HIS OCCASIONAL DISCONNECTION, we grew closer with every visit, and he grew more reluctant to leave me in Austin as time went on. I hated it too, but I had work and school demanding my attention. Joe called every other night or so, either from Rick's garage studio or a hotel room on the road. I spent most nights alone, but not all. I had needs, after all, and Joe's two visits a month didn't nearly meet them.

The first time he brought me to LA, I marveled at his Westwood penthouse—what I could see of it, beyond the mess and eccentric bachelor-pad touches. I tried not to judge, but the butler's pantry bordered on hoarder territory. Joe claimed to be in the process of spring cleaning (I shuddered to think what it had looked like before he'd started), and as proof he presented me with an artifact unearthed in the process—an eight-by-ten of Gene Kelly's lamppost scene from Singing in the Rain. My jaw dropped as I reached into my purse for the greeting card I'd brought him, depicting the exact same scene.

"Another sign," I squealed. Joe just smiled, saying nothing.

He had friends over to meet me, one by one, starting with Geno Michelini, the KLOS rock DJ. Geno was breezy, polite, and not at all judgy about the stripper thing. Later, I overheard him tell Joe I seemed nice. I was about to join them in the kitchen when he continued. "I mean, there's a lot to be said for a beauty like Lisa, but you're better off without the drama. Besides, this one seems smart."

I returned to the living room with a lump in my throat. Geno was used to voicing opinions uncensored on the airwaves. I respected his honesty and tried not to be hurt. Besides, I *was* smart. And Lisa was a real beauty.

Next, I met J. D. Souther, whom Joe called a good friend and great songwriter. JD and I had Texas stomping grounds in common, which led to a discussion on all things Southern. When I let slip an unflattering crack about Nashville fashion, JD's nostrils flared in defiance. "*Well*," he snapped, "Mama Judd sure looks good." I just pressed my wine glass to my lips, stifling a laugh.

I liked the General, Joe's soft-spoken college friend, who carried with him a mysterious undercurrent and a pocketful of LSD (two things that were possibly related). I felt most comfortable with Robbie, Joe's round-faced assistant, a man so chill and unruffled that the night I almost set Joe's kitchen on fire, making my first (and last) bananas Foster, he'd shrugged, dug in, and pronounced it delicious. Joe slept through most afternoons, leaving Robbie on call as my only company. He'd drive me to the store for tampons or kitty litter, then drop me back at the penthouse, where Rocky and I wandered in circles, wondering where we fit in with Joe's clutter.

Joe rose around 4:00 p.m. but rarely came to life until sundown. He and Rick did everything together, starting most nights with dinner at La Toque on Sunset Boulevard. From there we'd head to Rick's garage, where he and Joe made silly recordings and I played poker with Geno and Sean Karsian (another close friend of Joe's). More friends would drop by, and the energy would kick in around 1:00 a.m.—aka 3:00 a.m. Texas time—aka my bedtime. If Joe was having fun, I'd go inside and crash on Rick's sofa—sleeping accommodations on par with those at the penthouse.

Joe's master bedroom was a disaster of strewn clothing, storage boxes, unpacked suitcases, and other stuff. Piles of crap so huge I didn't realize there was also a king-size bed in there until my third visit. We slept in the smaller bedroom that served as Joe's office, on a futon on the floor between the desk and the bookcase. Though he tried to keep it tidy (if not exactly clean) it rarely met my standards. The night I found a half-eaten sandwich under my pillow, I had to take a moment alone in the bathroom to keep from snapping at him. The next day, I took over housekeeping duties for that one room.

I slept well most nights and hardly minded Joe's piano playing. The same haunting melody every night, drifting in from the living room to wake me, would then lull me back to sleep. One night, the playing failed to resume, and I got up to investigate. I found Joe sitting on the couch, disheveled and spacey, a legal pad slowly sliding off his lap. I took it as an invitation.

Our sex life was still somewhat awkward—what existed of it at all—and I leapt at the chance to jump-start things. Pushing aside the legal pad, I straddled his lap and moved in for a kiss. But I didn't get a kiss. I got shoved aside instead.

"Don't *ever* do that!" he snapped, roaring to life.

I stared at him, dumbstruck and flooded with shame, despite having done nothing shameful. I waited for an explanation or apology—*you startled me, I was meditating,* something—but he clammed up and acted distant and bristly. I went back to bed and curled in a ball, furious, confused, and tongue-tied.

I awoke to find him asleep beside me. I spent the next four hours going stir-crazy. Still angry, I decided to entertain myself any way I saw fit. The night I'd arrived, on that particular trip, I'd spied a lipstick-smeared wineglass in the kitchen. Curiosity, combined with the sting of fresh rejection, was enough (in my mind) to justify snooping. I searched every drawer, cabinet, and stack of papers in the butler's pantry for clues to the sleeping

KRISTIN CASEY
52

giant down the hall. I found pictures of him with other people—
some women, all pretty—but nothing to latch onto, as in, *Ah, I get
you!* Then, in a small chest of drawers in the living room, I found
something. Lisa, dozens of her, three contact sheets full. They
were studio shots, against a plain backdrop, in a peasant dress with
stockings and heels. She was absolutely stunning.

That night, I followed Joe's path—literally, he'd made a
path—through the main bedroom's clutter to a catastrophic bath
and dressing area. It broke my heart to see such luxury rendered
unusable, though it managed to serve Joe's purposes. The closet
doors were floor-to-ceiling mirrors, and this time I decided to run
with it. There had to be something I was missing.

It's not like I didn't enjoy the male gaze—I was a stripper, for
Pete's sake. I just didn't get it outside the context of work. Yet if
I hoped for an active sex life with Joe, adopting his style seemed
the only way. I tried to step outside myself as Joe stripped off my
clothes, to release all analytical thought—to cease thinking at all.
I took in the couple in the mirror without placing judgment or
expectation on them.

Then it happened. I sensed the vibe he was going for. And
damned if it wasn't erotic. In a detached sort of way, but enough
to pique my interest. Which Joe must've noticed, because the
next thing I knew we were all over the place—literally, all over the
building. He toyed with me in a dark corner of the underground
parking garage where my sex noises echoed off the concrete. On
the roof, he stripped me naked, impressed by my boldness. When
I joked about the door locking behind us, we raced back inside,
laughing. He tied me naked to the penthouse balcony, briefly, as
it was late and I was sleepy. The next time Joe did a bump, I asked
if I could have one.

"Sure," he said, his voice artificially light. If there was a
millisecond pause, I ignored it. It wasn't until afterward that
I remembered that cocaine killed my sex drive. Otherwise, I felt

amazing, fearless, and up for anything. Being blindfolded and spanked was new and exciting. Sex toys? *Sure!* Porn videos? *Why not?* Lingerie fashion show Polaroid shoot? *Let's do it!*

Nightly playtime became our routine, and once we got going, that was it. Phone, fax, and clocks were ignored during our erotic improv circus. The danger was losing track of time, and the first night it happened I groaned outright. I'd done enough meth and crack in my life to dread the onset of sunlight.

"I wish it could be two a.m. indefinitely."

"Twelve," Joe replied, untying my wrists. "If I could, I'd make it midnight forever."

Apparently, he wasn't immune to it either, that unsettled feeling that came from living without rules in a world necessarily governed by them. I don't know why I thought he would be.

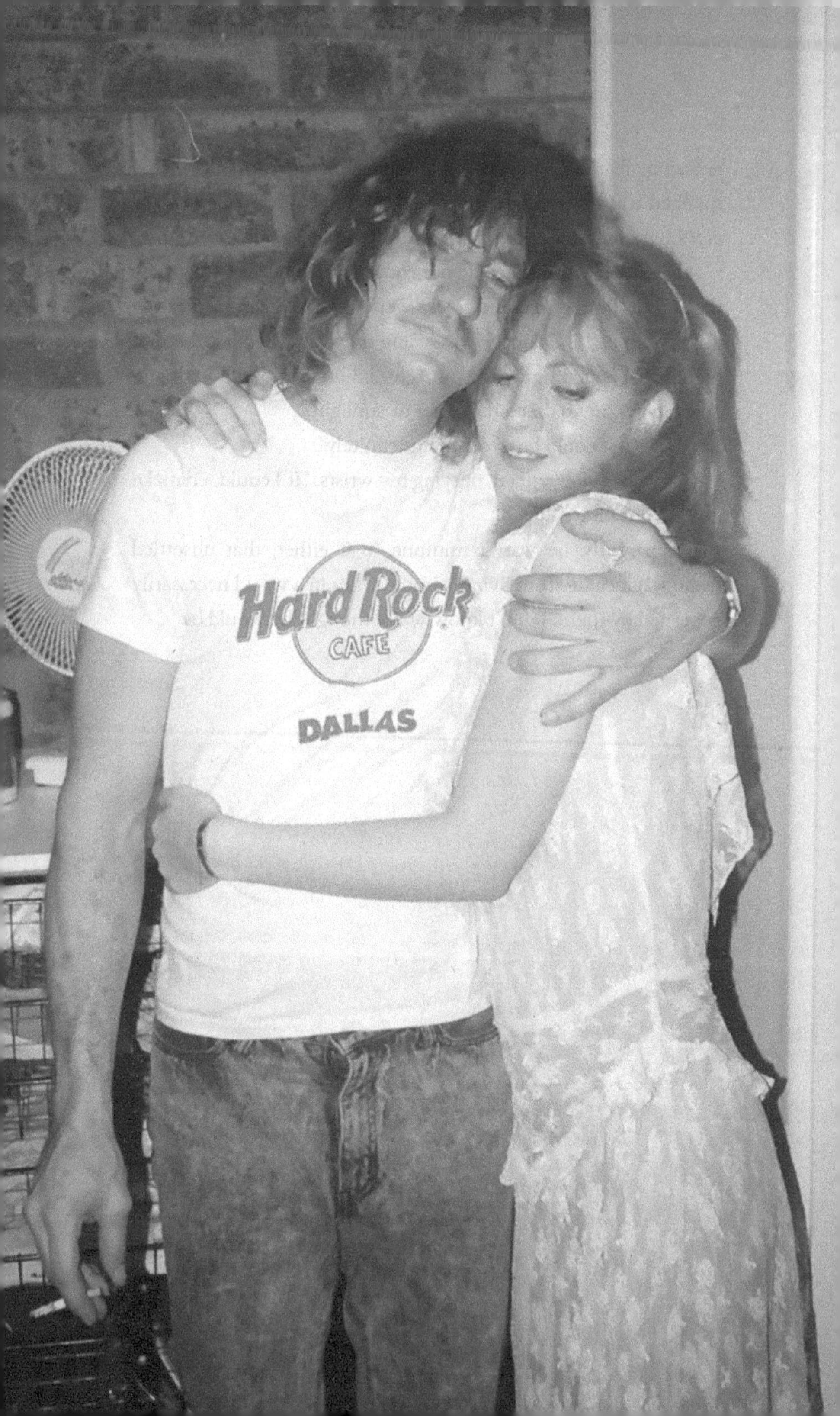
Hard Rock
CAFE
DALLAS

How to Make a Monster

I STARTED MEETING HIM around the country, catching flights on short notice whenever Joe beckoned. One time, changing planes in Dallas, I spotted his road manager on a connecting flight. We exchanged hellos as I passed through first class. Later, he came all the way back to my seat in coach to explain that he'd used mileage points to pay for his upgrade (though I hadn't asked). That night I asked Joe how the frequent flyer thing worked—*so someday I can sit up front, like Kevin.* Joe didn't answer, but from that day forward Kevin flew coach and I went first class.

Warm nuts in ceramic dishes, free champagne, and hot towels. More legroom than I knew what to do with. Well-dressed chauffeurs awaited my arrivals, holding signs of my name announcing to the world that someone in it thought I was special. I was relieved of carry-on items and instructed to point at my suitcase as it circled by in baggage claim. Joe usually waited at the hotel but sometimes surprised me in the limo, a screwdriver in one hand, the other pulling me to his side. It never got old;

I melted at the sight of him every time. I'd have followed him to Siberia. I'd have flown there in coach.

We kept a low profile on the road, a closed circle partying in our room, Rick's room, or hotel bars for a change of scenery. Rick's many girlfriends—mostly sweet and always pretty—were unfailingly short term. Mostly it was me and the boys, whose capacity for silliness far exceeded mine, though I served well as a built-in audience. One day, I entered our room to find them converting a bedsheet into a concert banner for their imaginary band, The Balls (whose first hit, according to Joe, would be "My Ex-Wife's Got Me" by—wait for it—"The Balls"). When the last pen went dry they pulled it from the wall, revealing five square feet of ink-speckled plaster, half the wall covered in red and black Sharpie.

CNN anchors were still prime targets, but after the obligatory beard and devil horns, anything not bolted down had comedic potential. Room-service lids were cymbals, drums, confetti (tossed three at a time on the nearest tile floor, for sound effects, basically), and then hats. Everything had hat potential, even real hats, which Joe liked to stack on top of each other. Hats were big. Joe, especially, never tired of hats. Prank calls, too, never got old. The boys made frequent targets of information operators, dialing 411 for an endless supply of unwitting contestants in their ongoing game: "How long can we keep this sucker on the line before they hang up on us?" The calls were recorded and replayed for anyone who'd listen (me, Kevin, Robbie, me, the roadies, then usually me again). The road with Joe and Rick was like an understaffed summer camp and I'd often catch myself wondering if there shouldn't be more adult supervision around here.

That said, work was Joe's priority and I was honored to be along for the ride. I'd bring a book to sound check and settle in on the periphery, somewhere Joe could catch my eye. Nothing compared to one of Joe's purposeful looks, especially in sight of his band and crew. I thought it was the most romantic thing in the world.

Preshow, Joe's dressing room was solely for us, a private place to chill, cuddle, drink, and do bumps. At showtime, we'd walk hand in hand to stage, where he'd leave me, with a kiss, next to guitar tech Kevin Buell, or Todd Bowie. They'd always have a chair for me, though I'd usually stand and dance or sway to the music. At the end of the show, Joe would sweep me back up and repeat the ritual in reverse—kiss, embrace, hand-hold, dressing room, cuddle, drinks, and hog rails (huge bumps). At the hotel were more drinks, bumps, Sharpie games, old pranks, new ones, and then at some point, *good night, Rick...hello, playtime.*

❀❀❀

PRIVATE TIME WITH JOE was like social time with Rick in its unrestricted running-naked-in-the-woods feeling. We were adults having adult-styled sex, but Joe's term for it had a whimsical feel. He called it "playing."

"Hey, babe, you want to play?" he'd say, as a statement more than request. That attitude made it all the more enticing, his commanding delivery part of the foreplay. We were often in Rick's room till 3:00 a.m. with little time left over for intimacy—sexual or otherwise—and in an effort to optimize our time together, I started doing more and more blow. To sleep was to be separated from the man I loved. Given the option, I couldn't allow it, and cocaine gave me that option.

Joe understood, to a point, and did his best to regulate my intake. He doled out bumps as he saw fit—a vexing policy that I did, in fact, see the wisdom in. For starters, the more blow I did, the more I drank, causing hangovers that usurped the next day's quality time. Also, I could be loquacious on blow, though Joe didn't always mind. He got a kick out of my alter ego—an airheaded, philosophy-minded Valley-girl chick given to spontaneous rants on any topic he lobbed my way. It was a funny shtick when I got it right, but the minute Joe initiated playtime, I shut my mouth and did what I was told. The fun of it, for me, was relinquishing control.

The first bump of the night still doused my libido, but the better part of a gram later, I'd be spacey and sexually pliable. A few words from Joe, a shift in attitude and dimmed lighting, caused my stream of idle chatter to be replaced by willing submission. I'd adjusted to Joe's way of doing things. My curiosity for the BDSM thing had segued to fascination, arousal, then abandon.

I trusted Joe and enjoyed learning new things. I'd always been a good student. That said, sex was a vast arena and I saw no reason to be pigeonholed. My past sex life had been a series of stolen moments with uncommitted partners. What those encounters lacked in emotional intimacy they made up for in fierceness and frenzy. Joe's sexcapades, by contrast, were elaborate and *involved*. Marathon events versus a good, hard sprint. I missed launching out of the gate and going full blown, and feared that the further down Joe's kinky path I went, the less traction I'd have to turn back. My issue wasn't with the level of intensity (which these days would probably be considered pedestrian, run-of-the-mill BDSM), but with the fact that it was the only kind of sex he seemed to want to have.

At some point, I chose to ride that horse in the direction it was going. It's not like kink wasn't fun, after all. It had grown on me, like the cocaine had. In fact, they went hand in hand. Without coke, I wasn't turned on by kink. *With* coke, kink was the only way I *could* turn on.

❦❦❦

WE WENT TO NEW York City in December. It was my first time there. As the limo sped through a tunnel, I popped my head through its sunroof, only to be yanked back down for a lecture on exhaust fumes. I laughed it off but Joe wasn't smiling. "You're not in Kansas anymore, Dorothy."

It wasn't just air quality he worried about, but thieves, liars, false friends, and social climbers, too. Los Angeles was full of them, but the problem was universal and naïveté made me a weak link, vulnerable to pushy fans and opportunists. New people and experiences thrilled me, but Joe rode my wave with an undercurrent of worry. He expected the best of both worlds from me—a street-smart ingénue—and bombarded me with a litany of cautions: *Be careful, watch your back, stay close, don't be so trusting.* I'd nod quietly, thinking, *Bright lights, big city, blah blah blah...* It was hard to take his concerns seriously.

Joe was a guest on David Sanborn's *Sunday Night* TV show. I was touched to be greeted by the brilliant saxophonist as warmly as his world-class guests. Watching Joe's performance from the wings, I felt a gentle tug on my hair. It was a grinning Al Green—the gospel-music legend—teasing me like a schoolboy. We covered our mouths and laughed together. I hadn't known life could be so magical.

On future visits we stayed at the Plaza, though sometimes at the Royalton, which was hip and chic and buzzing with models and other fashion-industry types. If I felt dwarfed by the Plaza's elegance, I was baffled by certain Royalton features: micro-elevators, hallways too narrow to carry more than one suitcase at a time, mesh wastebaskets (useless for dumping ashtrays, which was flabbergasting), a three-legged desk chair that stayed upright only until someone sat in it, and a bathroom counter sized to fit two toothbrushes and nothing more. The famously huge Royalton tubs were a treat, but the unmarked toiletries, a mystery. I feared an inquiry to the front desk would seem touristy, so after identifying shampoo and conditioner, I took a chance on bottle number three. Later, at dinner, I raved about my luxurious bubble bath to Rick, who informed me the thick blue liquid was actually Woolite, and then laughed until he cried.

Early one morning, Joe and Rick left for a radio interview. We'd been doing hog rails all night, and I was trashed enough to want to stay behind. Joe thought that was wise. He'd cautioned me about this unpredictable DJ, who might try putting me on air. I didn't know what a "shock jock" was but didn't intend to find out with all of New York listening in. I pulled the comforter to my chin, lay my head next to the radio speaker (for all its flaws, the Royalton headboard stereo cubbies were a favorite feature), and zoned out instantly. The next thing I heard was a phone on my left and then one on my right. I fumbled for the louder of two.

"Mmmello?" Hearing a weird echo, I thought I must be dreaming. Either that, or my voice had just come through the cubby speakers.

"This is Howard Stern, and you're on the air."

"Oh *shit*," I said, bolting upright.

"Whoa, you can't say that word here."

"Uh, sorry," I replied, as our entire exchange was repeated on delay from the headboard. Disoriented, I lowered the stereo volume. I should've hung up the phone. Howard took full advantage of my daze, asking the very type of personal questions I'd been warned about. I answered honestly: that was just my way, caught off guard or not. He asked about stripping, of course, and my sex life—Joe's and mine, to be exact.

"So, do you guys have threesomes and stuff?"

"Um, yeah...well, once."

Then all hell broke loose. I heard Joe screaming at me through the phone and stereo speakers, both. "Mayday, mayday! Get off the phone! Hang it up! *Hang up now!*" I did what I was told.

Apparently, Joe had just returned from the men's room, where he'd been when Rick decided to debrief Howard on Joe's new "stripper girlfriend." Howard had gotten me on the phone right away, then Joe returned and realized what was happening.

Back at the hotel he was angrier than I'd ever seen him, especially about the threesome comment.

"My *mother* was listening!" he bellowed.

Whoops.

Where I came from, threesomes gave a man clout, though admittedly I hadn't considered Joe's position. (I hadn't considered whether he'd want the threesome at all, an ill-conceived attempt to impress my new boyfriend by sharing a dancer friend as a gift. It was not something I planned to do again. Nor something I remembered well, or fondly, to begin with.) We were from different generations and disparate cultures. Austinites and Angelenos had distinct sets of priorities. Strippers and celebrities diverged on issues of privacy and public image. Some of this Joe clued me into. The rest I deduced on my own, bit by bit.

***

AROUND THAT TIME, WHILE Joe and I were in LA having a mellow visit, I was enjoying the simple routine, but Joe was brusque and irritable. The dry cleaners had called about a forgotten load he'd dropped off six months earlier, and I waited in the car while he collected it. When he emerged with three huge duffel bags in tow, I burst out laughing—*How could you not miss an amount of clothes the size of my entire wardrobe?* Joe scowled in response, and though I didn't know why, I knew enough to drop it. We then went shopping for a gift for his daughter, and when I complimented his selection of matching bedroom lamps, he ignored me completely. Back at the penthouse, I packed my bags. Joe was beside himself preparing for Lucy's visit, organizing ingredients for baking cookies (before finally sending Robbie out for a tube of ready-made dough). I flew home before Lucy arrived, feeling in over my head.

Joe rarely discussed fatherhood and I didn't ask. The pain of losing his first daughter and being separated from his second was far beyond my ken. I was in love with a man whose demons outsized my own. I had to wonder what good I was to him, in ways that really mattered.

On my next visit, Joe pulled over on Laurel Canyon Boulevard to tell me that he loved me. He wanted us to "make it" and if I could hang on through the craziness, he felt sure we would. I told him not to worry, that nothing about his lifestyle would change me or ruin us. I believed every word of it.

He said he had somewhere special to take me: the studio where Paul Shaffer was recording. I'd seen David Letterman's bandleader on TV and he seemed nice, if quirky. Meeting him, I understood why Joe had been excited to introduce us—Paul had a pure and beautiful energy, as if the walls most people put up (myself included) weren't there with him. While he and Joe talked shop, I observed a quiet, clean-cut, middle-aged man with sandy hair. He had ghostlike movements, and though tall in contrast to the diminutive Paul, the man seemed waiflike by comparison. His gaze passed from me to Joe to some far-off place, making me wonder if we'd fully registered. Later, outside having a smoke, I asked Joe about him. "He seems out of it."

Joe nodded. "That's Brian Wilson from The Beach Boys. He's been through a lot...but he's better than he was."

"Jeez, what was he like before?" I asked, but Joe shrugged, as if it were too complicated.

###

WE SPENT CHRISTMAS IN Austin, where I trimmed a four-foot tree with half a dozen tasteful ornaments and Joe taped tacky strands of shimmery green garlands to every wall and doorframe in my apartment. He gave me a string of gifts, starting with a small, blue-green glass globe that he said was so close to the color of my eyes he'd bought it as soon as he saw it. Later we went to Highland Mall for the most expensive item at Victoria's Secret, an off-white lace bed jacket with iridescent sequins and poufy sleeves. I paired it with lacey bobby socks and red pumps for Polaroids by the fireplace. The last shot was for Joe's coffee-table-book project— celebrities (and cute chicks) in Groucho glasses.

The gifts kept coming. Next up, a breathtaking vintage blouse of sheer black silk with intricate beadwork that fit like a minidress and was very flattering. "Where did you get it?" I swooned.

"It was Stevie's, she gave it to me."

"Stevie who?"

He laughed. "Stevie Nicks." Then, to my blank look, "We used to date. She gave me some of her clothes."

"Oh. I didn't realize. When did you date her?"

"Before Lisa. We toured together—it was a road thing, you know? Ended with the tour."

"Okay, well...more importantly, why give you women's clothing?"

He shrugged. "We were pretty high most of the time."

I laughed. I gave away my favorite stuff when I was high, too.

"That's also kind of why we broke up," he added.

"The drugs?"

"Yeah, well...there were a lot of 'em," he sighed. "We spurred each other on, and with people like us that lifestyle can get dangerous fast."

I didn't respond. I understood what he was saying, but all I could think was that I'd never let drugs come between me and the man I loved.

Later, Joe bestowed on me two more of Stevie's dresses: an antique lace peasant dress and a brown knit tunic with gold-and-orange detail, both perfect in size, color, and style. Raiding

Stevie Nicks' gypsy-chic wardrobe had been my fantasy since high school, but Joe's blue-green globe topped everything. *He saw the color of my eyes when we were apart.* Nothing beat that. I had never been happier in my life.

✦✦✦

I DIDN'T DO MUCH coke over Christmas, a happenstance supporting my "recreational user" self-image. In truth, though I'd been using for only a few months, my intake was all across the board.

On a previous Austin visit, Joe and I did hog rails through the weekend. Thirty-six hours in, I was running on fumes, greeting my second sunrise feeling ill, agitated, and paranoid. I was about to crawl into bed and pray for sleep when Joe ran out of vodka. I was fading fast but he was on a roll and needed supplies to ensure a soft landing. Neither of us used prescription downers—right or wrong, smart or dumb—so alcohol was vital to take the edge off, especially for Joe, with his higher tolerance. The two Miller Lites in my fridge wouldn't cut it. He needed vodka and needed my help getting it.

Somehow I summoned steam to navigate the grocery store and get our items to the register. Joe fished for his credit card while I fought back nausea. *Ten more minutes and I'll be between the sheets.* Unfortunately, that's not what happened.

The store clerk, a skinny, pimply teenage boy, rang up the orange juice, then balked at our next item. "I can't sell you this."

I'd just turned twenty-one, but instead of digging for my license I jerked my thumb toward Joe, old enough to be my father. "He's *forty*," I said sharply, dying to get home.

The kid stared at me like I was an idiot. "It's *Sunday*. You can't buy booze until noon."

Duh.

Joe glared at me, as if I should've known, as if I routinely purchased liquor at 8:00 a.m. I didn't; I worked in a bar, where I drank for free and then went home to sleep at 2:00 a.m. like a normal person. It wasn't my fault Texas had archaic liquor laws.

We left empty-handed and anxious. Having missed the sleep window, I now needed a drink as badly as Joe. By the time we got back home, my hands were visibly trembling. Then Joe came up with a plan, flipping through the Yellow Pages for a limo service. *Genius.* The car would have a stocked bar. We'd drive around Austin drinking for an hour, then swipe a bottle to bring home, leaving a hefty tip for the driver.

That's not what happened, either.

I crawled into the limo, willing myself not to throw up. My head pounded, my legs wobbled, and I had a hard time sitting up. Joe slid past and reached for the standard row of three crystal decanters, all empty. The bar wasn't stocked and my Miller Lites were long gone. I closed my eyes and focused on breathing slowly and evenly. Joe had a word with the driver, a dark-skinned black man with graying hair, who gave a thoughtful nod before driving us to his house. While we parked at the curb, I lay across the back seat with my eyes closed, fantasizing about hospital admittance—I felt that poorly. When our driver reappeared, he passed his personal stash through the partition. Joe thanked him and asked him to take us to the Four Seasons.

I struggled to sit up as Joe offered me the first swig from an unfamiliar bottle. I'd never had brandy before but forced down two sips, figuring I couldn't feel much worse than I did.

I was wrong.

By the time we got to the hotel, my salivary glands were on overdrive in a pre-vomit automatic reflex. I held the impulse at bay with single-minded focus and gentle, repetitive swallows, like a mantra distracting me from intense physical distress. Joe helped me to the lobby lounge, where I sat like a lump, meditating—

breathe, soft swallow, breathe, soft swallow. Securing a room took a remarkably long time while I rapidly deteriorated. When he finally collected me, I could barely walk and had to be half carried and propped up at the elevator. Still, we were almost home free, mere seconds from the salvation of blackout drapes, bed, and minibar. I envisioned saltines to settle my stomach, washed down with sips of chilled wine…but alas, it was not to be.

"I'm sorry, Mr. Walsh," said the front desk clerk, rushing over to block the elevator. "There's been a terrible mistake and we're unable to accommodate your stay."

This can't be happening, I thought, looking for a trash bin or planter in which to vomit. I figured sixty seconds if we were lucky.

Turned out, the flustered young man's boss had just alerted him that Joe was banned from the hotel due to an incident on a previous stay. A throwing-star competition gone awry, Joe later explained, when he and some radio contest winners had removed a large painting from the wall that, when finally rehung, did little to cover their amateur ninja damage.

My knees buckled, just in time for Joe to work it in our favor. "My girlfriend is sick," he pleaded. "She needs bed rest. No parties—you have my word."

His word wasn't enough. Management took pity on us but posted a security guard in the hall outside our room, just in case.

I was so relieved that I overcame the urge to vomit. Joe fed me melon and wine until I felt well enough to cross from the sofa to bed. My boyfriend had different ideas, and the next thing I knew I was bound naked to a balcony with melon juice dripping from my butt crack, where Joe had tucked a slice of honeydew. I'd never been less into his kinky scenes, but the river view was nice and I liked making him happy.

I had a low threshold for boredom and didn't want to lose the life I'd found. Reining in Joe never occurred to me. Instead, I vowed to keep up with him.

❖❖❖

I HAD NO INTENTION of returning to my hard-partying meth days, but I loved being high—inside the sweet spot of a buzz, weightless and floating, yet not so far out there that I couldn't access my bearings. Nailing the recipe was key. It was easy to slip up and overindulge, emerging days later mentally fried and remorseful. Joe didn't always get it right either and he had a term for that. He called it *monstering*.

"We're monstering," he'd tell Rick, to explain why we couldn't come over. Or, "That was quite a monster last week, huh, babe?" and, "I can't believe you did four hog rails in a row, you monster." It was our little joke, conveyed with both affection and concern—plus, if we were honest, admiration. The idea was that an occasional, accidental monster was unavoidable, but at least we were *aware* of it. Like, don't make it a habit…just make the most of it when it happens.

Our monsters were balanced with periods of normalcy: dining out, shopping at the mall, and watching TV, sober and clearheaded. Such was the case when Joe received Austin's key to the city, a campy-cool honor bestowed on him by the mayor in a private ceremony in his office with a photographer. Afterward, we went to Chinatown, a popular family restaurant in North Austin. I'd been feeling down that day, so Joe clowned around at the table to cheer me up and entertain my friend Daryl, whom we'd invited to dinner. The restaurant was slow, with two other occupied tables, and Joe was soon throwing himself into Dick Van Dyke–worthy stunts, twice sliding off his chair, and fumbling with a spoon until it went flying. I was giggling in no time, but the restaurant manager wasn't. Without a word to us, he called the cops.

The police weren't laughing, either, but they were smug—apparently seeing Joe as a real threat to society with his unkempt hair and leopard-print jacket. (Who knew what he was capable of?

Did you see what he did to that fortune cookie? Broke it right in half!)
They handcuffed him before I knew what was happening.

"He's only had one glass of wine!" I wailed, unaware that
a public intoxication charge did not require a Breathalyzer. The
irony was staggering. This was literally as sober as Joe *got*. That it
had all been an act to make me smile made his arrest feel all the
more tragic. "Don't worry, honey!" I yelled, as he was deposited
into one of three squad cars responding to a single flying spoon.
"I'm right behind you." And I was—unfortunately in another
squad car when they ran my license and found a three-year-old
traffic ticket I swore I'd paid. I tossed my car keys to Daryl, who
promised to meet us at the station. I was more worried about
Joe but tried to stay calm. *Maybe he doesn't have any coke on him*,
I thought. *Please, God, don't let him have any coke on him.*

He had coke on him.

I had the cash to cover my fine so I was released, but no one
would tell me what was going on with Joe, which seemed like a
bad sign. I had no idea how true that was. As he relayed it later, he
was literally backed into a corner and ordered to undress so they
could search him and his clothes. With mere seconds to hide the
drugs, it was a good thing Joe worked well under pressure (being
the same guy, after all, who'd subverted Texas's etched-in-stone
liquor laws). With a looming PI charge to lend him credibility, he
gave the performance of a lifetime, launching into a paranoid rant
about injustice and civil rights, while simultaneously yanking off
his jacket and flinging it wildly across the room. High-top sneakers
whizzed past his captors' heads as they moved in to restrain him.
He was tossed into a private cell, clothes and shoes bundled and
stored until the cops could figure out what to do with him.

Meanwhile, I called a stripper friend whose husband was a
police officer. Tim was off-duty, but I reached him at home and
he promised to do what he could. Joe was free within the hour,
without a body search, thanks to one call from Tim and $250 bail

from Daryl. He appeared none the worse for wear, aside from mild disappointment that his key to the city did not unlock its jail.

On the way out, he signed autographs for the station cops, then ushered me into the elevator with Daryl and our friend Quinten (who'd come with Daryl to the station). When the doors closed, Joe reached into the pocket of his leopard-print motorcycle jacket and pulled out two full vials of coke. "What do you say we have a little party on the Austin PD?" And that's exactly what we did.

Down Under

IN JANUARY, JOE WENT to Australia. He'd be gone months, probably through spring, and said he would send for me "at some point." We'd been long-distance dating for months, and now an entire ocean separated us. The distance was hard, the uncertainty crushing.

Moodiness set in, insecurity, self-pity, and the razor-sharp belief that we were over before we'd begun. At least once a day I'd berate myself for my childish feelings, then buck up for a few hours before sinking into despair again. This was my first relationship in four years, my second ever, and I didn't know the rules. Going on instinct and the awareness that nothing repelled like neediness, I took Joe's calls with cheerful confidence and zero complaints. I wasn't an idiot. Ending a relationship from overseas was as easy as hanging up a phone.

One night he called at 3:00 a.m., after I'd already passed out from a long night at work. When we finally spoke, he brought it up, putting me on the defensive.

"Is it really so hard to believe I was at home, alone in bed? You're the one traipsing around the world doing God knows what. I didn't fly off without *you*, you know. You left the country without *me*."

Joe laughed. He did that sometimes when I got fired up, in a way that suggested he was impressed. I never knew how to respond.

"You got me there, kiddo," he said.

Whatever he thought, I wasn't cheating on him. If only because the guilt of betraying the man I loved would wreck me faster than celibacy threatened to. But my sex drive was no small thing, and I secretly thought I deserved more credit. Instead of a trophy for my Herculean self-restraint, Joe dropped a bomb on me.

"It's probably unfair to put expectations on you, being so far away and all."

"What do you mean?"

"You have a right to get your needs met. I wouldn't like it, but it's up to you."

I pondered his statement. Was this a trick? A loophole to absolve himself of a recent indiscretion? Or leftover remnant of his generation's free-love, hippie-shit ethic? Unsure whether to be impressed or appalled, I stammered something indignant and changed the subject.

Casual non-monogamy was practically all I'd had, making it neither liberating nor revolutionary to me. But who was I to impose my will on an autonomous adult man? As for Joe's vision of the ideal relationship, I got a lot of mixed signals. Reading between lines was tough in person and impossible long-distance.

Meanwhile, being in love took the fun out of stripping. Work began to feel like a real job, and I reacted to every slow shift or rude customer, barging into Chris's office to wail, "I can't work like this!"

He ignored my pleas until one night I caught him buried in paperwork. "Fine," he sighed, waving me off like a gnat. "Get out. Go home."

I left, but instead of the one mile to my apartment, I drove six across town to Daryl's. In the process, I forged a new freeway ramp down a grassy slope, having missed the preexisting, conveniently marked and paved one. I was pulled over two blocks shy of my destination.

The arresting officers were patient and polite as I was handcuffed, processed, and deposited into a clean, private cell, where I curled in a ball and cried for four hours until Christine bailed me out. I called Joe and told him what had happened, and he replied by inviting me to Sydney. In the interim, I went to court and requested that the judge suspend my license. Probation, the alternative, entailed a process of permissions for every out-of-state trip for two years—a formality, my lawyer said—*No one's trying to stop you from following your boyfriend around the world. Calm down.*

Fuck that shit. Having to ask *at all* was repellent. I'd kowtowed to Chris, who had power to fire me; outside the club, I answered to no one.

Lockup had rattled me. The loss of my basic freedoms, however brief, felt dehumanizing. I didn't trust authority figures to look out for me, having been failed or betrayed by too many— cops, parents, teachers, coaches, priests, nuns, and two previous business partners (i.e., drug dealers). When I paid my fine ($600, in tens and twenties) my community service requirement was waived, finalizing one of the breeziest DWIs ever handed down in Texas. I was as grateful as I was ashamed.

My rebellious streak had a way of getting me in over my head, and scrambling out from under it was a way of life I wanted to shed. For years, I'd bounced from adventure to adventure, too busy ducking and weaving to wonder what any of it meant. Three years earlier, that recklessness led directly to a violent attack. After getting mugged, I moved across town and threw myself into work at Sugar's, an exclusive, insulated world in which I didn't have to process emotions or events. Traumas were left outside the door of that throbbing, glittery womb in which I gestated a new identity. I did not reconcile the past; I ditched it like an annoying little sister. I did not examine my flaws; I burned those traitors at the stake. Rising from the ashes was a new, improved me, but the DWI suggested that she, too, was an illusion, just another failed experiment.

Too many versions of me were scattered around Austin, shady shadow selves hiding in alleys and behind trees. It was getting harder to escape myself locally. Why not start fresh in another country, carve a new identity from the rib of the man next to me?

❋❋❋

MY FIRST TWO WEEKS in Australia were a boozy blur of crowded shows in heaps of pubs. Joe was touring the Sydney area with the Party Boys, a popular local band. The gigs were packed and lively, if in smaller venues than he was used to. Our accommodations were similarly downsized—a one-room guesthouse in Neutral Bay at the home of some friends of Joe's. The main house was tidy and spacious. Our detached bungalow was thrown together like a dorm room, with stackable wire basket drawers and a three-piece foam contraption mattress.

Oddly, we slept fine on it. Odder still, we slept every night. I hadn't had cocaine since Joe left the States, because if it wasn't around I didn't dwell on it. When it was, I very much did. Such was the case in Sydney, when after a few days of blissful ignorance, I discovered someone in Joe's circle had blow on weekends and was known to be generous with it. To our laid-back Aussie friends, cocaine was an afterthought. I tried to emulate their foreign ways, pretending I could take it or leave it. I didn't have much choice, considering Joe's coke budget was as scaled down as everything else.

He'd give me one bump the night of each gig, but that was it. Then, while Joe showered and dressed, I'd loiter in the main house, watching sports with the generous friend, always trying to look surprised by the offer and offhand about accepting it. I'd make moderation look easy if it killed me, dammit...except there was no moderating my drinking. Many a morning found me in the main house, waiting on the world's slowest coffeepot, pretending not to have the world's worst hangover.

The close quarters did have an upshot. Lack of privacy curtains or soundproofing meant Joe's kink scenes were out, and straight-up fucking was finally on the table (so to speak). I went for every opportunity, landed half, and called it a win. I had to assume Joe was satisfied too, when he caught my eye from the stage, singing about a couple who "were good in bed." I figured our sexual frequency would pick up at tour's end, and then life would be perfect...as soon as I scaled back my drinking.

I didn't scale back. My drinking got worse.

I was generally a happy drunk, but also one easily triggered. Cocaine dulled my insecurities, making me less reactive and testy. It also had a sobering effect, keeping me from being sloppy and embarrassing. Our diminished intake in Australia opened the door to stupid arguments. Most blew over quickly, but one issue became sticky: I wanted more sex than Joe did, and I was becoming vocal about not getting it.

When my cajoling became badgering, he sat me down to talk. "It's not that I don't desire you. *I do.* But your needs might be bigger than I'm wired for, so you have my blessing to have sex with someone else."

"Oh, God, not this again—"

"Just listen. You're young—I *get it.* But I'm working here, and spread a little thin."

"Don't... Don't you love me?"

"*You're my woman*—of course I do. I'm only cool with this if it's not behind my back. I'd need to be in the room."

His unconventional ideas were less shocking the second time around, and I was less inclined to shoot them down out of hand. Since puberty, I'd lugged around this insatiable sexual longing, like a heavy, wooden cross twice my size and impossible to carry. I finally had a boyfriend at my disposal 24/7 and still couldn't get enough. If he felt pressured or inadequate, wasn't this a favor to us both? Where I came from, threesomes were ubiquitous. How different was this, really? A twosome with a witness.

"Who?" I asked, expecting him to shrug or laugh it off as a joke. Instead, he suggested Trevor and I perked up.

One of Joe's Aussie friends, Trevor was handsome and polished, yet playful. He had clear blue eyes and tight dark curls interwoven with hints of silver. When Joe made the offer, Trevor came right over. Had Joe not been sitting there, flipping through magazines and cracking occasional jokes, I might've had more fun with it. Instead, I called the game early, too self-conscious to go all the way. I loved Joe for trying to meet my needs, even if he didn't understand them.

❋❋❋

I THOUGHT IT MIGHT be selfish of me to expect love *and* passion from one man. After all, I wasn't everything Joe needed, either… and I obsessed about my shortcomings.

Kevin Borich, the Party Boys' guitarist, and his fiancée Melissa were an ideal couple. He was handsome, roguish, and funny. She was a beautiful young model, angelic in every way. As many pubs as our guys played in, I never saw her drunk. I was too shy to just come out and ask for her secret to a blissful relationship; then one day it came to me: Who *wouldn't* love Melissa? *Duh.* And I was back at square one.

The Brothers were equally fascinating. Hamish, Angus, and Fergus Richardson sang backup for the Party Boys and possessed a more compelling presence than even the "perfect couple" did. In their early- to mid-twenties, the Brothers were boyishly handsome, naturally fit, and well mannered, yet waggish and exuberant. Their close bonds and joyous demeanor drew me in like a powerful drug. Twice on tour, Hamish pulled me onstage to dance with him during the show. Each time I'd felt both thrilled by the inclusion and abashed by my undeservedness.

On a strip club stage I had leverage. Everywhere else, I was lost, and not just dancing with Hamish. No one in Joe's world needed anything from me, which should've been freeing yet sucked me into space. I was liberated to the point of weightlessness. I missed work and being put on a pedestal. Joe's attentions could turn on a dime and our bickering escalated. We had a screaming match or two but reconciled because we hated fighting. We didn't resolve things; we didn't know how.

After a gig in Coolangatta, the band drove home while Joe and I opted for a commuter flight. Arguing all morning, Joe had resorted to the silent treatment as I shadowed him through the terminal. The small airport was practically vacant (due to a holiday or a worker strike, I forget) and the lack of witnesses spurred me on until I cornered him.

"Stop ignoring me. It's childish," I fumed.

"*You*'re chasing me and *I'm* childish?"

"You're childish for making me chase you."

"I'm trying to get away from you!"

"I get that. It's not happening."

"Stop yelling—everyone can hear you."

I rolled my eyes. "There are three people here and one is wearing headphones."

"I don't care," he growled. "Lower your voice."

"Make me."

He did, yanking me into the restroom, where he backed me into a stall and fucked me hard and fast up against the wall.

That shut me up. So much so that when he zipped up and left, I was too stunned to chase after him. *Well, that was interesting.*

The flight to Sydney was quiet and calm—we didn't speak but the tension had passed. Later, Joe blamed our fighting on the stress of low-budget touring. When the Party Boys run was over, we moved to the Hyatt and succumbed to old habits. Monstering hard, we crammed a month's worth of sex and drugs into a forty-eight-hour period. Physically, he rocked my world. Emotionally, it felt as intimate as an answering machine message.

###

IN NEW ZEALAND, OUR routine stabilized. Joe was there to produce a record for Herbs, a folk-reggae band known for heartbreaking harmonies and powerful lyrics. Their style was soulful, collaborative, and unrushed, like the band members themselves. I connected right away with Charlie (the bassist), Dilworth (the guitarist), and their manager, Hugh Lynn, a trim, serious, sage-like Maori with self-possessed magnetism. He showed us around Auckland, then his studio, where we met his staff and friends.

The local tribe held an official welcoming ceremony at their temple on a cliff. Two-dozen members pressed their noses to ours. They sang songs and the elders gave speeches. When it was Joe's turn, he introduced me as "the woman I love" then sang "Desperado" a cappella. It was the kind of sublime moment that made the high of cocaine seem petty and ridiculous. That there was none to be found in New Zealand was a relief. Later, we met more friends of the band, and one of them offered us speed.

I'd never snorted crank—having been an intravenous user in my day—yet I'd done enough blow with Joe that the straw felt natural in my hand and I barely hesitated. From there, we went to a rehearsal party that turned into a six-hour jam session. I danced with everyone who asked, from little kids to tribal elders, self-consciousness be damned. On the way home, we stopped at the Hells Angels' clubhouse, but finding them a surly and suspicious lot, we didn't stay there long.

Hugh had rented us a beach house in Omana Bay, a cozy wood-frame cottage separated from shore by a gravel road and ten million mosquitoes. We settled in with the help of Andrew, our temporary personal assistant. Hugh came by with a numerologist friend who insisted on doing our charts for free. She said my soul number (nine) indicated an old soul and my inner-self number (eleven over two) was identical to Joe's destiny. Hugh declared us "meant for each other." Joe didn't say anything. He'd been sullen all evening, and when our guests left, he clammed up entirely. He declined my every attempt to connect, from sex to a shoulder rub, back scratch, or the porn video he'd had Andrew pick up "as a joke." I stormed into the bedroom and slammed the door. Joe spent the night on the couch.

In the morning, he went hunting for clams, returning with just two in his bucket. He looked so forlorn, I offered to help, and we walked the beach until my feet became painfully scraped up. Squatting to investigate, I discovered a veritable carpet of clams stretching all the way down the beach.

"Right under my nose," Joe said, digging away.

"No wonder you couldn't see them," I teased. He chuckled, and life was good again.

###

In Christchurch, he stuck to me like glue, leaving my side only once to tape a TV interview. One morning, I awoke to him counting my freckles. When I stretched and rolled over, he feigned dismay and made a production of starting over.

"You're a freckle farm," he said. "No, a map of the universe. I'm going to name them, like planets." I giggled and he shushed me. "Quiet now. This is serious business."

"Right, sorry." Then, "How long might this take, exactly?"

"I've been working on it for days," he sighed. "They move around when you're asleep... It's very complicated."

He tried going dot-to-dot to form a picture, but it tickled and I squirmed. "Enough!" I cried, wrapping my legs around his neck. We spent the morning making love without any drugs, toys, or kinky scripts. As days passed, I became relaxed and unguarded. Joe even caught me singing to myself and gasped, he was so delighted. One night in bed, I snuggled him so relentlessly, he almost fell off the edge.

"Honey?" he whispered, nudging me awake. "Open your eyes." I did, to see two inches of mattress between him and a drop to the floor. Behind me was enough room for three more bodies. I scooched backward, sheepish.

When Herbs played a gig in Christchurch with Joe as "special guest," word got out he was in town, and fans started closing in. They hovered at restaurants and approached him in bars and everywhere else we went. Antiquing one day, we were suddenly surrounded. I stepped out of the way while Joe signed autographs, but two young women singled me out, asking pointed, personal questions in a rude, aggressive way. In a blink, Joe pulled me back to his side. The fans moved on, but I felt deflated. I didn't like Joe's fame appearing out of nowhere. Something that big and unpredictable just might extinguish me someday.

###

AFTER THREE WEEKS IN New Zealand, we returned to Sydney. Joe
had meetings with record exec Tim Murdoch and a promoter
named Sam Righi. The former was crazy like a strip club bouncer;
the latter, sophisticated and charming. As warm and friendly as
they were to me, I felt painfully out of place.

When his meetings were over, I picked a fight with Joe to make
myself feel better. I accused him of neglecting me. He refused to
talk to me for three days, then ran out of coke and took to bed
for two more, with extreme fatigue. If Trevor hadn't shown up
with a fresh supply, we'd have missed the Hard Rock Café grand
opening in Sydney. Joe pulled it together and we emerged from
Sam Righi's Rolls-Royce to a mob of fans and paparazzi. When an
MTV crew shoved a mic in Joe's face, I froze, then stepped out of
frame. Inside was more of the same: mics and cameras every few
feet, until a doorman swooped in and delivered us to VIP.

I hated being so self-conscious, especially on camera. Smack
dab in the middle of the best party in town, surrounded by
celebrities and revelers, I was determined to rise to the occasion.
A couple fat hog rails in the ladies' room and I was back in our
booth, chatting up INXS members like we were best friends.
When Toni Childs's guitarist made eyes at me from stage, I flirted
back without missing a beat.

Before bed that night, Joe and I went for a walk. I thanked him
for being so good to me. "I am grateful, even when it doesn't show."

"Thanks for that," he said, stopping to gaze in my eyes.
"I'm lucky to have you, too."

I buried my face in his neck. I could learn to be poised on
camera and mingle with celebrities, but Joe's loving, soulful eye-
gazes would always overwhelm me.

❖❖❖

IN APRIL, WE RETURNED to Auckland, where Joe played a benefit for Greenpeace (which I supported) and one for the Hells Angels Defense Fund (which I didn't). No matter how many times we visited their clubhouse, only one or two of those guys were personable in the slightest.

The Herbs and everyone connected to them were utterly genuine. While Joe worked in the studio, Margaret (the numerologist) and Natalie (Hugh's secretary) took me to lunch and other girlie gatherings. Some days, I'd sit in Hugh's office reading about Maori culture, or call his massage therapist, Lance, for deep-tissue work and conversation. Lance had Hugh's same quiet confidence, and I was extremely attracted to both men. It made me feel guilty and vaguely resentful, and I reacted by accusing Joe of flirting with Natalie. Her bubbly personality was invaluable in the studio, but since bubbly wasn't my nature (sober, anyway), I became jealous and irrational. Joe ignored my catty barbs, and I realized how awful I was being. I apologized and told him the partial truth: that I was afraid I didn't make him happy.

"You know I love you, Kristi. C'mon now, stop it."

"You seem unhappy, though. You never laugh or joke around anymore."

"I'm under a lot of pressure, trying to do right by Hugh and the band. This record has to be special," he said. "Besides, I'm tired of being everyone's clown."

I quit complaining. I'd been losing myself in him for months, never imagining he, too, might want to reinvent himself.

###

WE'D BEEN IN NEW ZEALAND three weeks when Rick the Bass Player arrived, on tour with Neil Young. We hung out like old times and had group dinners where Neil was the center of attention and Joe was relieved not to be for once. We attended an Ice-T performance, followed by dinner with the rapper and his entourage. Neil, Rick, Ice, and Joe gathered at the head of a long table while I studied Ice's beautiful girlfriend. Neither of us received any attention, yet she seemed perfectly content. I was bored and wanted a bump. Glancing at the floor, I'll be damned if I didn't find one. I slipped the folded paper packet to Joe, who pocketed it without offering me some.

With Joe and the band spending long hours in the studio, Hugh organized occasional diversions to recharge everyone. We went caving with the band, floated in isolation tanks alone, saw Rudolf Nureyev perform, and explored a labyrinth of World War II cliff tunnels with Andrew in tow. Joe remained distant through it all. He'd shed tears watching Nureyev dance. I'd cried in my isolation tank, for different reasons. Finally, I suggested a romantic getaway for us to reconnect. He arranged a weekend campout but invited Andrew along. At the campgrounds, I sent Andrew on a nature walk and corralled Joe into the camper loft for our best sex since Coolangatta. It didn't bring us closer. Joe's walls came down when he was good and ready, for reasons only he could fathom.

One week later, he doted on me at our favorite Japanese restaurant, attentive, sweet, and romantic. When he got up to sing karaoke, fans closed in immediately, so he rushed offstage and pulled me outside with him, laughing together like kids. Days later, we threw a dinner party at the beach house for the band and their friends. Afterward, we all dropped acid, and Joe took requests on an acoustic. When they left, we took more acid and made love until sunrise. The next day we took a helicopter to an isolated property called Butterfly Bay. It was for sale and Joe wanted to buy it.

The house itself was small and airy, nestled in a private beachfront cove. We wandered its parameters, trying to imagine living there, far from everything we knew.

"What about your career?" I asked.

"Maybe I don't need it," he said.

"*Retire?*"

"I could quit making records and trying to impress everyone. Be free of the headaches and ego trips. Be myself here, just me and you."

I played along. "I'd quit stripping, and then...what?"

"Anything you want."

I let myself dream. "I could write stories and screenplays."

"Write and *cook.*"

I laughed because I didn't cook. But I could learn.

We sat in the sand, at the crest of the cove, above sloping fields of brush. When it was time to go, Hugh shouted in our direction, causing thousands of butterflies to fly out, en masse, and flutter skyward. Joe and I followed suit, climbing aboard our helicopter, back to the real world.

###

THE HERBS TOUR KICKED off in a tiny club in Taupo, empty but for a handful of drunks. Things picked up at subsequent shows, and between times we went antiquing, filling both tour vans with Joe's impulse buys. As winter approached, the drafty vehicles became as cold as they were cramped. Traffic was unpredictable, less from cars than sheep crossing—and by crossing, I mean filling the space of both lanes and then hanging out there indefinitely.

No one complained, least of all me. With my legs propped up on a box of Joe's junk, I'd snuggle closer, shivering happily and enjoying the scenery. One day, Charlie pronounced me "family." My boyfriend proclaimed his love for me daily. We'd had one real spat early on in the tour that had blown over quickly. Since then, nothing but peace, love, and harmony.

We crossed to New Zealand's South Island during the worst storm anyone could remember, including the ferry captain. Joe watched over me on deck for two hours while I clung to a railing, nauseated and green. According to Charlie, the air quality inside Cook Strait was the purest in the civilized world. "Had I known that," I quipped at dinner that night, safe on solid ground, "I would've breathed more of it." The entire table—my tribe, my family—burst out laughing.

For the first two weeks on tour, I hadn't a care in the world. It felt too good to last.

Joe found my neurosis endearing. "That's just your nature," he said. "If there's nothing to worry about, you'll worry about *that*."

I knew he was right. I would've changed if I'd known how.

Calling my parents hadn't helped. Spurred by a sense of duty, it had done little more than remind me how disconnected we were. On top of that, they'd put down our dog. Obi was old, but of all my siblings, I was closest to him, and no one had told me till afterward. Thoughts of Obi—and Rocky, back home, being cared for by my neighbors—brought tears to my eyes. The tour was going well. The band was accomplishing things and fulfilling their dreams. Joe was relaxed and happy, living show to show, with his lady at his side. Meanwhile, I began to feel like a spectator, a disappointment to my parents and pets, and a wannabe writer who could barely bring herself to journal. Instead, I immersed myself in books—*A Moveable Feast, Duncton Wood, Oscar and Lucinda*—reading about real writers, fictional gamblers, and anthropomorphized woodland creatures.

On the drive to Queenstown—a picturesque town reminiscent of Lake Tahoe—Hugh, Joe, and I took mushrooms. The men were fine, but I got mildly carsick. Later, at the hotel before dinner, Hugh went door-to-door passing out acid. When I declined, Joe did too in a gesture of solidarity. A disparity in mood became apparent at the restaurant, where band and crew were seated already, amped up and tripping their brains out. They held it together until entrees were served, when a massive food fight broke out. A double-fisted, ten-person mêlée—everyone in our group except myself, Joe, and Natalie. We ducked under a table, and when Joe and Natalie laughed, I did too, so dissociated in that moment I actually needed a cue.

I told Joe I should probably go home soon, and when the band found out, they sought me out, one by one, urging me to stay. We were in Taranaki at the end of May, on the one-year anniversary of our first date. Joe arranged a candlelit dinner in a private section of the hotel's dining room, where we sipped champagne and watched snowfall outside. Joe said he loved me and was sorry for not having flowers. I buried my face in his neck, half laughing, half crying. What was wrong with me? I had *everything*—a fairy-tale setting with my own Prince Charming—yet I wanted only to escape.

That night, the power went out around 2:00 a.m. All the hotel guests migrated to the lobby, warming ourselves around the freestanding fireplace, drinking hot spiced wine and cocoa courtesy of the elderly proprietors. It was like a family reunion holiday, with kids and people of all ages, most of us strangers, though a mere few staying that way. They played cards and board games through the early hours, the younger ones well past sunrise. Joe and Charlie went outside to play in the snow. I drank tequila in the bar with the crew. Four months among the best people in the world, and I still felt like an imposter.

Most mornings, Thom (the percussionist) practiced a Maori stick-fighting technique in motel parking lots and courtyards. I'd watch from my room, nursing a hangover, envying his form and dedication. Hugh had this trick where he'd look at clouds and "will them" to disappear. He called himself the cloud eater, and I'd feign amazement, playing along. Charlie's singing had the power to convert, which it did to me, on a nightly basis. Dilworth was an ex-rugby player who'd lost a leg to gangrene before he tapped into his musical softness. He had a volcano inside him, according to Hugh, but they were all forces of nature, as far as I was concerned. They formed a bubble of loving protection around me and Joe, honing in when we needed it. The most profound example took place the morning after our one and only serious fight on tour.

It was quick and fierce, with hurled insults, dishes, and knickknacks. Whatever we'd fought about was forgotten by morning when Dilworth, Charlie, Tama, and Thom arrived bearing juice and coffee. They hugged me as they entered, then casually swept through the room, collecting broken glass and pottery. I pitched in and Joe did too. Someone hummed a tune, one of my warrior brother cleaning crew. There were no side-eye, judgmental looks or heavy sighs. No condemnation or taking of sides. Just acceptance, compassion, and familial love, reminding Joe and me what the bubble felt like, inviting us back inside.

They were the tribe I'd sought all my life, with a place for me at their table. But I felt like I had nothing of value to bring to it, and I told Joe to send me home.

With a Little Help From my Friends

RINGO STARR INTRODUCED HIMSELF by kissing both my cheeks. I flinched—I couldn't help it. *Did a Beatle really just touch my face? Twice...on purpose!?* Ringo chuckled and then shrugged. "I live in France," he said, by way of explanation. As if I needed one.

Joe had been eager to see his friend all day. He seemed nervous, but mostly excited. We'd been waiting in the sitting room of a posh hotel suite when Ringo and his wife swept in like royalty, with warmth that was genuine and disarming. Barb and I made small talk while Joe and "Richie" (as Joe called him) talked tour business. The first incarnation of Ringo's All-Starr Band was set to launch later that month. It couldn't come soon enough.

Though Joe didn't discuss his career concerns with me, I was aware his latest record hadn't done well. Low sales ate at his self-confidence, which in turn fed his bad habits. Going on tour with an artist he admired was exactly what he needed—what we both needed.

Between my DWI and Joe's more recent legal run-in, I'd practically been scared straight. Returning from New Zealand, Joe had stopped in Hawaii for some R and R and been detained

Top: Neil Young, Rick Rosas, Joe Walsh, Charlie Tumahai

Bottom: Joe Walsh and Stevie Nicks

at US Customs on suspected drug charges. A vigilant agent, combing through Joe's eleven suitcases, had unearthed a single paper packet from the Hells Angels' clubhouse. To our relief, lab results cleared him the next day. Powdered caffeine, it turned out, was not an illegal substance.

I'd never been happier to get screwed over in a drug deal. We thanked God for those asshole Kiwi bikers, then vowed to be more careful. We'd have help in that department. Ringo and Barb were clean and sober, and drugs and alcohol were prohibited on tour.

###

THE ALL-STARR BAND WAS exactly that—a group of established musical talents playing each other's hits, plus a plethora of Ringo's. The lineup included Dr. John on piano; Rick Danko and Levon Helm from The Band; Nils Lofgren and Clarence Clemons from the E Street Band; Billy Preston on keyboards; and Jim Keltner, a revered session drummer.

The wives—Cynthia Keltner, Sandy Helm, Liz Danko, and Dr. John's wife, Lorraine Rebennack—treated me like one of them, despite my younger age and lesser, unmarried status. Ringo and Barb were friendly and accessible. Barb regularly asked how I was doing and what I was reading and included me in group conversations. One day, she waved me over backstage from a room where she was chatting with friends. I entered in time to catch the tail end of her anecdote—a darkly funny punch line about alcoholic blackouts. Everyone cracked up, while I looked on in awe. I'd yet to make peace with my checkered past, much less be able to joke about it. Barbara had studied philosophy and was building a rehab clinic. I thought she was a rock star in her own right and would've hung onto her skirts all day if she didn't make me so tongue-tied.

Every day, Ringo greeted me by name, and every day, it caught me off guard. He created a family atmosphere on tour, hosting group dinners and riding with the band to and from gigs. Nothing got by him; he was attuned to everyone's needs. During a sudden downpour at an outdoor photo shoot, the first thing Ringo did was shelter my eleven-year-old sister (who was visiting for the weekend) in his personal limo. She didn't know The Beatles from a hole in the wall but happily watched cartoons in luxury all day. I entered his dressing room once to find a big bowl of pistachios—*pre-shelled*. I'd never seen anything like it. I always had to shell my own, I told him. Ringo burst out laughing and insisted I eat all I wanted.

A pervasive lack of snobbery surprised me at every turn. Dr. John gave me a new compliment every day. Levon and I had an instant rapport. He said I reminded him of his favorite aunt from Arkansas. Rick and Clarence were sweet and outgoing, Jimmy and Nils unfailingly polite. Only Billy was distant, but as the man responsible for my favorite four minutes of the show, Mr. Preston could do no wrong in my eyes. I danced my ass off to "Will It Go Round in Circles" every single time. "The Weight" was another favorite—of mine and most audiences'. Joe's rockers were major crowd-pleasers, and opening act Mason Ruffner had a sexy shredder called "Gypsy Blood" I couldn't get enough of. But the ultimate unifier was love for Ringo. When he left his drums and took center stage for "With a Little Help from My Friends," "It Don't Come Easy," or "Photograph," the entire crowd sang along, mimicking his peace-sign wave and simplistic dance step to the end in perfect unison. Compared to the hardcore punk shows I'd loved, it could've seemed corny. In truth, it was celebratory and bonding. There was something magical about Ringo, and his shows were intoxicating.

Tour producer David Fishof became one of my favorite people. He was guileless and cherubic with an ever-present grin that suggested no one was more delighted by this thing he'd set in motion than him. Hilary Gerrard, of Apple Records, never missed a chance to say hello or bestow upon me a little wisdom. First, he was adamant I "let" Joe marry me.

"I'll get right on that," I laughed.

"Everyone should marry at least once. How many husbands have you had?"

"Hilary, I'm twenty-one. *None.*"

"Well, then, marry Joe and leave it at that."

"Anything else?"

"Dehydration is the enemy—drink lots of water."

"Got it."

"And pursue your passion. What are you passionate about, dear?"

"Writing, I guess...and film."

"Good for you! Pursue that and *then* get married."

Hilary had done well for himself and I needed all the guidance I could get. I upped my water intake immediately.

Allen was another of Ringo's inner circle, a manager of some sort. I liked Allen because he was always having fun and making sure I was, too. In Dallas, after meeting one of my prettiest stripper friends, he pulled me aside to ask about her. "Is she single?"

"She has a boyfriend in Austin."

"Tell her something for me anyway."

"What's that, Allen?"

"Tell her, *fast cars, fast boats, and a house on the beach.*"

I laughed and promised I would.

Allen spoke the language of my tribe back home. Maybe I wasn't *that* different from Richie's camp, after all.

I sensed Dr. John and I had things in common. He had one foot in the demimonde. I wanted to crawl inside his head and see where else we connected, but it seemed an inelegant task. One day he asked me to fix the latch on his necklace, the one his special pouch hung from. He told me he didn't want anyone else to touch it, and that said everything I needed.

❖❖❖

IN AUGUST, WE WERE in New York City for a cluster of arena shows. Joe and Clarence did a *Letterman* taping where I ran into Paul Shaffer. I started to remind him of where we had met, but he just laughed and hugged me. "How could I forget you, Kristi?"

We smoked a joint in Paul's dressing room before the show. After, he took us to his favorite restaurant where they set up a table in the kitchen for him, away from the other diners. I caught a buzz from just two glasses of wine, and when Joe offered a bump to counteract it, our good behavior abruptly ended. We spent the rest of the night in our room at the Pierre, monstering through sunrise.

I crawled into bed, strung-out and feeling ill. Joe, wired to the gills, called the *Howard Stern Show*. Unable to sleep, I flipped on the radio and heard Howard say something about "Joe's gorgeous girlfriend with the great body." Since we'd yet to meet in person, I figured it was his way of apologizing for ambushing me the previous winter. I fell asleep feeling special, then woke up too hungover to make the show. The band went to Albany without me. Joe was brusque before heading out, filling me with shame for monstering. *Not on this tour*, we'd said; *Not around Richie*. I spent the day cleaning sex toys and sending out his laundry, trying to make myself useful.

Liz Danko called from her room, having missed the plane, too. I was tempted to confide in her but decided not to. She and I had smuggled vodka backstage at the first two shows, giggling like teenagers. She liked to drink, but others on tour had bigger demons. Maybe Liz did, too. I didn't want to tempt anyone with thoughts of cocaine, or ruin a freshly clean slate. Nor did I want to share our stash, if Joe scored one again. (The fear was justified when, later on in the tour, Billy correctly suspected Joe was holding. He hounded us for days while we hid in our room, ignoring his phone calls and door knocking.)

❋❋❋

THERE WERE OTHER STRESSORS on tour—health issues, for one. Hilary and Ringo had bad colds; Dr. John cracked a rib; Joe temporarily lost his voice; and Clarence suffered an ear infection and chronic back pain. They were accomplished musicians, but not young men, some trying to jump-start stalled careers. The night before the first show, Rick Danko spent four hours jamming in our room, polishing his bass skills. The practice paid off, but that he'd needed it at all unsettled Joe. Tensions were building. One day, Billy lashed out at his wardrobe assistant, an unassuming young man I gathered was also a special friend. The poor guy just stood there while Billy yelled at him over a minor infraction—a wrinkled shirt or missing button, something like that. Rick, Jim, and I were hanging out on his couch at the time. None of us spoke as we casually strolled from the room.

Joe said the guys needed to blow off steam—like the Herbs had, with their acid-fueled food fight. He and Levon devised a scheme, faking a feud that escalated throughout the day and culminated in a physical "brawl" backstage. They really threw themselves into it, with Levon wielding a fake knife and shattering a prop bottle over Joe's head. Everyone was in on it except David Fishof, who was beside himself, trying to break the men up and remind them of their friendship. When the prank was revealed, David's jaw dropped to his chest. Band and crew dissolved in hysterics. Laughter erupted over and over that night as the story was retold to everyone who'd missed it.

❋❋❋

JOE WANTED ME TO come out of my shell and socialize with his friends. "They're your friends now, too," he said. One night, during intermission, he asked me to find John Candy. "He's backstage, but I can't find him. Tell him I want to hang out after the show. Don't let him leave, no matter what."

"You want me to put John Candy in a headlock?"

"Tell him you're my lady," Joe said, running back onstage. "Just do it, trust me."

I found John between two curtain panels at side stage, tapping his feet and bobbing his head. I touched his shoulder, and he turned with strained resignation. The toe tapping ceased.

"Sorry to bother you," I shouted, leaning in and feeling him tense up. *This is going well*, I thought, plowing ahead. "Uh…see, I'm Joe Walsh's girlfriend and he said to introduce my—"

"Hey! You're Joe's lady?" John exclaimed.

"Yeah, I'm sorry to bother—"

He cut me off with a bear hug. "I'm so happy to meet you! Joe's one of my dearest friends—*I love that guy!*" John insisted I stay and share his curtain spot for the whole show, and he even scored us a couple of beers (I have no idea where from). On the bus later, we laughed as the band members one-upped each other with Little Richard anecdotes (which at least half of them happened to have). At the hotel, we gathered in Levon and Sandy's room, where John did a hilarious improv bit on the insanity of touring. Jim Keltner videotaped it.

Few on tour had it easier than me. "My heaviest lifting is the phone to call room service."

"Don't underestimate room service," Jim quipped.

"It is a marvelous concept, I agree."

Jim nodded. "A weirdly wonderful thing."

"Right up there with in-room massage therapy."

Levon balked. "Nope, not for me."

"You don't get massaged, Levon?" I was stunned. "Why not?"

Sandy answered for him. With a good-natured eye-roll, she explained that to her backwoods Arkansas husband, the concept of bodywork didn't fly. It just sounded *wrong.*

"No way something weird ain't happening there," Levon muttered, confirming her statement.

I laughed, though more at her ribbing than his paranoia. I would've loved to roll my eyes at Joe once in a while. Lord knows I'd have been justified. Like that time he fashioned a pair of tinfoil goggles and Viking helmet, then donned a reflective silver cape, and paraded the ensemble onstage. But his clownish image wasn't my business, whether he shed it or fed that beast for life. I had firm opinions on a variety of topics, most of which I kept to myself.

I observed people. I studied and analyzed them, then found a way to fit myself into their perceptions of reality. Drugs and alcohol loosened my tongue, but I rarely voiced dissent or challenged anyone. That's just how I was raised. At home, church, and school, a sharp intellect was for passing tests and getting good grades. Book smarts were fine, but critical thinking was the road to hell. The nuns kept us in check with a variety of shame tactics and unpredictable bouts of rage. At home, my mom did the same. Question authority? Yeah, right. Not out loud, anyway. Things I cared about—things that mattered, like politics, religion, and social constructs—weren't up for debate. I had no idea how to do what Sandy had done, but I was dying to learn.

The next day, our group gathered in the lobby awaiting transportation when Howard Stern's name came up in conversation. A debate ensued as to whether the shock jock was a jerk or just a showman. I spoke up, figuring my personal experience applied. Voting the latter, I relayed our disastrous on-air interview, followed by Howard's recent on-air flattery.

Suddenly Joe whirled on me. *"He was talking about Lisa."*

Everyone went silent. Joe didn't seem to care. He glared at me, letting the barb sink in.

One minute he was pushing me to befriend John Candy and Ringo's kids. The next, shaming me for thinking I measured up to his ex. I reacted the way I had as a kid—stone-faced, stuffing down my hurt feelings, and dissociating.

The next time Joe did Howard's show he insisted I come with, but only in my airhead Valley-girl persona. "It's the perfect deflection. Howard will be helpless against it." I didn't think it was a good idea. I agreed with his theory but thought I was too coked-up to pull it off, and I was right. Howard wasn't amused, he was bored. I didn't make Joe proud, I let him down.

###

THE BAND WENT ON to Canada. I flew home and threw myself into work. I missed Joe, but the confidence boost from being in my element was worth it. Two weeks later, we met up in Vegas, like newlyweds, fawning all over each other. From there, on to LA for the final two shows.

Backstage, the Greek Theatre was packed with guests and celebrities, something Joe said was common in LA. The first night, things were hectic and Joe was distracted. I'd invited Vicki and Christine, and barely noticed his inattention. The next night, we purposely didn't bring guests, hoping to enjoy the backstage camaraderie together. Jack Nicholson had other ideas, barging into Joe's dressing room to do bumps, rushing off, then reappearing with Harry Dean Stanton and a handful of fans. Harry and Jack took our chairs as his hangers-on spread out on the floor. Joe watched from the doorway, more amused than anything, as Jack held court. I leaned against a wall, studying Harry and wishing I had the balls to make him return my chair.

I couldn't get used to what passed for etiquette in LA. Before the show, Gary Busey had cornered Joe in the hall, practically shoving me aside in his rush to ask if he could jam with the band. Joe had been firm yet kind—*It's Ringo's gig, man, sorry.* Once Gary was out of earshot, he'd turned to me with a smirk. "Everyone wants to be a rock star," he said. "*Especially* actors." Later that night, I met Alan Rogan, Pete Townshend's right-hand man, who disarmed me with his warmth and wit, not to mention his ability to engage in a *two-way* conversation.

The tour's end was bittersweet, but I was excited to have Joe to myself. In two months' time, we'd head to Japan where proper etiquette was prized and monstering strictly prohibited.

Photo: Clarence Clemons and Kristin Casey

Woman on a Train; Up on a Plane

THE ALL-STARR BAND HAD consumed Joe all summer. We had eight weeks to unwind before Japan, and I expected to spend it shutting out the world, with copious sex and drugs. I was wrong.

First, Rick the Bass Player came down with a mysterious stomach ailment and we spent the weekend at his place, caring for him. Back at the penthouse, the phone and fax were blowing up with band business and other drama, including Dr. John threatening to quit. (He didn't.) Each new development sucked Joe deeper in and pushed me further out. I offered to take messages or man the fax machine, but Joe was juggling chainsaws and said I was throwing off his rhythm. I tried to give him space but there was nowhere to retreat. The office was off limits and the living room was blanketed in faxes and paperwork—floor, sofa, coffee table, everything. There was not one uncluttered space in that sprawling penthouse for a girl to bury her nose in a book.

My sympathy waned. When pouting didn't work, I monstered.

Joe was still in the habit of cutting me off around sunrise. The times we monstered around the clock were his call, never mine. Twenty-four-hour binges were at his discretion, usually due to being in the middle of some roleplay or kink scene he wasn't ready to finish.

That wasn't the case this time. Even when the calls and faxes ceased, Joe continued to shut me out, citing stacks of paperwork and contracts he had to read. Yet he didn't cut off my coke supply or send me to bed. Emboldened, I requested more hog rails and got them. I was being girlish and cheeky. Joe was surly, yet the bumps kept coming. I held my breath for an argument that never came. Instead, he rented a Bentley.

"We're moving to the Bel Age."

I didn't ask questions, just went to pack a bag.

Later he explained that we needed a change of scenery to get our brains back. As logical as that sounded (or at least not illogical) in my case the opposite happened, when a portion of my gray matter evaporated en route to the hotel. It was a surprisingly pleasant experience...for me, that is.

Tackling LA morning traffic, while grinding out on blow, was asking for trouble. I'd learned the hard way that too much noise, motion, and sunlight could trigger a bout of paranoid anxiety. What came over me this time, however, was mental euphoria and hypersexual arousal. I had no idea why or how (though the high-end luxury of that finely crafted automobile didn't hurt), only that it was sublime on every level. Not to Joe, but I couldn't help that. Sorry, babe. *I'm running with this.*

With my long-suffering boyfriend behind the wheel, white-knuckling a jammed-packed Sunset Boulevard, I danced in my seat doing a striptease (literally), for him and anyone who might glance over. No one did—outside the car or in. Joe's eyes never left the road. He fought rush-hour traffic and my nymphomaniac advances all the way to the hotel.

"Pull over, let's fool around."

"No."

"C'mon, it'll be fun—"

"*No*. Just, no!"

I left him alone but continued dancing in my seat. At the Bel Age, Joe retrieved my clothes from the back seat and floorboards, tossed them at me, and stormed into the hotel.

"You're no fun," I shouted, laughing to myself, untangling my bra and getting dressed. The valet guy waited outside, expressionless.

In our room, we immediately crashed out. Joe was up before me—a first—still acting bristly. I still didn't know why. He went to Rick's without me and was gone so long I called to check on him. There was a woman's voice in the background.

"It's no one," Joe said. "A friend from my building. We're watching the game."

"The blonde woman who has a crush on you?"

"Yeah, so?"

"You left me alone in a hotel room all day to spend time with another woman? Really?"

"*Back off*," he snapped. "Don't tell me what to do. It's none of your business who I hang out with."

"Never mind... Forget I said anything. Do whatever you want, Joe." Then I hung up.

❖❖❖

WHENEVER JOE WENT FROM zero to sixty like that, I reacted like a flooded car engine—I both revved up and stalled, at once. Confrontation of any kind sent me straight back to childhood.

Discipline in my home had been verbal, never physical, beyond some half-hearted spankings (that even my six-year-old brain could tell my dad was uncomfortable giving). Dad rarely raised his voice, and when he did his bark had no bite. Mom's tone was different. More bobcat than hound dog, her reprimands drove home what a burden I was—or, at least, that's what it sounded like. Like my behavior was somewhere between tiresome and maddening, my presence unwelcome at best. She had five kids and a lot of individuation to keep in check—what her generation called discipline. I called it something else (silently, in my head) but it was effective nonetheless.

My mother was a child of the fifties, a Daddy's girl and obedient Catholic. Being tidy and correct was integral to her identity. Being devout led to a large family. She envisioned a Norman Rockwell existence. I gave her Pippi Longstocking on acid—a toddler so strong-willed I once screamed myself purple rather than relinquish my favorite (unwieldy) stuffed animal so she could change my diaper. The ensuing meltdown, to hear my mother tell it, was a display of such unrestrained rebellion as to be incomprehensible to her. My eyes rolled back into my head and my lips turned blue. I don't recall the incident, but it sounds like me—someone who'd sooner kill or be killed than release whatever security blanket I'd found as a stand-in for what my mom couldn't give me.

From her perspective, I had a temperamental problem that was her duty to eliminate. From mine, the problem was less about my reactive temperament than *her* rage and depression, which I was reacting *to*. I had a temper, this was true, and also anxiety, shame, and confusion. The more she tried to squelch their expression, the more entrenched those emotions grew. Lacking any other coping mechanisms, I learned to stuff my feelings and dissociate from them. To be honest, I thought I was kind of a genius for figuring out how. Anyway, the bits that leaked out in her presence were nothing compared to what I held in. In that respect, her disciplinary style could be called a success.

I was chastised for falling and scraping my hand, then berated for giving myself subpar first aid. (I'd neglected to dig out the last few pebbles and snip off a lingering wisp of torn flesh.) I was punished for peeing my pants when the neighbor boy forced me to walk to the corner store with him and wouldn't take me to a bathroom or show me the way home. I was reviled for putting my shoes on the wrong feet when Mom was in a hurry to leave for church. If I missed a spot with the Windex, threw a striped blouse in a load of whites (it was half white, after all), or clumsily dropped a roll of Charmin in the toilet bowl as a kid, she'd eviscerate me in a dagger-sharp tone—*What's wrong with you? Can't you do anything right? Why must you make my life so hard?* I tried to do better at reeling in my feelings and clumsiness. One night, she let me join her and Dad in our new swimming pool, after dinner. I don't recall where my siblings were, but I was beside myself at sharing a rare bit of fun with my emotionally elusive mom. I splashed around goofily to get her attention, promptly thwacking her *hard* in the eye. She didn't say a word that time. She didn't have to. I was mortified. I just couldn't do anything right.

On rare occasions, as a little girl, I'd glimpse the truth of it—which one of us was in the wrong. Who was the first to break the terms of the universal mother-daughter contract, and which one of us, on at least one occasion, treated the other the way most people wouldn't treat a dog. On a campout at Lake Mead, I'd needed to go potty, but instead of walking me to a private spot away from our three-family group, she led me to the far side of a rocky slope on the perimeter of our site. There she commanded me to poop on a big flat rock, a few feet from my preteen brother and uncle, fishing with their backs to us. I couldn't do it, of course (my entire intestinal track ceased functioning at the very idea), and begged her not to make me, but she said I had no choice and walked away. I ended up pooping in the lake later on, unable to hold it anymore. One of my aunts read my face and announced to the group I was pooping. I didn't know what to do. I couldn't stop, but everyone was watching. I looked to Mom in desperation and saw her awash in the same shame I was in.

Growing up, I came to understand the onus wasn't on my parents to meet my needs but on me to *need less*. Eventually, I approached all relationships that way, trading cumbersome stuffed animals for adult-styled security blankets: booze, sex, drugs, money, men, adventure, and lust—sometimes, all at once.

❋❋❋

WHEN JOE RETURNED TO the Bel Age, he suggested I go home to "regain perspective." It wasn't bad advice. I went to Sugar's six nights a week, getting drunk on tequila, cash, and attention. I refused to call Joe, and when he called me I didn't rehash things. Within a month, he was begging to see me.

He wanted me in Memphis for Albert King's record release party. "Take the next flight out. Please, honey, I *need* you." When I arrived, his abundant affection all but erased the painful separation. Before I'd had time to unpack, Joe bestowed his most romantic gift yet.

"I had Gary name one of his ducks after you."

"What ducks? Gary who?"

Joe explained. His friend Gary Belz owned the Peabody, the hotel we were in, which was famous for the ducks that lived onsite. They spent their days in the lobby fountain and nights in a custom rooftop home. Guests gathered every evening to witness their march from the lobby fountain, down a red carpet, to the elevator. "I had Gary name one Kristin," Joe said.

"Nuh-uh!"

"Uh-huh! Go downstairs and ask."

I did. "Why, yes, we did just name a duck Kristin," the concierge said. "By chance, was that in honor of you?"

"Yes," I said, blushing a little. I was about to walk away when something occurred to me. "So, tell me...how many names do each of these ducks have, anyway?"

The concierge chuckled. "Well...you know. Most have more than one."

"Ah," I said, and we shared a laugh. "Okay, I see how it is." The concierge winked and I headed back upstairs. In truth, I didn't care if my duck had ten names. It was still incredibly romantic.

❊❊❊

ALBERT KING'S PARTY WAS an invitation-only gig, for friends and family mostly. Joe went early to visit with the guest of honor. I arrived later with Kevin Allison, with whom I'd developed a mutual friendly tolerance. When Kevin introduced me as "Joe's lady," a young male employee rushed me to a front-row table. I'd have preferred to sit in back but there were no seats left.

I was no stranger to dive bars, yet I'd never blended in worse than that night at Club Unity. At Antone's, it wasn't uncommon to see Albert King–level greats playing any night of the week. It was less common (in fact, probably unheard of in Central Austin) to be the sole white patron surrounded by big, beautiful divas decked out in sparkling diamonds, sequins, lamé, and poufy wigs. I felt like a trespasser, like I didn't have a right to be there. I decided to quit worrying about it and try to be inconspicuous. Joe sent word he'd be sitting in with Albert and would see me after the show. I sent word back: I was having a fine time.

The place was jumping and drinks were flowing, with lively conversation at every table but mine. "That's a beautiful ring," I remarked to the woman on my left, whose ruby, sapphire, and emerald cluster covered half her middle finger. Her response was an equally impressive combo of gems: straightened spine, lowered chin, and slow, subtle side-eye. I stared ahead, committing to memory her spot-on body language (for the next time I needed to intimidate someone).

When Albert took stage, the room was united in thrall. When Joe stepped out to join him—as corny as it sounds—I fell in love all over again.

❋❋❋

HE WANTED TO TAKE Amtrak back to LA. Trains were relaxing and sleeper cars sexy, he said, which sounded great, until he invited a third wheel. Kip was a young, friendly, unassuming Yuppie who reminded me of Alex P. Keaton from *Family Ties*, minus the grating personality. I told Joe I didn't mind, because how could I say no? We'd been at our best in Memphis—loving, carefree, and in sync. After Joe's godlike performance at Club Unity, as far as I was concerned, he was the sexiest man alive. I got a duck named after me; I questioned nothing.

And Joe was right about train travel. The gentle vibration, whizzing along the rails, felt simultaneously futuristic and old-fashioned. Unfortunately, its erotic potential was stymied by Kip. Well, that's how I saw it, but Joe had different ideas. In the bar car, he encouraged us to socialize, in a weirdly pointed way. *Just ignore me and get to know each other*. Kip and I complied, and since we were close in age, our conversation touched on college and high school experiences. Joe joked that we made him feel old. Later, in our sleeper car, he reintroduced the theme as a segue to his real agenda.

Instead of giving Kip the smaller bunk, Joe suggested he share the double bed with me. I stared, dumbfounded, as he explained: "I'm old and can barely keep up with her, but I want her to be satisfied. I thought you could ring her bell tonight while I conserve my energy."

Ring my bell? *Jesus fucking Christ.*

Kip was even more surprised than I was, but also more agreeable. *Sounds fun, I'm game*—like we'd been paired up in a church picnic's three-legged race.

I felt too on-the-spot to gauge my feelings, much less articulate them. Back in Sydney, I'd been gung-ho about Trevor, but we'd discussed the idea beforehand. Joe probably thought springing Kip on me would be erotic. It was the furthest thing from it, yet I seemed incapable of saying that. I also feared declining would make me a prude or a buzzkill. I'd gone cold, there was not a drop of arousal in me, and yet it didn't seem like a valid reason to turn him down. Kip and Trevor were attractive men, with whom I had no real chemistry. *Is that my fault? It must be.* It was all so confusing. I only knew I needed to be sexually adventurous. I couldn't risk boring my boyfriend, couldn't risk being a B student. When it came to sex, an A-minus felt like an F to me. If that meant doing after-hours extra credit, so be it.

I parroted Kip: *Sure, I'm in.* It was easier than breaking rank. If Joe called all the shots then whatever went wrong was his fault, whereas taking a stand would make *me* accountable. Acting on blind faith was a remnant of my upbringing. *Ignore your instincts. Defer to authority and paradise awaits.* That night, paradise was an awkward, unsexy event that flattened all the magic we'd built up in Memphis.

❋❋❋

I FLEW TO AUSTIN to pack for Japan. While I was there, Abe's band played Antone's again. We hadn't seen each other since that one night, more than a year earlier, but had stayed in touch through postcards from our individual travels. I considered Abe a friend and was a huge fan of his band. I'd just turned twenty-two, and Joe sent a dozen long-stemmed roses with a card that read simply:

I love you. Twenty-four hours later, it took everything I had to peel my body off Abe's and slam the brakes on our make-out session.

We'd connected like magnets after the show, stepping outside to catch up and gravitating to a discreet stairwell across the parking lot. There, I'd been overcome with equal parts lust and guilt, pulling him to me, then pushing him away, more indecisive than I'd ever been. I ravaged and refused him, over and over again, that sweet, sexy, incredibly tolerant, and increasingly confused man. Our chemistry was as powerful as ever. This thing with Abe felt like the fulfillment of my deepest longing—the gnawing, aching, vacuous hunger that never, ever left me. I'd fed it booze, drugs, and sex throughout my teens. But I was an adult now, a woman in love with a good—no, *incredible*—man, and yet still inexplicably half empty. The passion Abe stirred in me was the promise of satiety, albeit with a bitter aftertaste.

I'd never felt so torn, chest to chest and all the rest, backed against a wall, overcome and overwhelmed: *Don't think—just feel and breathe.* We inhaled each other, groping, gripping, grinding as I stopped and restarted a dozen times, and Abe let me, turning over the reins—*whatever you need, whatever you need.*

I needed to stop. We did, at the last possible second, before crossing that final boundary, the one specific act from which we could not turn back—as if penetration alone qualifies as cheating. I'd already gone too far, I told myself, but at least I hadn't done that.

"I can't do this to him," I said, catching my breath, feeling like an ass. *I couldn't take it if he did it to me,* is what I thought. "I love him too much," is what I said.

Abe said he understood. I was glad one of us did.

❋❋❋

THE FLIGHT FROM LA to Tokyo was over eleven hours long. One hour in, Joe offered me a bump. It was the first I ever turned down. Odder still was his insistence. Turned out, he had a lot on him—enough to fly to Japan and back without the aid of a jet.

"Well, that's a switch."

"What?" he replied, so plainly bewildered I didn't know whether to cry or laugh. It was like having my chosen lottery numbers hit the one time I forgot to buy a ticket.

"Listen," I whispered. "At this moment, you and I are stuck inside an airbus, miles above the ocean, with a hundred strangers. Even if we could snort that much blow in ten hours, *why?*" But the role reversal was too tantalizing to waste. Being pestered for my attention was more addictive than cocaine. We spent the next few hours talking in whispers, writing "Dear *Penthouse*" letters, and swapping legal pads to pen sequels for each other. We played rummy to five hundred points, and made a list of hotel aliases. ("Mr. Edd" was put to immediate use in Japan.) But with seven hours left to kill, I reached for my book and Joe headed downstairs to wander the aisles of coach class.

Two hours later I found him, mid-row, center section, talking with a lanky, impassive man in his thirties. Pete was an oilrig worker from Houston about to spend six months at sea. We chatted about life in Texas and commiserated over long-distance relationships. He reminded me of a young Sam Shepard.

"Six months is a long time," Joe said, and I agreed. Pete shrugged. *It is what it is.* Joe gave me a look. "We should help him out, don't you think?"

I knew exactly what he meant, and this time was not entirely opposed. Not that I was horny—I wasn't. The combo of cocaine and public transit had had a definite cold-shower effect. But I was bored, and the logistics of Joe's plan were intriguing.

The timing was ideal. Dinner service had been collected, the overhead lights dimmed. It was a half-full flight, most passengers asleep behind their eye masks. The crew was curtained off, oblivious to our threesome entering the lavatory one at a time. Within seconds, we'd struck the perfect configuration (one man standing, one sitting, with a reversed cowgirl in between them), but once the puzzle pieces were aligned (and adjoined), the novelty wore off. The men felt the same, and we broke apart laughing, shushing each other before slinking out, back to our seats.

We touched down in Tokyo with half a gram left over. Against Joe's advice, I tucked the vial inside me, corked with a tampon. Going through customs, I felt sick with anxiety—cocaine-induced on every level. At the hotel, I snorted the last of it because Joe didn't want any. He fell asleep while I fidgeted next to him for hours, hating myself.

❀❀❀

THE NEXT DAY WAS no fun for either of us. I'd gotten almost no sleep. We were both starving, but there was no room service. Or air-conditioning. Our first meal was at the rehearsal venue: stale chips, M&Ms, and eggs (hotplate provided). After rehearsal, we returned to the hotel with plans to attack the minibar, except neither of us had a key. The front desk apologized—every time I called—yet never sent anyone to open it. What the hotel *did* have were spiders, huge ones. Considering the size of everything else in Japan, it was almost funny.

Everything from bathtubs to bus seats were miniaturized. To others, they were downright microscopic. Clarence "the Big Man" Clemmons, wasn't pleased. One day he returned from shoe shopping empty-handed. "They laughed at me, Kristi," he said, morosely. "They took one look at my feet and laughed at me."

By day three, Joe was sick with fatigue, worsened by an unrelenting heat wave. He withdrew completely, leaving me isolated and homesick. I agreed with Clarence—Japan was not a good fit. The cultural decorum rubbed me the wrong way, mostly because I thought it sucked the life out of concerts. I quit attending them mid-tour, after one crowd's bizarre nonreaction to Nils Lofgren leaping into their midst while *playing guitar with his teeth*.

As the least traveled person in our group, I thought I might be cynical. "I'm literally complaining about excessive etiquette," I remarked to one of the roadies.

"Don't let them fool you," he said. "No one likes Americans here. It's their tradition to fake it. When you think about it, it's like they're lying to our faces."

It was a fair point. I disliked not knowing where I stood with people. I was so insecure, I needed reassurance from strangers that my presence was welcome, that I was liked or at least interesting. One day, Sandy told me, "You get more attention in Japan than Ringo."

Actually, it was my hair, Levon explained. "The men here stare at it everywhere we go—sidewalks, trains, elevators. They wait until you walk by or look the other way before they gape, totally fascinated." That's when I decided I liked Japan.

When Joe's energy picked up, we went sightseeing, to castles, temples, and ground zero. We went to hotel bars with Kevin Buell and Joseph, Billy Preston's new assistant, but kept our drinking to a minimum. One night, I almost overdid it. We were out to dinner with a few of the guys and I caught myself flirting with Rick Danko. Joe didn't notice (neither did Rick, funny enough), but I put down my sake for the night. I wasn't trying to bed Danko. It wasn't *his* attention I was after.

I'd dropped fall semester classes to go to Japan and was starting to regret it, but then suddenly Joe became attentive again. The band had a day off and he wanted to go shopping.

"A toy store? Seriously?"

"It's six stories tall. You'll love it!"

"It's like you don't know me at all." But he did, since I followed him everywhere.

Joe's mood was so improved he got a scolding from the cab driver—his second since arriving in Japan. It appeared the second cabbie didn't appreciate Joe's spastic, backseat-driver behavior any more than our first cabbie appreciated the unintelligible nonsense he shouted at random (extremely startled) pedestrians.

After we left the toy store (packed with the calmest shoppers ever), Joe went to Sony for some newfangled type of camera. He used it to shoot everything within view at the restaurant where we had dinner—his steak, my fish, our waiter, Rick Danko, the table centerpiece, and random stuff under the tablecloth—until I told him to stop wasting film on my shoes and kneecaps. Back in our room, Rick hooked Joe's camera to the TV and a slide show appeared on the screen. "Oh," I gasped, delighted by a stream of crisp, colorful images taken minutes earlier... including one straight up my skirt.

"Joseph!"

Rick burst out laughing as Joe scrambled to advance the frame. "Sorry, honey. I should've explained how these work." He paused. "And asked if you were wearing panties."

He doted on me for the rest of the tour. After playing the Budokan, we had dinner with Mr. Udo, Japan's biggest promoter. He'd reserved an entire teppanyaki restaurant, which served the best meal I'd had all tour, maybe ever. We had drinks with an English promoter that, Joe said, "held the keys to Europe," then ditched him to watch *The Witches of Eastwick* together in bed. At the Hard Rock, Joe slapped down his AmEx card in the gift shop. "Two of everything, please." We spent our final night in the hotel bar with the crew, drinking Scorpions, our official Japan drink (for reasons I don't remember).

In the lobby awaiting airport transport, Joe suggested I go spend whatever coins I had on me—over $200 worth—which couldn't be exchanged like paper currency. The hotel boutiques carried little at that price point, but I got lucky and found a darling leather coin purse imprinted with an eerie circus scene. Spotting Barb across the lobby, I went to show her, then caught sight of her new three-piece luggage set *in the exact same circus design*. I tucked the new pouch away, my good taste confirmed.

❖❖❖

BACK IN LA, WE went straight to Rick the Bass Player's house. We did our first hog rails since flying overseas, and then Joe visited with his daughter. I watched TV, where on every channel the Berlin Wall fell, over and over. I was happy to give Joe and Lucy a wide berth. As much as I craved his attention, I couldn't imagine how much she might.

My parents had not divorced or traveled much. Dad worked long hours, but at the end of the day, he loved being with his kids. Mom worked long hours, often on call, which meant she couldn't even relax on days off. As a kid, I had no concept of her life outside motherhood. I only knew my mom didn't like the part she spent around me. I thought she hated me. Being an analytical kid with zero analytical skills, trying to understand her psychology, knowing nothing about the human psyche, well...it was like mapping the universe through opera glasses. Basically, whenever I sensed tension or conflict, I assumed it was my fault.

I appreciated everything my mother did for the family. Every holiday was done to the hilt. Easter dresses were sewn from scratch with fabrics chosen to match each child's personality. No Halloween costume was too complicated to ask of her. My ruffled gingham bedding with matching curtains had sprouted from her sewing machine in the corner in our cramped laundry room. Her hands were never idle, and she made sure her kids' weren't, either.

I was never at a loss for books, games, and crafts of all kinds. She broke her back to ensure I had a structured, active life. If my mother ever forgot to pack a variety of sunscreen and the favorite foods of seven individuals for a week of outdoor camping, I never knew it. I was fair-skinned, and sunburns were serious business. But demanding I relieve my bowels, semi-exposed at a large family gathering, taught me my body didn't belong to me. The damage was internalized. A sunburn was on the surface, where anyone might see, and where it might reflect on the quality of her mothering to teachers, neighbors, and relatives.

I craved softness and affection, big and small signs of her approval. I wanted to be appreciated and cherished. At three, I got stage fright during a mother-daughter fashion show. I froze on the runway, my panic compounded by the knowledge I was disappointing her on a day she'd been nicer than ever. She kept us physically protected, busy, and organized. Softness wasn't on the list. She didn't have it in her, not enough for five kids and Dad, plus all those hospital patients. If there was one thing I *had* deduced about her, it was that she resented being asked. She felt she had given me everything any offspring should need, so I could take my demands for nurturance to my room until I could be less of a selfish brat.

I exhausted her. She lost her temper with me and I started losing mine with her. Had she the skills to manage fear and resentment, she'd have surely passed them down. My father once joked that I "came out screaming and haven't stopped since." He seemed to find that endearing, but Mom never did. Joe could be just like her: moody, demanding, blamey, ragey, and impossible to figure out. Other times, he was my dad all over—playful, joyful, delighted by me, and yet nobody's savior. A provider, not a protector, Dad never seemed to notice I was hurting. When Joe ignored me in Japan, I felt ten years old again. I'd been born into a large family—invited, as it were—then shamed for exceeding my allotment of resources. I never knew how much I was allowed to want—not as a child, and not as an adult.

Joe was spread thin. I got more attention than his *only kid* and still it wasn't enough. Though Joe said I was the oldest twenty-year-old he'd ever met, in some ways I was immature. To say Joe was youthful at forty was an understatement, but he could feel weary and ancient, too. Still, our biggest problem was coke. I wasn't using every day (yet), but once I started I couldn't stop. Joe could moderate, but without *some* blow every day he barely functioned. It didn't take a genius to figure out why he got sick every time we left the country. He needed a strong woman to inspire him. I needed constant love and affection. We gave each other feast or famine.

Joe came with me to Austin, needing the peace and quiet. We saw my friends, watched TV, and went to bed early. One day, he announced that he had an interview at UT for a music department teaching gig. I waited in the car, fantasizing about campus life—the film student and music teacher meeting for lunch in the student union. On the way home, I asked how it went.

"They asked me to submit a résumé," he said, then fell silent.

The next day, Paul McCartney invited us to his concert at the Forum. We caught a flight to LA. Joe never mentioned teaching again.

❋❋❋

OUR SECOND CHRISTMAS TOGETHER, he agreed to spend a day with my relatives if I spent Christmas Eve with his friends. Isaac Tigrett had cofounded the Hard Rock Cafe chain. His wife Maureen was Ringo's ex (and mother to their three kids). She and Isaac were living on the top floor of the Stoneleigh, in Dallas, where Isaac was building a new Hard Rock.

I'd seen Maureen in the audience on Ringo's tour. We hadn't met but she'd been impossible to miss, like a sparkling diamond in a sea of dull pencil erasers. Joe described Isaac in similar terms. I asked him what he meant. "You'll get it when you meet him, but for starters, I won't have to point him out. He'll zero in on you. He's freaky like that."

Minutes later, at baggage claim, my gaze was drawn across the room to a brown-haired man who turned and fixed his bright blue eyes directly on me—Isaac. He was tall, broad-shouldered, and handsome, with high cheekbones and a trim beard. He had charisma—Paul Newman meets Orson Welles with a pinch of Jesus thrown in. His home was just as warm, colorful, and richly textured. His wife, energetic and birdlike. Maureen made us welcome, despite her apparent surprise to hear we'd be staying the night. Her daughter Lee joined us for dinner, and Maureen even produced Christmas gifts for us, her unexpected guests. Later, in our room, I changed into a short robe just as Isaac dropped by. I rushed to redress, but Joe said not to bother. "It's just Isaac."

We sat on opposite beds—the men on one and me on the other, holding a pillow to my chest. Isaac's eyes were penetrating, but he was buzzed and seemingly unaware of his intensity. Maureen, however, did notice, having come in search of her husband before bed. That's when I realized my robe was, in fact, inappropriate—though not from anything she said. She was much too gracious for that, bidding us good night as Isaac followed without being asked. It left quite an impression—that of an unfazed, empowered woman, fully aware of her worth.

To be Treated

We celebrated New Year's Eve at our favorite restaurant, La Toque. It was my first time doing up the holiday in style and Joe encouraged me to go all out. "Be a girl," he quipped, handing me a small wad of hundreds. "Find something that makes you feel beautiful."

I did. A form-fitting spaghetti-strap cocktail dress covered in delicate beading and gold sequins. I paired it with dainty, dangly earrings and my hair in a loose upsweep, Joe's favorite style. I emerged from the bathroom shimmering in gold from head to toe.

"You look like a million bucks," he beamed. "Literally." And I didn't disagree.

The dress was the second most glamorous I'd ever owned. The first—acquired two years earlier—had been in my possession a mere twelve hours. It was a gift from a Sugar's regular, who'd whisked me away from the club to Vegas for an all-night gambling bent. His sole intent: to blow as much money as possible before the soon-to-be ex-wife got it. We caught the first flight out, then kicked off his spending spree at a Caesars Palace boutique. He thought I needed something more suitable for high-dollar tables than the cotton stretch mini I'd worn to work. Minutes later, I was the dubious owner of a $1,000 black satin, crystal-encrusted, plunging-to-the-navel Halston gown. It was an absolute stunner, in which I felt fairly ridiculous, lacking the hips, height, bosom, and Bond Girl bravado to pull it off. I did my best, sitting stiffly next to him in the role I'd signed up for—feigning interest in the ups and downs of another woman's childish, vindictive husband—dreaming of the day I'd get dolled up like that to hang on the arm of a man I loved.

Two years later, there I was. At La Toque, we were seated at a table for eight with Rick the Bass Player and his date. The extra chairs were for a myriad of friends stopping by through the night for champagne toasts and plates of appetizers. Midway through the evening, I noticed Dan Aykroyd on my right. His wife, Donna, was deep in conversation across the table, leaving her husband open as fair game. Danny, as I elected to call him—possibly with his permission, although God only knows, as I was really on a roll by then—proved a most amiable hostage, bombarded with my earnest opinions on the state of an industry in which he'd had huge success (to my zero experience).

"Seriously, Danny, check out the Austin film scene. This fat-cat studio system y'all got out here is just plain obsolete," I insisted. "You got to stay ahead of the curve and get in on the ground floor of the indie scene."

"Is that so?"

"Totally!" I smacked the table. "Hollywood has sold out. There's no artistry anymore, no *depth*…just soulless hacks churning out an assembly line of superficial, formulaic crap." I dropped my chin and pointed at him. "You're too good for them, man."

"That's kind of you to say."

"It's a fact!" I declared, smacking the table again. I lowered my voice to a loud whisper. "Listen, Danny, Austin is where it's at. Remember that—*Austin*."

"Austin, you say?"

"Austin!"

"Okay, then… I'll look into it."

"You heard it here first." To be sure, I repeated myself a few times, and Danny's gaze never wavered. He seemed bemused, but it was hard to say. Our table was on its tenth or twelfth bottle by then. "You're kind to indulge me," I said, patting his hand, signaling his release. "My apologies…champagne makes me subversive."

He laughed. "Nothing wrong with that."

I decided to force down some ravioli before launching my next antiestablishment coup. Two bites later, Bob Dylan walked in. He was with his producer Debbie Gold, a savvy East Coast chick I'd recently met at Rick's and been too intimidated to talk to. Debbie pulled up a chair straightaway while Bob cast furtive looks around the room. Other diners in our section were absorbed in food, drink, and revelry. Bob finally took a seat between Joe and Rick, though not without a few more backward glances. I decided my lecture on Austin's indie-music scene could wait until Mr. Dylan was more receptive.

I knew next to nothing about the reclusive icon, aside from radio hits and the awed tones in which Joe's generation spoke of him. What I noticed was a vast chasm between Bob's reservedness and the easy receptivity of my good friend and comrade, Danny. If it weren't for alcohol and cocaine, I'd be closer to Bob's side of it, myself. I had always wanted to be vivacious. At best, the world overwhelmed introverts; at worst, it dismissed us. Coke and booze helped me bypass all that. They leveled the playing field.

As midnight approached, the wait staff corralled us outside to count down 1989. Amid plastic horns, drunken cheers, and passing car honks, Joe wrapped me in his arms for a long, tender kiss, with a dip. When the crowd broke into "Auld Lang Syne," he scooped Bob between us and linked our arms so we'd all three sway in unison. Soon, I felt Bob relax. I glanced over and he smiled, then joined in the last few lines of song.

I wasn't a superstitious person, but if there was truth to the notion that New Year's Eve celebrations set a tone for the coming year, it would seem in 1990 I'd have nothing to fear.

❀❀❀

BY NOW JOE'S WORLD was far more compelling to me than school, and I dropped out once again. College would always be there, I reasoned, but Joe might not. I'd be a fool not to grab every chance to be with him. He felt the same and flew me out whenever he could. When apart, he called daily, one night from Wisconsin at 3:00 a.m.

"Hey, babe," I said, rubbing my eyes. "What's up?"

"I'm calling to ask for your hand in marriage."

I had not seen that coming. "*What*? Wait, I mean, yes. Yes!" We had a good laugh, then I was serious. "My hand is absolutely yours, the very moment you say the word."

"Okay, just...someday, you know." He stammered, nervous all of a sudden. "We'll talk about it again...down the road."

I was getting used to that side of him, the impulsive leaps and sudden backtracks. That he'd asked was all that mattered. "Joseph, my answer has been yes since the day we met. If you don't ask again for twenty years, it will be yes then, too."

"Glad we got that settled," he said, sounding relieved. Then, "There is one other thing."

"Name it."

"I want a son."

Gulp.

"No need to answer *that* yet," he laughed. "Just keep it in mind."

As if I could help it. I lay awake long afterward, thrilled to be considered marriage material and stupefied he thought me remotely parental. I wished to fulfill Joe's every need, but the only family portrait of us I could see was me and baby center frame, with a blurry, unfocused Joe in the background. I'd seen stripper friends' relationships crumble after a kid. Those who didn't split up were exhausted, sexless, and perpetually on edge. My own mother had made it look like a miserable job. Why on earth would I subject myself to that?

Joe scoffed at my concerns, citing many happy freewheeling friends who were married with kids. To prove it, he took me to the Hells Angels clubhouse in Manhattan's East Village. Though it was off limits to outsiders, Joe had an open invitation. He said the New York chapter were true friends and "good people." I wouldn't know. Hells Angels were not exactly accessible. Joe's friends Butch and Joan lived in the six-story apartment building above the biker gang's headquarters, with their son who was maybe eight or ten. They were a nice enough couple, if politely reserved and disinclined to anything resembling conversation. Of the other six or eight bikers hanging out that day, I only met Eddie, the chapter president, and he barely said a word to me.

For the rest of the night, Joe was the center of attention, literally surrounded shooting pool on a table he'd gifted the biker club himself, years earlier. I was not offered a turn or a seat to observe, instead being slowly nudged into the next room. I took a seat on the U-shaped sofa where three bikers passed a joint that I declined every time it came around. When their urging took on a sour note, I took a short, quick toke. *Go along to get along,* I thought. *No harm done.*

I was wrong.

In no time, I was disoriented, spacey, and addled in a way pot had never made me. I hightailed it to Joe, bumping into furniture all the way.

"Hey, babe...you okay?"

"I don't think so," I whisper-croaked.

Joe alerted Butch who immediately took me to his apartment, practically carrying me upstairs, while Joan secured their dogs behind a flimsy plastic barrier. I lay on the couch with one eye on them, but they curled up on the linoleum, as uninterested in me as I was them. When equilibrium returned, I found Joe and Butch downstairs watching TV. Underdog Buster Douglas had just knocked out Mike Tyson, the previously undefeated world champion.

***

IN MARCH, WE HIT the road, starting with four sold-out gigs in Ohio. Despite snowy conditions, the bus was warm and cozy for me and the nine men inside: band, crew, and Joe's opening act, Jack Tempchin.

By now, just about everyone in Joe's circle had conveyed approval of our union, the lone holdout being Chad, his drummer. Over eighteen months, I'd come to know Chad as thoughtful and even-keeled. He could take as long as he wanted. Meanwhile, Jack and I formed a playful bond. His glass-half-full attitude was infectious and offset my nagging awareness that Chad's reticence was not unfounded.

Joe wanted to move in together but hadn't set a date. I had to get my coke use under control, he said. (Whether he planned to himself was not a topic I felt entitled to broach.) I agreed I must do better and cobbled together periods of restraint, each sabotaged by a binge I never saw coming. In Ohio, I did well and Joe was at my side every minute not onstage—once, even then. In Detroit, he yanked me from my perch atop an equipment case, to the mic, where I stood spotlit and in shock, a smoldering cigarillo awkwardly at my side.

Joe grinned. "I want you to meet my girlfriend," he said, to a smattering of applause. "Is it any wonder I play so good? Just look at her!" I covered my beet-red face as the crowd exploded. Later, Chad pulled me aside to say he was glad I was with Joe. "It really does seem like you're good for him." I told him I hoped to be half as good for Joe as he'd been for me.

In mid-March I went home for a few days, then rejoined the tour in New York. As I entered Joe's room, he grabbed my hands and pulled me toward him. "I missed you so much," he said in a tumbling rush. "I've decided I'm ready to live together on a trial basis." He rattled on without pause, going so far as to suggest a fall wedding in Europe (where he had tentative tour plans). I smiled and nodded. For no reason I could fathom, the moment felt wholly unreal.

Joe was the romantic, and I, the practical one. While the concept of soul mates was real enough to me, the realities of commitment were alien. Joe was the marrying kind—he'd done it three times—whereas my longest previous bond had lasted four months. I sometimes inquired into Joe's breakup history, in an attempt, I suppose, to bolster our immunity. Asked about his most recent divorce, he said they'd argued about Christmas decorations, specifically the foil condom packages he'd hung on the tree in lieu of traditional ornaments. Jody hadn't seen the humor and they'd divorced soon afterward. Obviously, there was more to it, but my takeaway was clear.

Don't expect him to grow up. Don't try to curb his behavior or keep up with it. Be on his schedule and wavelength naturally. Taper off cocaine, yet remain high-energy. Be responsible, empowered, and strong about drugs, yet submissive sexually. Neither buzzkill nor cokehead should I be, just toeing the line in between. Oh, and also have a baby, please.

❀❀❀

AROUND THAT TIME, SMOKEY Wendell became Joe's new tour manager. They'd worked together briefly in the seventies before Smokey was hired by John Belushi. (Tasked with keeping the comic off drugs, Smokey by all accounts did, quitting shortly before the night of John's fatal overdose.)

Joe said Smokey had been in the Secret Service for ten years. He placed full trust in him, so I tacked mine on, too. Smokey seemed capable, fearless, and smart—even smarter than he let on, I thought. He was pleasant to be around and easy on the eyes— tall and strong with olive skin and short, black, silver-threaded hair. His softly handsome features and jovial demeanor belied a smoldering intensity—another asset, I figured.

Smokey had more on his plate than tour managing. The drug situation, for starters. We crossed many state lines, and some by the skin of Joe's teeth (i.e., Hawaii), and needed someone on our side who was cunning and savvy. Smokey was also privy to the private aspects of our relationship—there was no way around that fact. My presence on the road affected Joe's work and if we took a negative turn, Smokey dealt with the fallout. He had to know when to step in, when to butt out, and how to enforce peace all around. He had his work cut out for him. Sometime mid-tour, Joe stopped talking marriage and cohabitation and started stirring up shit, picking fights and pointless arguments. I'd finally been embraced by his inner circle, only to be ostracized by him.

In New England, the band played a brutal schedule of seven shows over five nights. Rick's wrists were killing him, Chad's hands bled, and Joe's vocal chords were shredded. He rose to the occasion for every performance, but offstage he was impossible to be with. The whole band avoided him. One day, he laid into me for no apparent reason in front of Rick and Smokey. I was humiliated and unable to defend myself against his nonsensical accusations. Then he turned and targeted Smokey, accusing him of outlandish things before storming from the room. No one said a word. Smokey riffled through his briefcase and Rick stared at the floor. I waited an hour, then found Joe in our room, calm yet unapologetic. I didn't try to reason with him; I just took advantage of the opportunity for angry sex, which, while not ideal, was at least fun for me. Afterward we fell asleep without a word, facing away from each other.

Another time, in another hotel, Joe sent me to score a little pot from Jack. While I was there, Jack convinced me to smoke some, unaware of what a lightweight I was. At the elevator, I couldn't recall which floor I was on, my room number, or what alias we were under. I tried to return to Jack's but got lost looking for his room, too. I finally thought to have the front desk call Smokey, who returned me to Joe, frazzled yet horny—that's just what pot did to me—which, inexplicably, pissed off Joe and sparked another argument.

The worst, by far, was in Pennsylvania, a battle of wills from zero to Armageddon in two seconds flat. With so much resentment stored up by then, one snarky remark and my fuse was lit.

"How dare you talk to me like that?!" I bellowed.

The blowback was swift. Joe's voice was twice as aggressive as my own, and before I knew it, I'd thrown the TV remote at him. It hadn't come close to hitting him, yet without missing a beat, Joe grabbed a one-liter bottle of vodka and chucked it at me. It hit the wall behind me and shattered on contact, fat chunks of glass embedding deep in the plaster.

"Are you nuts?" I screeched. "Seriously, are you fucking mental or what?"

A screaming match ensued until I couldn't take any more. I tried to leave, but Joe blocked my escape, which freaked me out and made me cry. This caused him to bellow louder, right up in my face. Frantic, I grabbed the nearest thing (a glass of red wine) and doused him with it. *"You're trying to drive me to the edge and I'm not going to let you!"*

We finally petered out, but I kept my distance for days, fearing the position I'd put myself in. Joe's love could feel healing and euphoric, like a premium narcotic. But also toxic and explosive, it could send me into a tailspin. I'd been there as a kid and I couldn't take it again—expecting healthy, safe, reliable love from someone who was incapable of it.

I racked my brain for the cause of Joe's anger. Two nights earlier, Gene Simmons had brazenly flirted with me despite Joe's presence. He'd kissed my hand like he was savoring a pork rib, and though Joe hadn't reacted then, he *had* just launched an Absolut bottle rocket at my head. The incidents may've been unrelated—I was done second-guessing him—but when I finally gave him a chance to explain, he made even less sense.

"Blowouts are to be expected in a relationship. They can be healthy, even necessary."

I was too tired to argue or continue avoiding him (no easy feat on a tour bus, that). Sensing that I was ready to reconcile, he followed me around all day, professing his undying love. When he asked if I would meet his parents, that was it—he won me back.

First, we had a business dinner to attend. Having grown more comfortable around industry big shots, when one of them cracked a sexist joke at my expense, I ignored it. Later, the same man called our room at the Plaza and invited himself over "to party." Joe was out of earshot, but David Fishof happened to be over, so I covered the receiver and relayed the situation. David took the phone from my hand and hung it up without a word. That minor gesture meant so much, he may as well have slayed me a dragon.

I'd been taking care of myself since my teens, and not all that well, quite frankly. Despite Joe's unpredictable temper, I felt protected in his world. Smokey helping me back to my room and Jack's purposeful positive attitude…these things were a big deal to me. Giving them up would defy my every good instinct.

That night, Joe and I monstered, soothing our recent wounds with an all-night dopamine surge. I crashed at 5:00 a.m. and awoke twelve hours later, half panicked about meeting his parents. But George and Helen couldn't have been sweeter, and after dinner and a Broadway show, we put them in a cab and I turned to Joe. "I think it went well, don't you?"

"They really liked you," he said, emphatic.

After the tour, we recuperated in Austin, renting movies and going hot-air ballooning. Joe went shopping and returned with matching "pre-engagement" bracelets. *That's not a real thing,* I said, but I loved them anyway. He had a hernia operation scheduled in Minnesota. "Come with me, and when I'm healed we'll go apartment hunting in New Jersey."

"Whatever you say, babe." We were moving in together... I didn't much care which city.

✿✿✿

A PRE-SURGERY CHECKUP AT the Mayo Clinic turned up an "inconclusive" spot on Joe's lung. They promised to call with results the next day. Get some sleep, they said. Try not to worry.

Joe was a two-pack-a-day smoker. I smoked just as much. My grandfather—also a smoker named Joseph—had died in his fifties of lung cancer. His death had caused my devout grandmother to question her faith for the first time ever. I eschewed religion entirely, but when Joe asked me to pray with him, I did without hesitation. He also made me promise that if he had cancer, I'd get pregnant right away.

"My son and you will be well taken care of—count on it."

"I'm sure we will," I said.

The spot turned out to be a calcium deposit. Joe said I was off the hook "for now" and I laughed harder than his little joke deserved—*whew*.

We had time before surgery for a few days in LA, where Joe went cold and distant. I had *just* agreed to be cornered into motherhood, then *bam*—shut out again. Back in Minnesota, another 180. "I'm sorry, I'm a dickhead. Please, forgive me. I'm freaking out about surgery...and stuff." I forgave him because the "stuff" he was referring to was big.

Joe was checking himself into rehab. Smokey had talked him into it.

I was proud of him and excited for us both. As much as I loved cocaine's effect—the joyful confidence I couldn't otherwise access—it was our main source of contention. For that reason, above all, the coke had to go. I was ready and certain I could quit, as long as Joe did.

Joe was skittish the day of surgery. I lit him a final cigarette while he rummaged through his briefcase, retrieving a blank nametag and Sharpie pen. Fifteen minutes later, he entered the hospital with it on his chest: HELLO, MY NAME IS HERNIA IGLESIAS. I thought it was funny, but when no one else laughed, it riled me, and suddenly I didn't want those pasty drones anywhere near my boyfriend's intestines. Joe, for once, was cucumber-calm while I was ready to take a flamethrower to the place. Smokey held me back until it was over, and I rushed to Joe's bedside supremely grateful for the stellar medical care. He was groggy and in pain, but smiled when he saw me. I held his hand for six hours as he faded in and out of sleep.

Two days later, his docile side disappeared upon transfer to the dependency ward. Their "no phone calls" rule was a deal-breaker and he refused to be admitted, yelling at the staff and demanding to see me ASAP. I raced from the hotel to find him packing a bag. "Please, honey, give it a chance." But he remained defiant until a doctor came to talk through his concerns and agreed to let me stay past visiting hours.

Back at the hotel, I was too keyed up to sleep and hung out in Smokey's room instead. For three hours he shared outrageous stories about Nixon and Ford in the White House, as well as wild times with Belushi and stints with Jimmy Buffett and David Crosby.

Smokey was a gifted storyteller, and my steady stream of laughter prevented further obsessing on all the unknowns of Joe's recovery. Still, I was relieved to know Smokey would fly home in the morning. Joe's courageous, soul-baring overhaul was taking place right down the street, making it the worst time to acknowledge the primal longing Smokey stirred in me.

If Smokey felt it, too, he gave no clue. In my head, a stream of images resisted my every attempt to force them out. Nothing good—absolutely *nothing good*, I told myself—could come of repeatedly imagining Smokey's full, soft lips on mine.

⁂

I WOKE EARLY TO meet Joe at a morning lecture on the science of addiction. It was surprisingly interesting, all the patients agreed. Later, Joe told me their group meetings were actually fun, but having me down the street was what gave him strength to stay on.

Four years earlier, I'd kicked meth on my own, but not before reaching out to a trusted UT physician. The doctor had had a heart of gold, yet no experience with addiction. When he offered to check me into a mental health hospital, I bolted. Going through rehab alone was unfathomable. I'd stay in Rochester as long as Joe needed.

The next day was Family Day, and Joe had listed me as his sole family member. At a large group meeting, I heard parents, spouses, and patients detail their painful struggles, but to me it wasn't relatable. Their lives were falling apart in ways ours weren't. Also, all the alcohol talk was frustrating. When would they teach us how to quit cocaine? Later, in a private session with Joe and his counselor, I was told it was my turn to speak.

"Mine? I don't understand…"

"It's important for Joe's recovery to see how his behavior affects loved ones."

Under normal circumstances, confronting Joe would be a
dream come true, but in that context, it felt like kicking a man when
he was down. Dr. Oh assured me it could only help Joe, so I shared
a story I thought not too damning about Christmas with my family.
Joe had gotten drunk and been obnoxious. Everyone had pretended
not to notice, but I'd been embarrassed. My voice cracked and I cut
the story short, but Dr. Oh said I'd done very well.

Joe agreed. "You did tremendous," he said, in the hall, giving
me a long, full-body hug.

The next day Joe was pensive. He'd made a leather belt for me
in art class, which I liked and fit me well. And yet, for a world-class
musician, certified blacksmith, and ham-radio operator, childish
crafts seemed...unhelpful. Joe checked himself out soon after.
I said I understood and that he'd done tremendous. He said he
loved me and that we didn't have to move to New Jersey.

###

I WENT HOME FOR a few days, then met up with Joe in LA. He
greeted me at the penthouse, where fresh air and sunlight
streamed in through windows I hadn't known could be opened.
At ten days sober, he looked better than I'd ever seen him.

That night, on the way home from a David Bowie concert,
we scored a gram and split it. Joe was disappointed in himself but
vowed to try again. *One day at a time*, we said. In the morning,
we had coffee and ran errands. We bought groceries and made
dinner in Joe's kitchen—the first time we'd used it for that.
Afterward, we went to Rick's and did a bunch of blow. Then to
the China Club with Jeff "Skunk" Baxter from Steely Dan and the
Doobie Brothers. Wayne Newton was there and talked Joe into
jamming with him onstage, classic blues and "Rocky Mountain

Way" despite Joe's reluctance to do his old stuff. Later, at home, he played me a new song in progress. It blew me away.

We celebrated our two-year anniversary at L'Ermitage, and then Joe went to Australia. On his way home, he met me in Hawaii. He greeted me at the plane with a purple lei, then took me to a jewelry store, where he slipped an opal-and-diamond ring onto my left ring finger. "Someday, I'll put a real engagement ring there. Till then, this means the same thing."

The rest of our trip took on a honeymoon feel, with romantic beach dinners, fruity rum drinks, sunset strolls, and ocean swims. We made love every night and I didn't even think about doing blow. One day, Joe surprised me with a scuba lesson, something I'd always wanted to do.

"Just don't freak out underwater," he said, "but if you do, it's okay."

"Don't be silly. I'm very excited."

"I'm just saying," he shrugged. "It happens."

Monty, our guide, was cool and good-looking, with long, gray hair and deeply tanned skin. His surfer garb and mannerisms passed for a local's, though he was originally from Manhattan, and had worked years of overtime to afford the relocation. Monty was my type all over, but my love for Joe had never been stronger. I was high on his presence and drunk on the sight of him. No other man registered, not even sexy surfer/sage Monty, not even when claustrophobia hit, and he held my hand underwater, distracting me with sea urchins and fish that ate from my fingers.

Back in LA, we met up with Sam Kinison at the China Club. It was two days after the alleged rape of his girlfriend and, though somber, a night out with friends lent Sam some of the normalcy he was craving—despite the gapes and stares from other patrons. News reports made Sam out to be callous and unconcerned, but that wasn't true at all—Sam was a wreck, and his darkness rubbed off on all of us.

A few days later, while I was having a bad acid trip, Joe was again unsympathetic and detached. It lasted for weeks on end. There was no more talk of moving me in. I pretended everything was normal. On Catalina Island, with Rick the Bass Player and his date—a lively and athletic, fresh-faced blonde—I took a stand. In lieu of being held hostage by Joe's insouciance, I decided to mirror her. We raced around the ferry like kids and danced around the living room of our rented condo, drinking wine, doing blow, and dropping acid. Joe stayed on the balcony all night, listening to waves and picking at the strings of his acoustic.

He'd been all over me in Hawaii—marriage this, forever that. From goddess to pariah in six weeks flat, I was mystified and sick of it. I went to bed cursing him loudly in the darkness through an open window—*You're a dickhead, Joe. A cock-sucking asshole.* The barbs elicited no response from their intended victim, though Rick the Bass Player cracked up at every one.

In LA, I gave it one more go. I told Joe I was confused about our relationship, what he wanted, and how I factored in. His reply came out of nowhere. "I think we should move in together for eighteen months and then get married." I stared at him, but he just turned back to his recording equipment, laying fart noise effects over a piece of classical music.

How High the Moon

ONE MORNING IN AUGUST 1990, I awoke at the penthouse and
turned on MTV. I liked to start my day that way, watching lazily
over Joe's shoulder, with his back pressed to my belly. This time
the images weren't soothing and I bolted upright with tears in
my eyes. A helicopter had crashed into a mountain. Stevie Ray
Vaughan was dead.

In my work bag back home, was a frayed piece of paper
with my favorite stage songs listed on it—eighty or more titles,
ten of them Stevie's. His signature guitar slinger sound was
the first I'd ever stripped to, the first to make me feel sexy and
uninhibited onstage. His live shows had helped me move on
from the punk scene and the trauma of being mugged. If I had a
personal coming-of-age story, Stevie Ray Vaughan was all over its
soundtrack. He was a favorite Austin son.

Joe and Stevie had hung out back in Sydney. I'd been too
hungover to join them but had met Stevie once before, after a

show in Austin. He'd just gotten sober and couldn't have been sweeter, nor could his fiancée. I thought of her and shuddered, alone at the snap of God's fingers.

Joe's flirtation with sobriety had come and gone. What little control I'd once had plummeted. Away from Joe, I abstained from coke—I slept *seven nights a week* in Austin. With Joe, I averaged five out of seven and we spent three weeks a month together. Austin had become a pit stop for me, a place to dry out from my "real life" with Joe. He struggled to impose limits. I struggled to adhere to them. We failed as often as we succeeded.

I didn't think in terms of addiction. We just had "bad habits" that were exacerbated by an erratic travel schedule. We'd taper down when I moved in and settle into a routine. In my fantasy we didn't need to quit. We'd regulate instead, partying on weekends—Friday through Sunday—followed by four days of recuperation. The details could be worked out later. I was a big-picture thinker, and to me the plan made sense.

Fate intervened. Joe had a new band, and we were headed back to Japan.

❖❖❖

JOURNAL ENTRY:
September 29, 1990

First show Tokyo, now in Osaka (with Joe's band The Best). We've had two huge fights already, one my fault, one his. I bought him a YSL pen; he bought me a fur coat—holy shit!

Skunk's here. He's kind and super smart. John Entwistle is an ass (or just unfriendly, I dunno). He's hooked up with a wardrobe girl. His bass playing is incredible. Simon Phillips on drums—what a doll. Keith Emerson is nice (but his solo is too long). And the Brothers (singing harmonies)!

❖❖❖

I BARELY KNEW JOE's new bandmates and it seemed that would stay the case. None of their girlfriends had come, and without Ringo's magical vibe, the tour felt workaday in comparison.

The Brothers were a bright spot, and Skunk's calm, cool demeanor had a soothing effect on me. John wasn't really an ass, just reserved when he wasn't drinking. Singer, Rick Livingstone, was friendly and talented, if an odd fit with his eighties-era glam aesthetic. The other guys pulled me aside to ask if I could help refine Rick's style, or at least confiscate his homemade armbands. I agreed that the misappropriated shoestrings were uncool, yet good enough for Japan. Besides, *have you seen the shit my boyfriend wears?* In truth, I wasn't assertive enough to undertake their request. Armbands aside, the men got along fine—much better than Joe and I did.

Japan may've been a port in my cocaine storm, but a tidal surge of alcohol craving caught me totally off guard. The phenomenon was not new to Joe, who'd toured internationally for decades. His long-term cocaine use, interspersed with dry spells, sparked a need to compensate with drink. The cocaine dry spells I'd endured thus far (in Australia, New Zealand, and Japan) had been blips on the radar—an annoyance versus health hazard. I'd never exhibited signs of withdrawal—fatigue, mood swings, or increased alcohol cravings. He got them every time, while I'd sailed along feeling fine.

All that changed in Japan.

For the first time, I displayed signs of dependency, a knee-jerk compulsion for round-the-clock drinking, which I indulged aggressively. With Joe doing likewise, it was a wonder we didn't kill each other. Smokey had to step in the middle of two separate in-your-face screaming matches, and after the second one, I'd been so keyed up I stormed from the hotel. I sat on a park bench replaying the scene in my head, feeling aghast and perplexed. I had never fought with such explosive rage before. Joe had, but to have *two* loose cannons going off at once just might end us. I stared at the grass, despondent. When I looked up, Joe was standing there. He took a seat, neither of us speaking. Minutes passed and a calm came over me. After a while, he walked off.

It was all I needed to know. He hadn't given up yet.

Back at the hotel, in the gift shop, I perused designer pens. Joe collected them—all kinds, from gold and silver sets to flimsy souvenirs. I selected an Yves Saint Laurent, but before I could give it to him, he presented me with a much larger package.

I'd been given a fur coat once before, payment for a bachelor party I'd done. The best man, a furrier, had paid me in mink (for the easiest ten-minute performance of my life). I'd left it at a consignment store without insuring it first; then the store's owner tried to tell me she'd been robbed. I knew she was lying and had stolen my mink coat herself, but I couldn't prove it. *Easy come, easy go.* Plus I was hardly the fur-wearing type. I treasured Joe's gift for different reasons. I intended to keep it forever.

On our final night in Japan, nerves were frayed to a man. Joe cancelled the toga party planned for our room, and we hung out in John Entwistle's instead. For some reason, John chose that night to become openly affectionate, greeting me with a kiss on the lips, and later planting a string of them up my arm. Joe saw it all, wholly unconcerned.

I was so grateful to be together, I barely finished one drink and was still subdued at the airport the next day. I was thinking that Joe could've made me swim home and been justified, when he walked up with another gift. Inside the blue velvet box was an elegant pearl choker. A single strand of perfectly graduated pearls, flawless and breathtaking.

For most of the flight to Oahu, we cuddled and cooed like smitten teenagers until John, seated behind us, begged us to knock it off.

❋❋❋

JOURNAL ENTRIES:

October 3, 1990

   In Hawaii again. Had dinner with Monty (scuba instructor). Tonight is The Best concert.

October 7, 1990

   Smoke alarm, 7:50 a.m. Stuffed all sex toys under the bed just as hotel security arrived.

October 8, 1990

   The Best concert was excellent. Joe got glowing review. Then Monty came over and I asked if he'd thought about our offer. He said he'd love to fool around but not with Joe in the room. "It's just not my thing." (Bummer.) Joe went deep sea fishing, caught a tuna—my hunter!

October 10, 1990

   Back in LA for Ringo's party, and OH MY GOD, Joe says I can quit work if I want to. I love him so much…it's immeasurable. I'm happy, I think. (It's scary.)

❋❋❋

AT THE ALL-STARR BAND's record release party, Joe navigated paparazzi while I chatted with friends in the corner. Ringo came by with his face-kissing thing and Barb told me I looked lovely. After Joe did a round of obligatory sound bites, we joined Jeff Lynn and George Harrison in Ringo's booth. I journaled later about my relief at finally feeling comfortable in Joe's world, not so overwhelmed by flashbulbs and glitterati. Beyond the travel and luxury adventures, I felt his love was the ultimate gift. *The most important thing!* I wrote. *Hope I don't screw it up.*

❖❖❖

WE WENT TO CHATTANOOGA, Tennessee, to record Joe's next album. I wasn't sure what to expect from the process but hoped to be supportive.

The vibe was intense and the band serious, both in the studio and in our room, which served as their after-hours think tank. I relegated myself to bed while the men powwowed in the living room. At the studio, I stayed in the lounge, afraid to disrupt their creative process. I read books, hung out with Smokey, or chatted with Rick's and Kevin Buell's girlfriends. I didn't go sightseeing, despite being in such a scenic part of the country. Surrounded by hiking trails, waterfalls, and rock formations, I was unable to tear myself from Joe for a single afternoon. I'd never been so clingy or willing to endure boredom. All that mattered were the sporadic five-minute breaks Joe took in the lounge with me throughout the day.

I knew nothing about songwriting. I'd penned one short story and a couple of poems that said what I wanted in a way I found pleasing. I didn't know if they were technically good, but I liked them well enough. Other pieces, that I'd slaved over, came out sounding as forced as they'd felt. Joe had two weeks to write and record an entire album.

He'd told me once that some songs came to him in small pieces, others in chunks, half-formed and in need of shaping. Recalling the melody he used to play, over and over on the penthouse piano, fresh from the breakup with Lisa, I wondered if she'd been his muse. Was I supposed to be that now? And if so, how should I go about it?

"Give me space," he said when I asked how I could help. "Be *with* me, not all over me."

It seemed I was not only a piss-poor muse but annoying to boot. I tried to be unobtrusive peeking over my book from bed. Every night on the couch, he'd write on, then discard wadded-up legal pad pages, slowly filling the floor space with tiny yellow lyrical tumbleweeds. As the week wore on, I blamed myself for his struggle. I was uninspired and uninspiring, my inner light (whatever that was) dulled by cocaine. I failed to be the ethereal rock goddess he deserved...the career-making muse he needed.

⁕⁕⁕

WE LEFT CHATTANOOGA FOR Seattle, where my mood lifted but Joe's didn't. Nothing I did brought him out of his funk, not my new purple lingerie or submissive roleplay. No wonder I didn't inspire him. Outside of a sexual arena, I had little confidence and nothing much to offer.

He finally perked up at a Warren Zevon gig. After the show, I told Warren how impressed I'd been, gushing in a way I rarely did (unless I was drunk, which I wasn't then). Warren responded with a silent stare. Unnerved, I let the men talk, then later asked Joe what I'd done wrong.

"Nothing. That's just Warren. He's always like that."

For the second time that night, I let go, uncensored. "Oh, give me a break with the 'just Warren' shit, Joe. It was just plain *rude*, okay? Your friend Warren is a dick." Joe laughed and wrapped an arm around me, but I wasn't done yet. "I bet Stevie Ray Vaughan never acted like that."

"Okay, hon," he said. "Let it go. I get it."

I did, but an idea had formed. Maybe Joe should move to Austin, where musicians had less attitude. A man as sensitive as Joe (I thought) needed a nurturing tribe to feel creatively inspired. I never brought it up. Back in LA, we monstered, then after minimal sleep, Joe yanked the covers off me. "Get dressed. I need you with me today."

I rubbed my eyes, trying to gauge whether he was excited or panicked. "What's going on? What's the big deal?"

His answer got me out of bed, excited as hell.

JOURNAL ENTRY:

November 6, 1990

In the studio with (most of) the Eagles. They seem nice. Henley's from Texas, we chatted about Austin. He offered me a chicken wing. When I said I don't eat meat, Timothy wrote me a list of his favorite vegetarian restaurants and their best dishes. Felder said I look just like an old friend of his.

They jammed and Joe sounded awesome. A guy standing near me called it "brilliant." This is going to be big.

ALAS, IT WAS NOT to be—not yet, anyway—and Joe and I flew to New York for a *Letterman* taping. We arrived a day early to catch Les Paul at Fat Tuesday. I journaled that Les's guitar playing was "better than cocaine," which didn't keep me from going overboard with the real thing. I rationalized that it was Joe's birthday, as if monstering before a show taping was ever a good idea. Joe was completely fried, and it showed. I blamed myself, as did he.

We spent Thanksgiving at my parents' house. Their basement guestroom blocked all light and most sound, which was ideal for Joe, who hibernated there all weekend. He spent one night watching TV with the family, charming my grandma and getting her to sit on his lap. He skipped my mom's holiday feast (with her blessing), then conducted late-night kitchen raids for turkey and trimming.

My family made Joe comfortable, while I spent the weekend begging for sex and plying him with cocaine, scored from a high school pal. Joe steadfastly refused (the sex, not the coke), saying it was disrespectful to my parents. Also, he was creeped out by a framed portrait of the pope over the bed. "It's just wrong," he said, looking disgusted, as if *I* were too kinky for *him*.

❀❀❀

JOE FLEW HOME. I went to Austin, missing him right away and feeling embarrassed, or ashamed, I guess, for being cloying and excessive. Whatever I'd done to upset him—it was all a little murky, to be honest. But just because I couldn't pinpoint exactly what I'd done wrong didn't mean I hadn't done *something*. If he thought I was a burden, who was I to negate his feelings? It was hard to trust my own judgment. I had to take his word for it.

Something had to change, and when ACC's course catalogue arrived, I went through it, circling classes I had interest in. Later I called Joe to apologize.

"It's okay, but thanks for saying it."

"I want to be more responsible. I want to *do* something with my life."

"That's great, honey. I'm proud of you for thinking like that."

"I'm considering going back to school full-time." Silence. "Which would make me less free to travel...."

"I see."

The rest came out in a rush. "I'm terrified of losing you, scared you'll move on and forget about me, but I can't live in limbo. I have to move forward, on my own in Austin, or in LA with you."

"Mmhm."

"This isn't an ultimatum. I'm just filling you in."

Joe said he needed time to think. He called three days later. "Sell your car and pack up the cat. Let's buy a house and move you in."

Fools Rush In

Our realtor was the quintessential SoCal professional. Cresting middle-age, remarkably well maintained, she was efficient, personable, and unflappable.

"Kristin's a pretty name," she said. "Do you spell that *en* or *in*?"

"*In*," I said, appreciating the attention. Joe was a million miles away, next to me in the back seat, gazing out the window as our realtor navigated Studio City like she knew it in her sleep. "My mother named me after Ricky Nelson's wife," I continued. "They're not friends or anything. She read an article about him while pregnant and liked the name."

"Ricky Nelson is my cousin!" our realtor exclaimed.

"Oh my God," I squealed back. "It's like we're family!"

Joe made a sideways "you girls are nuts" glance, but I didn't care. House hunting was like Disneyland to me, though we'd yet to see an E-ticket property. Most were either too traditional or coldly modern for our taste. We wanted privacy with brightness and warmth. Something unique, yet spacious and practical. Home sweet home with a touch of rock and roll. The closest we found was Tuscan-style, with a courtyard fountain and extensive tile that had once been owned by Martin Scorsese. Almost perfect, yet too small. Joe said we needed space "to escape each other once in a while." He was only half joking.

"You're a cute couple," she clucked, walking back to her car. "Let's regroup after the New Year. I'll have fresh listings for you then."

That weekend, Joe had a boys' night out, with my blessing. It felt like a practice run for our impending cohabitation. The first two and a half years of our relationship had been feast or famine. Joined at the hip for weeks at a stretch, we'd separate for seven to ten straight days. I was ready for a natural ebb and flow to things, a little daily back and forth.

Joe had finally cleaned out the big bedroom, so I had somewhere comfortable to sleep while he hit the town with Sean Penn, Harry Nilsson, and Harry Dean Stanton. At 4:00 a.m., he stumbled in, grinning drunkenly, before falling into bed and smooshing his backside to my body. "Snuggle bunnies," he murmured—his term for our nightly cuddling—and I complied happily. I spooned him, my breasts pressed to his shoulder blades and belly flat against his back. I entwined our legs, kissed his neck, and traced my nails along his arm and hip. He faded into dreamland, and I didn't give one thought to boys' night out.

A couple days later, we went to Santa Barbara to visit Richard Richardson (Joe's friend, a music store owner) who lived in a big, old house with a massive wine cellar. Rick the Bass Player had been teaching me about wine for two years, slowly refining my palate, but nothing prepared me for the scope of Richard's collection. I trailed him through his basement racks, agape at the inventory— what I could see by flashlight, anyway. No explanation was given for the lack of electricity, and the question on my lips was washed away by a '67 Chateau Lafite-Rothschild (chosen for my birth year, at Richard's insistence). That one bottle could've paid two months of my rent, making me wonder how high Richard's electric bill was, and if one case from his cellar might not cover it.

What stuck with me most was that I felt sad for him. This dimple-cheeked English teddy bear of a guy owned a beautiful, potentially incredible, house that was kind of going to waste. To willingly live in the dark like that... I mean, it just seemed crazy.

❋❋❋

JOE HAD A GIG in New York City on New Year's Eve. We flew there on MGM Grand, the fledgling airline so exclusive and luxurious I thought they'd mistaken us for royalty. I spotted supermodel Linda Evangelista in the lounge, wearing sunglasses and looking bored. I wondered if her jet-setting lifestyle made it hard to find love, or if she made too much money to care.

The day of the show was hectic for Joe. He said he'd see me at the venue and that I should stick with Smokey until then. That suited me fine. Though Smokey was on the clock, it felt like hanging out with a friend. My secret attraction was alive and well, but so was the expectation that it would pass. Outside the hotel, Smokey pointed out a woman across the street, tall and plain, clad in a parka, scarf, and ski cap. When the light changed, everyone else crossed, but she stayed on the corner. Smokey asked if I knew what she was doing, and I said waiting on a friend, obviously.

"She's working," he said with a smirk.

I was incredulous. "But it's freezing!"

To work the street in those bitter temperatures was a harsh and sobering thought. I knew I had it good. Maybe not Linda Evangelista good, but a privileged life, nonetheless. I also knew it could disappear overnight and that I had no safety net. I'd been there before, after Dad's bankruptcy when I was fifteen. That's when I'd started drinking regularly. Security and stability were transient things. Life turned on a dime, there was catastrophe around every corner. The odds of street work in my future were not high, but higher than the supermodel life. I didn't dwell on the thought, but I didn't smirk about such things, either. The reins of my life had never been firmly in my hands, but I could try to be more present, I thought...now and then. A little less high, a little less drunk when special moments came around. I capped it at two beers that night.

From the rear of the Cat Club, I took in the scene, the cycle of energy between Joe and his fans. I'd never create anything so grand, but that the man responsible for it wanted *me* at his side, well—that was big. Joe once said I'd saved him from nothingness, but it was he who'd saved me.

I made it backstage as the countdown began—*three, two, one, Happy New Year!* Everyone cheered and kissed their partner as Joe craned his neck, looking for me. "Where's Kristi?" he shouted. "Where's my baby?"

His baby was held up by a security guard who'd mistaken her for a crazed fan. When I finally broke free, Joe scooped me up in his arms, the only place I belonged or wanted to be.

❈❈❈

IN JANUARY 1991, WE found our new home—a split-level, ranch-style house on a quiet, dead-end street four blocks up the hill. The back and side yards were Saltillo tile, with two grassy areas for the vegetable garden Joe wanted. Beyond the blue-gray swimming pool was a sloping, massive sprawl, overgrown shrubs and ivy cut through by a narrow walking trail. Privacy trees cushioned the lot on three sides then opened up for a full view of the Valley. At 2,500 square feet, it was perfect for our needs, and also just dated enough to be a fun remodeling project.

It was functional, flawed, and full of potential—much like the couple hoping to buy it. Joe said he would, under one condition. "If I have to spend a million bucks on a house and pool, I better see you skinny-dipping daily." I squealed and threw my arms around him.

After wrapping up the new album, he flew to Kansas to judge the Miss USA pageant. When he returned, he closed on the house and carried me over the threshold. I giggled uncontrollably as he fumbled with the lock, trying not to drop me. For the next two weeks, he sidestepped my every mention of moving in.

It was the exact scenario I'd hoped to prevent—too late to register for spring semester, another half year wasted. "I'm not getting any younger here," I quipped, but neither of us were laughing.

I dropped it when Joe's Uncle Buddy died. We'd flown to Wichita the previous month, expecting the worst, but the crisis had passed and we'd returned to LA, staying at the Bel Age. One morning at 2:00 a.m., while we were walking down the hall to our room, Joe had been pensive, and I was trying to engage him in lighthearted conversation. I told him I'd heard Vanilla Ice was throwing a party somewhere in the hotel. When he asked who that was, I broke into a chorus of "Ice Ice Baby," thinking it might make him laugh.

His mind was somewhere else. He stopped walking and shuddered.

"What is it, Joe? You okay?"

He looked up. "Uncle Buddy just died."

I didn't know what to say. We continued to our room. The next day, Smokey called to say he'd booked us on a flight to Wichita. He'd gotten the call from Joe's family. "Uncle Buddy died last night."

"What time, exactly?" I asked.

"Around five," Smokey said. "Eastern." The very time Joe had shuddered.

✦✦✦

AFTER THE FUNERAL, WE returned to LA, where Joe suggested a housewares shopping spree. I didn't bother stating that shopping for a home I might never live in didn't sound like fun to me. I wanted the house to have everything it needed, and I didn't expect it to happen without my assistance. I'd spent two and half years showering at the penthouse without so much as a plastic liner to keep the water in.

I vowed to have fun with it. He did not make it easy. First, he shot down every set of towels I showed him. "I want brown," he snapped. "I told you: plain, dark brown."

"Yes, but you need a second set when they're in the laundry. And look how pretty the mint green is."

"Put them in your bathroom, then."

"My bathroom?"

"The upstairs hall bathroom is yours—mint green your brains out. For me, *brown*."

I stacked both colors at the register, then added mauve, navy, and burgundy. *'Just brown,' my ass*, I thought. I would make that that house livable if it killed me. (Besides, he was giving me a bathroom, and that was something.) My mother had swooned to hear of our housewares spree—*my fantasy*, she'd said—though it wasn't the fun I'd made it out to be. Still, I managed to get his approval on three bathroom rug sets, soap dishes, tissue box covers, trash bins, hampers, candles in every color, and one standing towel warmer. Cookware was Joe's decision. Placemats and napkins, by mutual agreement. He selected a toaster, wok, blender, coffee maker, and flatware pattern. I picked out a fabulous set of cactus-stem wine glasses. Next, I looked at china patterns, but of a hundred on display, I liked only one—loved it, actually, for its bold yet sophisticated design. It occurred to me that Joe would think the whole idea of fine china silly, and I decided I was done shopping. Then Joe called me over to the same display wall and pointed at that very same plate.

"Don't argue," he said. "It's the only one I like."

I just smiled, thinking, *It's a sign.*

A Woman Knows

BACK IN AUSTIN, I sold my beloved '82 Cutlass Supreme, with double-tinted windows and burgundy velvet interior, packed up my apartment, crated my cat, and boarded a one-way flight to LA.

It was spring, a perfect time for fresh starts. Optimism bloomed in me like bright orange poppies along the Pacific Coast Highway. The move was not only a relationship landmark but a personal homecoming. Being forced to leave San Diego in my teens had instilled a restless dislocation in me. Eight years of gnawing uncertainty lifted and released with the first coastal breeze to hit my skin as an official Californian again.

Something lost had been found...and then some. I had true love, big fun, and a semblance of security. What more could a girl want? I would've been satisfied with the first two. I would've settled for the first one.

I still doubted my deservedness. I was reading *A Course in Miracles* and trying to learn to love myself, but I needed someone to prove I was worth the trouble first. Joe took that leap by moving me in—and it was big one. Arriving at the house, I walked around in a daze. *This is my home. This is my home?* It took a while to sink in.

The heart of the house was on the bottom floor—a large living area we dubbed the playroom, with a fireplace, full bar, and French doors to the backyard patio. Outside, Joe placed an all-in-one workout contraption that we used twice and never again. Inside were a pool table, jukebox, dartboard, slot machine, stereo, and our combined record collections (95 percent his). We strung twinkle lights as window treatments and plastered ceiling beams with *Got Any Gum?* stickers. After hanging a few gold records on the wall, Joe pronounced it done and moved on.

One floor up was the living room, dining, kitchen, and study; the latter furnished with Joe's treasured mementos, reference books, platinum records, his late father's office desk (Joe's birth father had died when he was a baby), and a stately leather wingback chair, angled just so in the corner. It was meant to be his personal sanctuary, but he surprised me. "You can come here to write," he said. "Use my father's desk for that anytime."

Our contractor, Rian Jarvis, oversaw a list of renovations that changed and lengthened daily on the new homeowner's whims. We knocked out a wall to enlarge our bedroom and make it part Zen-like retreat with rice paper accents, tatami mats, and a rock garden where the closet used to be. The ceiling was redone with a swirly-spikey plaster design, like two hundred square feet of meringue topping.

The ceiling treatment *alone* took two men a full week of hard labor. Rian was a skilled craftsman and savvy contractor but also a friend, and he convinced Joe to wrap it up. Rian tried to include me in the delicate conversation, but I had no idea how to talk about money, much less rein in Joe's spending. For the first time, I wondered if we were living beyond our means, but Joe didn't talk about money either, and I wasn't sure I wanted him to. I left the men and went to decorate the one space that was mine. Ten minutes later, Joe appeared with a finishing touch for my bathroom.

"What's that?" I asked, fully aware of what a toilet seat looked like. Also, that I preferred the existing white one to the black-etched monstrosity Joe intended to replace it with.

"It's from the Record Plant," he said, referring to the famed recording studio. "Used by some of the greatest musicians in the world. *Jimi Hendrix sat here.* This thing is priceless."

I chewed my lip. If he noticed the contrast between that dingy piece of memorabilia and my shimmery mint color scheme, he didn't say.

"Thanks, babe," I mumbled, unsure why it bugged me so much. Exiting the bathroom, I saw the bigger picture, and I was suddenly fine with it.

The movers had arrived from Texas, and Rian's men had placed most of my furniture. Joe's and my possessions were officially comingled; his throw pillows on my sofa, my lamp on his dresser, his double screwdriver dripping condensation on my breakfast table. We *lived together*. I wandered out to the driveway and stood soaking up the sun. It was a perfect seventy-two degrees. Rian's men were painting the garage door trim, and I was mesmerized by their meticulousness. In a rush of euphoria, I realized I was both cared for and being taken care *of*. I felt excited contentment, like coming home from a long journey and walking into a surprise party.

Joe walked up holding a crossbow.

"What the—"

"Cool, right? Let's christen the place."

The painters dropped their brushes and scattered as Joe demonstrated proper stance and hand positions.

"I'm not sure about this… Is Rocky out of the way?"

"Rocky's fine. Aim high and don't hit a window."

I aimed it at the only structure without any. Rian's crew returned to find two arrows jutting from the garage door, inches from their freshly painted trim.

Joe loved it. "Makes a statement."

"Yeah, *there goes the neighborhood.*"

Once Rian and his crew had left for good, Joe continued tweaking things, adding personal touches here and there on a nightly basis. Every day for weeks, I'd wake to find phones, lamps, and light fixtures installed in different rooms than they'd been eight hours earlier.

"I'm not complaining," I said. "Just curious… *This* is what you do while I'm asleep?"

"Pretty much."

"When will you be done?

"Never," he said. "If I finish, we'll have to move so I can start over."

I let it go. I liked not knowing what each day would bring.

❖❖❖

I ALSO LOVED THE homebody routine: collecting our mail, grocery shopping, spooning him to sleep, and waking to study every inch of his body and commit it to memory. I'd comb and trim his eyebrows, then rub between them with my thumbs, trying to smooth his furrows. One time I went to bed, still coked up, scowling in my sleep, only to wake with those same creases on my face. They lasted for two whole days.

I was twenty-three and (usually) crease-free, but I didn't feel pretty in LA. Joe told me I was beautiful every morning, no matter how disheveled and makeup-free. He also loved watching me get dolled up, standing in the doorway captivated by my hair-and-makeup process. One day, watching me paint my nails, he remarked, "I love that you're always so perfectly groomed."

I laughed. "It's the least I can do, considering you let me quit work and gave me my very own bathroom."

We befriended our neighbors, Bert and Penny, and had them over regularly for cocaine and cocktails. We'd swim and shoot pool, and on one occasion we dropped acid. It was a first for Bert, he later revealed (right after I nearly traumatized the man by walking him through our backyard, which, unbeknownst to me until just then, was in the midst of a massive spider infestation). Another night, Penny called our house in a panic. Bert was on a rampage, talking crazy and waving around a knife to block her escape. Joe went over and calmed Bert down—I have no idea how—then brought Penny back to our place for the night.

Bert had a huge home, much bigger than ours, complete with separate guest quarters. Penny could've easily moved into the guesthouse for a few days, time enough to pack her things and figure out where to go. Bert was refusing to let her step foot on the property at all, and it was legally within his rights. As they were unmarried, Penny's presence was dependent on Bert's good graces—and he had apparently gone temporarily insane (though he did let her back in eventually). Things were no different on my side of the fence, but I wasn't worried. *Joe would never do that to me.*

Tidying the playroom one day, I came across some papers in the stereo cabinet, a contract of some sort that awaited our signatures. Joe's habit of turning every enclosed space into a junk drawer made for a constant organizational battle. I usually put such things in his downstairs office (a three-hundred-square-foot junk drawer with windows), but upon closer inspection, I returned it to the drawer. It was the first cohabitation agreement I'd ever seen, and the concept made sense to me. In fact, it seemed rather generous—not that I'd know the difference. I didn't think in those terms, but apparently Joe's lawyer did. He'd put in writing that if we broke up, I'd be provided funds to relocate and finish college. I planned to sign it whenever Joe asked, but he never did. He never said a word about it.

❖❖❖

RICK THE BASS PLAYER lived two miles away—one, as the crow flies—and when they weren't hanging out in person, he and Joe communicated via CB radio. Not a day went by when they weren't in contact. I adored Rick and never tired of his company. Like most of Joe's friends, he was sweet and entertaining, without expecting all that much from me.

Joe planned a small housewarming dinner for a few close friends. Setting the table, I realized that despite our extensive housewares spree, we hadn't thought to buy a tablecloth.

"No problem," Joe said. He ran to the linen closet and returned with a fitted bedsheet.

"Please tell me you're joking."

"What? It's clean."

I thought he was nuts, but Joe's friends had known him too long to be fazed. When everyone arrived—Rian, Smokey, Rick, Chad, Joe Vitale, and producer Bill Szymczyk—I turned the kitchen over to Vitale. I didn't cook and no one judged me for it. Not even Joe.

Our fridge contained mostly La Toque leftovers, vodka, beer, wine, OJ, and Jerry's Famous Deli condiments. Tony's Liquor and Deli was another neighborhood favorite, and I especially liked their wine selection, despite its equally impressive markup. We started a tab at Tony's and had them invoice Joe's accountant, making everything from Polaroid film to batteries, booze, and deli platters free to us (or, at least, that's what it felt like). For post-monster nutritional emergencies—a frequent 4:00 a.m. thing—Ralphs's produce section provided a plethora of vegetables to juice. Our Champion juicer was the smartest purchase we'd made (the final count being three, since the first two juicers went unwashed so long that petrified pulp rendered them easier to replace than clean).

I kept our home tidy of clutter: sex toys, cigarette empties, record sleeves, coke-encrusted jewel cases, and X-rated Polaroids that somehow found their way into every room. Joe's longtime housekeeper, Angelina, did the real cleaning (except juicers, for whatever reason). She was a plump, motherly Guatemalan woman I adored. Which is why, upon hearing her screams one morning, I flew from bed to the kitchen despite having just fallen asleep. That morning we'd wrapped up an extended monster, and, in anticipation of her schedule, I'd carefully tidied up the evidence before going bed. Joe and Romero, Angelina's husband, were out front fixing a sprinkler. They reached the kitchen before me, and by the time I burst in, they were laughing hysterically. Angelina, with one hand to her heart, was muttering away in Spanish. Scanning the room, I spotted the source of it all in the microwave—a ten-inch-long, fat, pink, veiny dildo.

I shot Joe a look and stormed upstairs.

"C'mon, it's funny!" he called after me.

By the time he caught up, I was fuming. "Now our house-keeper thinks I'm a pervert!"

"Nah, don't worry," he said, putting his arms around me. "I told her I'd done it as a practical joke on her and Romero. Don't be mad, please?" I sighed and let it go. The real issue was bigger than one dildo (so to speak) and too complicated to explain to him.

❈❈❈

BESIDES LA TOQUE AND Tony's Deli, our most regular haunt was the Pleasure Chest adult store. Their inventory filled the storage space under our eight-foot-long window seat—porn videos, sex toys, bondage equipment, leather accessories, and all manner of battery-powered gadgetry—and I'd lost interest in it.

Kink was a fun experiment that had run its course for me. Pleasure Chest excursions, while initially intriguing, were now akin to wallpaper shopping. I'd trail behind Joe feigning interest, then throw myself into it at home with a "when in Rome" attitude. The combo of hog rails and fresh stimuli had a way of bringing out my inner Caligula. Gadgetry wasn't my *thing* per se, but it's not like the stuff didn't work. Neither was I immune to the charms of a well-orchestrated power exchange, but I was no life-styler. I was a dabbler, with a taste for men on the dominant side, but I found most roleplaying hard to take seriously. I wanted my passion reciprocated, to express my love through spontaneous physicality and feel Joe's love for me the same way.

I wanted above all to be desired, and with an intensity so uncontained and unquantifiable it defied scripts. To me, nothing felt more natural. To me, lust was more sacred than words. Passionate sex was how I gave thanks to the universe. It made me feel spiritually connected *and* grounded in reality. I wanted to be fucked to a place where words lost all meaning, not mind-fucked with verbal instructions and tauntings. The way Joe orchestrated things made me feel backed into a corner, as if he needed me there, where I couldn't stir up the power to hurt him.

In the end, going along with it was easier than stating my needs or delving into his. And in my silence, I denied us the chance at something more intimate.

After everything he'd given me, I didn't think I had a right to want more. I also sensed Joe's pattern: that he was drawn to passionate women, therefore always at risk of disappointing them, and none more so than a wildly horny, much younger girlfriend. Joe protected a fragile ego by suppressing my intensity. I abandoned my autonomy for fear of embarrassing him. I couldn't afford to lose him. I hadn't just fallen in love—my identity rested on my role as his partner, despite how poorly I filled it.

I disappointed him at every turn. Stymied creatively, I compensated the only way I knew how. In my world, sexual intensity had value. It meant *I mattered* and that I had a sliver of power. If I couldn't get Joe to lose control over me, the paradigm imploded. I needed to be ravaged to feel validated. I put the onus on him instead of developing myself as a writer (the one side of me he unconditionally supported). I blamed Joe for being controlling because taking control of my own life terrified me.

❋❋❋

IN MAY, JOE FLEW to New York to do *Letterman* again but had Smokey stagger our flights for reasons that made no sense. When I asked why he was going a day early, he bristled and refused to give me a straight answer.

At the Plaza, he acted happy to see me, and I played along even though I wanted to cry. I left him with Rick, Smokey, and Spero and went to the bedroom to unpack, where I noticed an out-of-place nightstand askew from the wall and bed. When everyone left, Joe came in, but before he undressed, he explained that since we were sharing a two-bedroom suite with Smokey, and our door didn't lock, he'd ensure privacy by blocking it with the nightstand. Then I understood why it had been off-kilter in the first place. Another woman had been there the night before.

I never let him see me sweat. I faked a good mood the entire trip while the trial of the century played out in my head. My heart fighting for Joe's innocence, my head compiling the evidence.

Sexually, I gave him everything he wanted and got a fraction of what I needed in return. If he had an ounce of libido to spare, *of course* I'd be the default recipient. That's what I'd told myself for years, even after learning he'd fooled me at least twice. He'd confessed to cheating the day after I moved in: once with the blonde penthouse neighbor, and once with Lisa, his ex. He was telling me so that we'd have a fresh start, he'd said, swearing *never again*. So I'd forgiven him. And if he'd been going to the Body Shop strip club lately, well, that was Sean Penn's influence. I'd worked in one myself, after all—the poster girl for sexual progressiveness.

It's not like Joe had developed an inappropriate friendship with the girl in that eight-by-ten glossy...the one I found in his briefcase with her phone number on it. Struggling actresses handed those things out all the time, right?

I wondered, too, about that friend of Rick's, the bookishly cool New York chick I'd met on a previous trip. Brusque with me yet openly affectionate with my boyfriend, she shared private jokes and used intimate body language. I was brainy, too, and had stripped for five years—the art of flirtation was *my business*. Did they think I was an idiot?

I had less to go on with the Japanese girl, just her name handwritten on letters scattered throughout our house on Blairwood Drive. A faceless fan who'd written Joe for years— "a nobody," he'd insisted. *We met once and she got obsessed. No big deal. Right, Rick?*

"Yeah, yeah, yeah," Rick had mumbled. "A harmless fan, no big deal."

Then there was Hope, another "nobody," I supposed. Some girl backstage at a show in LA. A tan, toned, attractive blonde, in a tight skirt and loose-knit sweater, with lips like Taylor Dane. She'd asked me a string of innocent questions, except the final one sounded rehearsed and pointed: *Is it hard dating a rock star?*

"Not at all. Why?"

"With so many woman chasing him, I'd think you'd be worried about affairs."

He'd never, I'd said—guffawed, in fact (since, after all, he could barely *keep up with me*).

Case closed, I'd thought. Until, weeks later, Hope's name showed up on a hotel receipt from Santa Barbara. I found it in Joe's pants doing laundry, instantly recalling his bullshit explanation for going to our favorite resort without me. I'd backed down to avoid a fight, but standing at the washing machine, I realized I'd known all along that he was taking another woman.

I snorted the coke I found in his same jeans pocket, then dialed the San Ysidro Ranch.

"Why hello, Miss Hope. I hope you and Mr. Walsh enjoyed your stay, and how can I help you today?" I hung up without answering him.

I never pressed Joe about Hope in Santa Barbara, or the nightstand business at the Plaza. Back in LA, he was loving and attentive. A few days later we had friends over. Joe, Rick, and Geno gathered at the bar across the room. I was eating a snack in front of the TV, watching a mindless celebrity news show, when the puzzle came together. The video clip was brief, but the content unmistakable—my soul mate exiting a limo at a Manhattan charity event, then helping a beautiful woman climb out after him. The reporter called her a beauty queen—Miss New York, apparently. The date of the footage was posted on the screen, the night Joe had been in New York without me, when he'd first blocked his door "for privacy."

The next day, I snuck downstairs to watch his pageant video from February. It came as no surprise that he'd scored Maureen Murray higher than any other contestant. The verdict was in. He was guilty as sin, and still I didn't say anything.

Are You Satisfied

I CONSOLED MYSELF WITH coke. I didn't confront Joe or talk things out; that wasn't my way. I didn't face obstacles and overcome them. I didn't mature; I didn't cope.

When Abe called to say he was playing the Palomino Club, I told Joe I was going and didn't invite him. He gave me a strange look but didn't argue. I never went anywhere in LA without him, but things had changed. I even bought my own blow, just for me. Something else I'd not done before.

I'd paid for cocaine in the past, for both of us, on rare occasions. Joe didn't always have cash on him, and since he paid for everything else, I was happy to pitch in. I'd socked away $5,000 of stripper income before leaving Texas. We'd chipped away at it, but I had plenty left. On the way to the Palomino, I bought a gram from Rick and indulged at the club liberally. After the show, Abe brought me into the dressing room and got his bandmates to leave us alone, only to discover our spectacular chemistry was AWOL. I was fired up all right, fueled by drugs more than desire. Abe noticed immediately. I sat on the edge of a counter and he stepped up between my knees. I wrapped my legs around his waist as we made out, hoping to spark our usual heat. Abe slid his hand down the front of my jeans, then put on the brakes entirely. What should've been a lush rainforest was dry as Death Valley. I was the furthest thing from horny.

"That's not like you," he said, concerned. "Are you all right? What's going on?"

This wasn't how it was supposed to go. This wasn't how we were. He was right that I wasn't myself at that moment, yet I had no idea how to reach her. "I did some coke," I admitted, hanging my head. Sexual chemistry was my favorite drug and *our* chemistry was pharmaceutical-grade stuff. I knew coke killed my sex drive, so why had I done it?

Abe was worried about me, which made me feel worse. Demoted from an object of desire to one of pity, I left as soon as I could.

◈◈◈

I FELT BETRAYED BY cocaine. Like a trusted friend that had secretly been nickel-and-diming me, it had now stolen my wallet. Cocaine hadn't just robbed me of my greatest pleasure—it had chipped away some of life's color and texture.

The previous year, in Japan, Simon Phillips had turned me on to electronica music—a heady experience, but also a punch in the gut. My rock music knowledge had never been vast, but alternative trends were my passion. I'd turned Joe on to the Butthole Surfers and Toy Dolls. (In return, he'd played me the Flying Burrito Brothers and Dan Fogelberg.) Suddenly entire genres got past me. I was totally out of touch.

The same light bulb went on at the opening of Lee Starkey's Melrose boutique. I'd worn my Stevie Nicks beaded blouse, hoping to fit in with her fashionable crowd, but the drapey silhouette was passé. Bare midriffs, hip huggers, and seventies chic were the rage. More than a fashion faux pas to me, it was Exhibit B in the case of the cocaine robbery. My scope had narrowed to the size of a straw, blacking out music, fashion, and nature. Not going hiking in Chattanooga was one thing. I'd yet to hit the beach *once* in LA—me, a lifelong water baby.

I'd watched Lee work the room at her party, as captivating as her mother. I'd hid out in the bathroom alone, doing hog rails one after the other. I'd never wanted to quit drugs so badly nor been more afraid to try. I depended on coke to overcome shyness and melancholy, to think clearly, speak freely, and fit in slightly. *Cocaine to detach, cocaine to interact.* Cocaine to connect with others, escape myself, and rebel against society. Dependency made me ashamed and then relieved me of the same. When Joe and I fought, his coke got me over it. When he was a dick, it rewarded me for tolerating his shit.

When I wasn't turning to drugs for comfort, I turned to Smokey. He lived in Detroit but was with us just as often—we depended on him a lot. On tour during shows, Smokey and I would watch from the wings together or find someplace quiet to shoot the breeze. Our friendship developed backstage and at hotel pools, talking for hours while Joe slept through the afternoon. We commiserated over road fatigue, shared private jokes and detailed personal histories (however much of his I could believe, since—when it came to Smokey—I could be really naïve). Joe's humor was unique. Smokey's, more my speed. His Kissinger impression slayed me. My Mrs. Kissinger—a female version of Henry, basically—made Smokey laugh harder than I'd ever heard him.

He'd been on The Best tour, and with us in Hawaii, when Joe spent the first two days in bed. With nothing to do, I'd occupied myself around the hotel, purposely avoiding Smokey, whom I didn't yet know very well. On the second day, I headed to the pool and found him lying out, oiled head to toe, in nothing but sunglasses and a Speedo. I could've pounced on him, right then, but hung back at the gate, fighting the urge and drinking in the sight—his broad chest and umber flesh, dripping with oil and sweat. The gold rope chain around his neck glinted in the sun, winking at me, for Christ's sake. The scene was like something out of a slick brochure for a swinging singles cruise, in a time machine to 1970s San Tropez. It was just so overtly, nakedly erotic I thought I'd go insane.

Instead, I suppressed my inner cavewoman—no small feat, that—and feigned cheerful casualness, plopping down next to him. "Hey, sailor," I joked. "Come here often?"

An elegant Asian woman two lounge chairs over suddenly stood, collected her things, and marched from the pool area. She was fortyish and petite, with a flawless pedicure, a designer bag, and Chanel jewelry. As her high-heeled sandals clicked down the path, Smokey burst out laughing. Apparently, she'd been eyeing him for an hour, about to make her move when I cock-blocked her. I apologized profusely, but Smokey said he couldn't care less.

I was secretly glad to have scared her off, though it hardly solved my dilemma. As much as I envisioned a future of blissful monogamy with Joe, I also craved variety and intense, unpredictable encounters, and was genuinely ticked off that I couldn't have one with Smokey.

❖❖❖

THE *ORDINARY AVERAGE GUY* tour started in June. The Doobie Brothers shared billing on a handful of dates, and the two bands took turns lobbing practical jokes back and forth during each other's shows. The antics escalated from flying rubber chickens to strippers, flashers, and zoo animals. Joe suggested I sneak onstage to dance around (fully clothed) with the Doobie Brothers, saying, "You've got better moves than the strippers we sent up there last week." (Touched as I was by the praise, I only had enough nerve to dance way in back, by one of their two drummers.)

In the years since Hamish had pulled me onstage in New Zealand, I'd shed my perennial outsider identity. It was easy enough after a few bumps, but most of the credit was Joe's for making me a part of something—when he wasn't trying to wall me off, that is. On the *OAG* tour, old patterns resumed. The same issues, triggers, and name-calling—*You're a cokehead, you're an asshole, give me space, give me sex!* Our ability to make up and move on, however, was gone.

The band played Austin on the Fourth of July, where Joe booked a hot-air balloon ride. Behind his back, I requested a "do not disturb" from the front desk. Joe's ride arrived, but when they wouldn't put the call through, he left. When Joe woke up he was furious at me, but I was too embarrassed to explain why I'd done it. A surge of irrational fears, of heights and abandonment, had kept me from going with him or letting him go without me. I was sinking into depression.

By Pittsburg, we'd reached peak tension. Together in our room, I felt an awkward, painful solitude. He scribbled on legal pads. I tried to interest him in a shared activity—room service, SpectraVision, or a game of rummy. He shook his head and kept on writing. It occurred to me that I missed journaling. If he refused to hear my thoughts, I'd record them on paper until they felt real... until *I* did. I asked Joe for a legal pad. When he claimed not to have a spare, I threw up my hands. "Fine. I'll get one from Smokey."

I knocked on the door across the hall. "Hey there," Smokey said, stepping back to let me inside. It felt like coming up for air.

"You busy? I don't want to impose..."

Nine times out of ten, Smokey answered the door with the phone receiver pressed to his ear, the cord trailing like a snake behind him. I'd told myself I'd leave if that was the case, but it wasn't, so I sat on his bed and vented. Smokey took a chair by the window and listened. I don't remember what he said or thought, but I do recall feeling heard.

"Well," I finally said. "I should let you get back to whatever it is you do when not gluing me back together." He smiled and assured me I wasn't falling apart, just being human.

We stood to hug like we always did, meeting at the shoulders and chest, then suddenly everywhere else in a full-frontal press. We were locked together from knees to neck, firmly and unmoving. My cheek pressed to his chin as I inhaled his warm skin and that faint musky scent that had driven me wild for months. A longing came over me, years of pent-up frustration. Yet I was frozen, unable to read the situation or trust what my gut was saying. I tried to gauge Smokey's stance and grip—anything to suggest he felt what I did—but there was nothing. Except that he hadn't let go of me yet.

I could not, *would not*, make the first move, but I could open the door and let him through. I relaxed my grip and ever so slightly turned my head toward his. As I did, he mirrored the movement, turning his head toward mine, until our faces met lip to lip. That's when I knew.

The last thought I had before losing my mind was that we would always be equally to blame for this...a perfectly coincided moment of weakness.

When it was over—our passionate kiss and one other, exquisitely intense, dropped-to-my-knees moment—I pieced myself together, crossed the hall, and went straight to bed. I'd forgotten to retrieve any paper, but Joe hadn't noticed or even looked up when I'd entered.

◈ ◈ ◈

TWO DAYS LATER, I awaited Smokey on the bus, half inflamed, half frantic, both thrilled and pained by this game-changer we'd set in motion. The force of my guilt was equaled only by my entitlement. *I should bolt right now, but there is no goddamn way I'm letting this moment slip through my fingers.*

The bus was parked behind the outdoor stage at a bustling fairground. At midday, it was hot and sunny out, cool and quiet inside the bus. Forty minutes late, Smokey finally arrived, barreling down the center aisle and pinning me to the mattress in back. I wrapped my legs around his waist and dug my nails into his back. Outside, Joe played his heart out. I recognized the song before Smokey muffled it, growling like a bear in my ear as he climaxed. In, out, done, and gone, he left the bus and me, alone, shivering in the air-conditioning, burning up with adrenaline. I reeked of shame and sex and something else I couldn't name, then later pegged as sorrow. I was officially a cheater, grieving my first true monogamous bond. I washed up at the sink, trembling with dishonor and desire. I wanted him again already.

A few days later, I popped across the hall again, this time with a barely believable yet uncontested excuse of showing Smokey my new outfit. He whisked me inside, maneuvering me face-first into the corner behind the door. He flipped up my skirt, yanked down my panties, and took me from behind, on the spot. I was absolutely undone, in cavewoman heaven.

I was back in our room minutes later, Joe apparently none the wiser. The next day on the bus, someone snapped a Polaroid of me and Smokey. Joe was out of earshot when I showed it to Rick and asked, "What do you think?"

"I think it looks like you're having an affair," Rick said, not missing a beat.

His deadpan delivery made it tough to discern humor from commentary. But it simply had to be the former. Only Smokey and I knew the truth, and *I* wasn't talking.

Wouldn't it be Nice

THE OAG TOUR WRAPPED up around the time fall semester began. I was enrolled at Pasadena City College until a day in biology class when I passed the microscope to my teenage lab partner and drove off campus for good. I'd craved love and adventure all my life. Now that I had it, I couldn't be expected to sit through freshman courses (suspiciously similar to the math, history, and sciences I'd already passed in high school).

Joe was sympathetic. "If college isn't working for you, find something that does."

I considered volunteering—no doubt compelled, partly, by guilt over being a three-time college dropout. I didn't, because the idea of being depended on by people with real needs made me hyperventilate a little. (It's important to know your limits, I felt.) I was a capable person and fast learner who'd worked steadily since age sixteen, including as a speed freak. I felt vaguely uncomfortable not earning my keep, at least my own spending money. A nearby flower shop on Ventura had had a HELP WANTED sign posted for months. How hard could that be? The worst I could do was kill a blossom or two.

They hired me at noon and I turned in my apron at three. Whatever fair compensation for soul-crushing boredom is, six bucks an hour wasn't it.

"I just want you to be fulfilled," Joe said. "Whatever does it for you."

I had many interests—writing, sewing, and martial arts,. among them—yet none strong enough to tear me from Joe and the fun that followed him around. I didn't want to miss anything.

Patrick Swayze came over while I was out of town, at my folks'. He spent all night making music in Joe's half-finished garage studio. Patrick was remodeling the house next door, and after meeting in his driveway, I'd said *come by anytime*, neglecting to specify a time I was home. Another time, years earlier, Joe got a surprise visit from Keith Richards at a hotel in Indianapolis. I'd left Indiana that morning to put in an appearance at work—probably earning a fraction in cash of what those two put up their noses that night.

I was at home the night Wolfman Jack dropped by. Uncle Wolf (as he asked to be called) was one of Joe's sweetest friends, and he referred to me as "the woman of the house" in a way no one else had, Joe included. "It takes a special kind of woman to handle celebrity-sized egos like mine and Joe's. You're strong like my wife. I can tell," Wolf said. He proceeded to profess his awe for her, women in general, and the power of female sexuality, which he likened to a righteous mythological weapon against puffed-up male narcissism. Before he left, he asked if I could help him score. I made a run to our dealer and returned with a gram for him alone, but Wolf refused to take it until I did some.

Pointing at a long, narrow piece of glass on the counter behind the bar (which we kept there for just that reason), he said, "Dump it there, do as much as you want, and I'll do the rest."

"Okay, Uncle Wolf," I laughed, "but this may not end well for you."

❀❀❀

My FAVORITE CELEB GUEST was the goddess herself. I met Stevie Nicks after she called to invite Joe to dinner and then extended it to me as well. "Both of us?" I asked. "She actually said that?"

"Of course. When I told her I was in a relationship, she insisted I bring you."

"Oh my god! That's so sweet! What'll I wear?"

Joe laughed. "Calm down. It's Stevie, not the queen."

"Yeah," Rick added. "Besides, she's probably more nervous about meeting you."

He and Geno were across the bar, beating me at poker. I gave Rick a look, but he loved teasing me and refused to explain the cryptic comment.

"Joe, what's he talking about?"

Joe shrugged. Finally, Geno took pity on me. "She's still in love with him. Has been for years. Doesn't she keep a special room in her house just for you, Joe, no one else can use?"

"I don't know…maybe."

The men awaited my reaction, but the info only made me like her more. The chick had great taste.

At La Toque, Stevie waited at the head of our favorite table, looking as expected—a luminescent gypsy angel in black lace and leather. She greeted me with a hug, but when her darting eyes wouldn't hold my gaze, I found it comforting to see the nervous habit in someone else for a change. She had a necklace snagged in her hair and fiddled with it to no avail. I offered to help and she sighed, grateful. "Please, it's been driving me nuts for an hour."

She and Joe talked while I worked, careful not to damage one strand of her precious platinum hair. When I presented her with the pendant—a silver claw clutching a hematite marble—Stevie insisted I keep it as a thank-you gift.

During dinner, half a dozen of Joe's friends showed up, apparently all having plans to dine at La Toque that night. It was quite a coincidence. One by one, they joined us, pushing tables together until we were a party of ten. Our quiet, three-person dinner was officially hijacked when Geno, at the far end of the table, joked about her "One-Winged Duck song"—trying to get a reaction. It worked, and Stevie's head snapped up. "That's dove, idiot," she barked. "White-winged *dove*."

Afterward, we took Stevie back to the house, with Geno, Rick, and Rick's date. The men gravitated to the bar while Stevie took a spot on the floor. Rick's date and I looked at each other, then followed suit. (I got the sense that's how it was with Stevie— she did what she wanted and you could either come along or not.) When I commented on her remarkable skin, Stevie shared her youthful secret. "European products, expensive as shit and totally worth it." From there, the conversation deteriorated into a rambling monologue, causing an amused look to pass between me and Rick's date. I'd never seen anyone talk so much and say so little who wasn't on coke or meth at the time, but Stevie had been in my sights all night and not done a single line. Maybe that's just how she was, I thought. Incredibly, *ridiculously* ditzy.

She left the same pile of jewelry in three separate spots around the playroom. Each time it was returned, with firm advice to place the valuables in her purse. Each time she promised to do so and each time the cache reappeared somewhere else. Around 2:00 a.m., Stevie abruptly left the room. We followed upstairs to the living room where she sat at the piano and we formed a semicircle around her. And that's where we stayed for the rest of the night, literally.

At 4:30 a.m., Joe whispered in my ear that it was time to call it a night. I agreed, just as I had the first two times he'd said it. Yet despite my hints, Stevie remained oblivious. Finally Joe pulled me aside and growled, *I don't know what to do...help me!*

He was right. I was the woman of the house, after all.

"Stevie," I purred, sliding next to her on the bench. "I could listen to you play forever, but Joe and I should really get to bed."

"Of course! It was so nice to meet you," she said, her smoky voice light and sweet.

I sighed with relief as Stevie continued playing. I raised an eyebrow at Joe. He raised both back at me. Geno observed with curiosity, Rick with absolute glee—on the verge of laughing hysterically. I pulled Joe aside. "Should we offer to call her a car?"

"She has one," Geno interjected. "Followed you home from La Toque, been parked in your driveway all night."

I stepped out to have what would surely be an awkward conversation with her driver. Instead, he nodded knowingly. "Just get her outside. I'll take it from there."

With renewed hope, Joe concocted a story about something outside Stevie *simply must see*, something magical in the sky or our shrubbery. The moment she'd cleared the front door, her driver was there, as promised—*Perfect timing, Miss Nicks, I know you like to be home by sunrise*—and guided her into the back seat. It was the only time all night she let someone else take the lead.

The next day, Stevie called in a panic. Her jewelry was missing—her late grandmother's heirloom jewelry, to be exact. It had huge sentimental value, and a retail of *thirty grand*. Joe and I tore the house apart—trash bins, drawers, sofa cushions—to no avail. Stevie begged me to keep looking, so I did. Joe paced and chain-smoked until I gave up. Day three, Stevie's final call: *Never mind!* One of her house staff had found the jewelry in her purse that night and locked it up safe.

❖❖❖

JOE AND STEVIE HAD a right to their eccentricities. They'd followed their dreams, invested their talents, made sacrifices, and taken risks. I didn't have their courage. I envied their wealth and accomplishments, but mostly the creative expression forever at their fingertips.

The fancy electronic typewriter in Joe's study did not compel my hands to reach out. It made them clench into fists. To me, it was less a writing tool than a lie detector test meant to confirm my lack of talent. One day Joe made an amazing offer. Until I could put my stories on paper, he would give me his.

He placed a tape recorder on the bar, where we did the bulk of our partying. Then, whenever the urge struck, he'd hit record and start talking, sharing his best rock-and-roll memories. My role was sounding board first, transcriber second—to draw him out, then edit the anecdotes, as coauthor of his memoir. Talk about starting at the top! But the plan came crashing down the first time I hit play and recoiled from the grating sound of a clueless cokehead interrupting her funny, tolerant subject with inane asides and irrelevant questions. It was cringeworthy. I was *that* girl—the girl you avoid at parties—and Joe's magnanimous plan evaporated along with my self-confidence.

At eleven years old, it occurred to me that I might want to be a writer. I'd read a book of stories by Roald Dahl, two of them personal essays—giving birth to a love of memoir. At thirteen, I read *The World According to Garp* and knew for sure. If it took a lifetime to write something one-tenth as good as that, it would be a life worth living—even just in the trying.

That same year, I was one of three students chosen from my class to enter a local writing contest. The night before it was due, I decided I could do better and started over on a new topic. Suddenly the words flowed in a way they never had before. Unused to the feeling, I didn't trust it and turned to my parents to confirm I was on track. But it was late and they were tired—*Seems fine,*

Mom said, skimming it and handing it back. Deflated, I'd gone to bed and turned in my original essay the next day. It scored an average grade, which, to me, meant last place.

Two years later I showed my dad an essay I'd written for sophomore English. A short piece about relocating to Texas. Earlier that year, I'd come out of my shell with a new group of friends, months before being uprooted. There'd been no discussion or comforting words. Just, *Prepare to say goodbye to everything and everyone you know in San Diego.* I'd shown Dad the essay at his request, quietly thrilled by his interest. He'd handed it back without a word—literally, not one—nor change in expression. If feelings weren't Dad's thing, disgruntled feelings topped the list, but I didn't know that then. Instead, I thought I must be quite a bad writer if he couldn't even say, "Seems fine, Kris." Another type of kid might've plugged away undeterred, but I'd never been very resilient. I needed tremendous encouragement. By the time I received real praise on my writing, from two teachers my senior year, I was a binge-drinking alcoholic with a sky-high fear of failure. I wanted to believe them, but I was too far gone by then. Eventually, I penned a few short pieces, nothing recent. But at Joe's encouragement, I planted myself in his study and tapped out some ideas. Whether they had any potential, I'd never know. When they didn't blossom into John Irving–level stuff, I quit working on them.

For my birthday in October, Joe gave me a top-of-the-line electronic sewing machine with all the latest bells and whistles, plus ten free lessons. The sewing machine of my dreams never left its box. I slid it under the typewriter stand and went to snort hog rails at the bar.

❉❉❉

AROUND THAT TIME, WE got a bad batch of coke that burned like hell inside my nose. Joe gave up after two bumps, but I was convinced the pain was worth it. When the ice-pick sensations spread from my nose and face to a whole-head debilitating pain, I lay down and rolled to one side, to snort lines off the plate. I pretended not to notice Joe pacing behind the couch. If he wasn't going to stop me I wasn't going to stop, no matter how much it hurt. My sinuses sizzled and buzzed, delicate mucosa stung and throbbed. For a brief moment I wondered—*Is this how it feels when cartilage dissolves?* Still I did more, until it was gone—the coke and my septum, both.

I saw a doctor who was kind but solemn. "Keep it up and your nose will collapse. Septal surgery is painful and expensive, and you should try to avoid it." I promised him I would. There were other methods of ingestion. Intravenous was out of the question, and freebasing a hassle. The rectal area was rumored to work, but after a period of fearless (and hilarious) experimentation—packing straws with coke and blowing it up each other's ass—the novelty wore off. It was too inconvenient.

We found another dealer: a loud, crazy Englishman on Beverly Glen. Gregarious and well connected, Gary owned a hair salon and pet-grooming business, and had dirt on half of Hollywood. With a personality as big as his gut, wild white hair, big lips, and a rubbery nose, he was clownish yet weirdly attractive. The accent didn't hurt, plus he was irreverent and filter-free. I adored Gary, but when Joe did a short tour that fall, I didn't call him. I stayed home, grieving my septum in isolation—not one line, over seven days. When Joe returned, we went straight to Gary's.

Our excitable dealer was more so than ever, showing off his fresh score—a blinding white, densely packed snowball of coke that broke apart in sheaths like an iceberg. It sparkled and winked, flirting shamelessly. We bought as much as we could afford.

❦❦❦

CHRISTINE CAME TO LA on a job hunt. We put her up in our guestroom and dragged her to La Toque to meet J. D. Souther. The fix-up was Joe's idea and I'd okayed it, realizing my mistake the moment I introduced them. *I* liked older creative types. Christine preferred young, athletic men. We'd known this about each other for years. "You forgot, that's all," she said. In truth, I hadn't bothered to remember. I'd been high the day Joe concocted the matchmaking plan, declaring it brilliant without any consideration.

The incident was not an anomaly. I wasn't the same person Christine had befriended five years earlier. I acted put-upon and dismissive, as my low-maintenance houseguest embarked on a major life transition. Her agreeable self-sufficiency was a slap in my face. Her well-meaning concern, a nail in our coffin— *I'm worried about you,* she said. *How dare you!* I thought. I couldn't bear to see my life through her eyes. I knew I was out of control, but since I couldn't change course, anyone who brought it up had to go. I was relieved when she found somewhere else to stay, hating myself for it, but not enough to stand in her way.

I wouldn't have been surprised had Rocky left with her. Though never an affectionate cat, in Austin he'd been playful. Every morning he'd attack my feet through the bedsheets, then would sit on my chest, tickling my nose with his whiskers. After the move, he quit all that. At Blairwood, Rocky viewed the goings-on with distrust and aggravation. I gave him gourmet cat food, limo rides to the vet, and a huge yard in which to frolic, but my cat was unhappy and I knew it. He kept his distance in LA, entering the bedroom only when Joe was out of town, and not to play or sit on my chest but circle the futon, restlessly, as if to say *hurry and pack before that man with the bad white powder comes back.*

***

IT WASN'T JUST FRIENDS and pets witnessing my descent. One night, we ended up at the house of Charlie Horky, the owner of our limo company. Charlie was a doughy, clean-cut guy that I secretly thought a bit shifty, though I liked his wife, Marcy, who was unpretentious and kind. That night, too strung-out to follow the conversation or tolerate indoor lighting, I slipped into the backyard.

Riding out the tail end of a monster, I felt like death warmed over. Joe failed to either register my condition or care enough to do anything about it. My only option was to wait until he wanted to go home. I sat at the edge of the pool and dangled my legs in it. Marcy appeared and pulled up a chair, then proceeded to confirm my top fear: that I wasn't hiding anything from her.

"Are you feeling okay?" she asked gently. "I mean, you've only recently moved to LA and I wonder if you're finding it...overwhelming."

"I'm okay, thanks." I was impressed by her boldness, as much as I wanted it to stop.

"You don't seem like it, though. I don't mean to be intrusive, but frankly, I'm worried about you."

I had no idea what to say. Frankly, I was too. *And?*

"Do you think about your future? Where's your life going, Kristi... Do you know?"

The few times I'd been around Marcy she'd seemed happy and composed, like she had it all mapped out. In my twenty-four years, I'd never once known where I was going, much less how to get there. I'd fielded questions like hers before, from well-meaning peers, nosy strangers, and frustrated relatives. They were the same questions I'd asked myself as a kid—unanswered so long, I'd stopped asking them.

We didn't talk about career planning in my family. By the time I was fifteen, we barely talked at all. I was told, "You're going to college." Not asked, "What interests you?" or, "How can we parlay your talents into a career?" I'd never met with a guidance counselor. I'd gone to UT because UT had let me (and done so, very cheaply). My parents hadn't gone to college, my grandparents either. As for its tangential benefits—the art of critical thinking, a lifelong network of connections—my family had no awareness of such things, so how could they inform me? But I needed that. For someone with low self-esteem and minimal self-belief, something beyond *you're going, period* would've been helpful, to say the least.

I did not know what my future held, only that life in LA was better than it had been anywhere else. "I'll figure it out," I told Marcy, making circles with my legs, creating waves in the pool, hoping I appeared unconcerned.

Marcy was silent, elbows on knees, wringing her hands gently. The rock on her finger was at my eye level, and to me it looked bigger than the moon.

###

WE GOT INVITED TO the Magic Castle on Halloween—a real coup in LA—and I threw together last-minute costumes (a football player and cheerleader) in the spirit of the exclusive club's big night. After navigating the mansion's labyrinth of hallways, we ordered a round of drinks and were treated to a private magic show and short palm reading.

I was fascinated by psychic ability. Among the fakes and charlatans, surely some spoke the truth, and I had a good feeling about the Magic Castle's palm reader. I arranged to meet her for a longer reading at a coffee shop in the Valley. There, she studied my palm for a long while. When she finally spoke it was earnestly. "Listen carefully. Sock away as much money as you can. *Save every penny.* I can't stress this enough, you need to be better prepared."

She didn't elaborate and I was too unnerved to ask.

Her other predictions were banal; I'd have two careers, two kids (possibly adopted), and two marriages "of the heart" (not necessarily on paper). Were that all she said, I'd have brushed off the doomsday business easily, but the rest was eerily spot-on. "You have resentment toward one parent for something they didn't give you. You love detail and organization, but can be lazy. You have a positive nature, yet don't believe in yourself. You're too giving and should practice better self-care. You're a good person for travel, which you do a lot. You're creative and should have a creative career. You missed your first opportunity, but another will come along. Your sex life is very kinky and you have an extremely high sex drive. You don't do moderation *at all*."

I left, promising to heed her advice, but having no job or paycheck to save—no incoming pennies whatsoever—I did the next best thing and got a credit card. Then, because I didn't do moderation *at all*, I got two more.

###

I WAS NO PSYCHIC, but I'd had premonitions, most in regard to Joe. Recognizing his voice on the radio six years before we met was the first. The others were less remarkable.

Whenever Joe traveled without me, he'd call home at random times—noon one day, 3:00 a.m. the next—so I never knew when to expect it. And yet I often did, sometimes to the minute, with a sudden urge to reach for the phone seconds before he called. More than once, I'd woken from a dead sleep with my hand hovering over the receiver, as if I could feel him dialing, right before it rang. One night, he'd stayed out all night without calling, something he never did. I was asleep at home, dreaming he was with Lisa. I woke up and he wasn't there, so I called Rick.

"Sorry, babe," Joe said, when Rick gave him the phone. "Lisa came over and I guess we lost track of time." He assured me nothing inappropriate was happening and I said I believed him. (There was no way to know, and I'd learned to pick my battles.)

"You'd like Lisa," he said the next day. "If you met, you'd be instant friends."

I raised an eyebrow—*Sure, babe. That'll happen.* A few weeks later, it did. At a party in Santa Barbara I looked up and there she was, as beautiful as I remembered. Also as likable as Joe had promised, despite being at the tail end of a monster (when no one is at their best).

Recalling Stevie's graciousness, I offered Lisa a bump. Then, after accidently spilling most of Joe's stash in the toilet, I burst out laughing—cackling, really—despite that I was now just as fucked as Lisa. I'd been monstering myself and fading fast. Now we had barely enough coke left for us both, much less Joe, who was waiting in the hall. Oddly, my fate barely fazed me; I enjoyed Lisa's misfortune that much. I also couldn't help but like her and the cognitive dissonance got to us both.

First priority was getting to our dealer. I offered Lisa a ride with nothing but good intentions, then spent the next ninety miles messing with her head, describing my every sleep-deprived hallucination. The poor girl grew more unsettled with every camel, rhino, and ostrich I saw outside the car. Maybe because I was driving at the time, going sixty miles per hour. I made it up to her at home, dumping out a string of hog rails without asking Joe. I thought it only fair he let me control our stash, considering what he and Lisa had done behind my back last year.

For the most part I took a philosophical view, that no one person could be all things to their partner. I had to accept that I wasn't everything for Joe. Not to mention vice versa.

✳✳✳

MY FLING WITH TERRY Reid began in the fall of 1991. I'd met the English singer the previous year at a dinner with John Entwistle. After I moved to LA, he started coming by the house, first with Rick and then on his own.

Terry was blithesome and boyish, with a thick British accent and no end of wild anecdotes. He was a rock legend and huge talent, though not a household name. Back in the day, Led Zeppelin had tried to recruit him, but at sixteen he'd been too young to tour legally. *"Mum wouldn't sign the permission slip!"* Terry would exclaim with every retelling of the story. He'd recommended Robert Plant for the job and the rest, as they say, is history. The tale was legendary and Terry told it often, as something of a calling card. I found the habit endearing.

Terry wore his heart on his sleeve. He wasn't cagey or a game-player. Joe's affections were unpredictable. From boundless to aloof, or just plain mean and feral, the inconsistency eroded our stability. Smokey was bearlike and fearless, had a way of making me feel safe, but he could also be cold and out of reach—*polar* bearlike, really. Terry was all puppy. I needed someone to nurture, and that boy needed nurturing.

Joe sensed our heat and would sometimes leave the room to eavesdrop on us through the intercom. There was nothing untoward to hear, just billiards, poker, and my smooth, slow brushstrokes through Terry's long, silky hair. He'd vent about his stalled career, and I'd lend a sympathetic ear. We didn't acknowledge our attraction, even when Joe left the room. Until one day...I did.

Whatever it was Joe said or did that propelled me to start up with Terry, I only remember being glad for the excuse. Grateful for the self-righteous anger that would override my guilt. Except it didn't, and instead of passionate and free I felt anxious and jumpy from the moment Terry touched me. I'd invited him over when Joe wasn't home, but I couldn't bring myself to go very far. "No problem, love," Terry soothed. "We'll have another go, another time."

I nodded, wondering what the hell I was doing.

❋❋❋

Despite the fights and the affairs, I was deeply in love with my boyfriend. As his birthday approached, I was determined to do something special, but Joe wasn't biting.

"What's to celebrate about turning forty-five?" he grumbled.

"Plenty, but that's beside the point because you're forty-four."

"Yeah...forty-four now, about to turn forty-five."

"What are you talking about, dude?"

He gave me a look. "What do you mean what am I talking about? *Dude*."

"Joseph!" I laughed. "You're forty-three. You were born in 1947 so in 1991 you turn *forty-four*." He sat up in bed and cocked his head, doing silent mental equations. "Happy birthday, honey," I said, pleased with my gift—one whole extra year of life. Also a flask, bought the next day and engraved with his birthdate (in case he needed it for the math).

To me, Joe was young and impervious. Other than requiring more post-monster recuperation than I did, he never complained of middle-aged aches and pains. He didn't have six-pack abs, but he had gymnast arms, track-star legs, and unfailing sexual energy (despite his claims to the contrary). His sensitivity about aging made me feel protective, but the feeling came and went. Later that month, my ambivalence came to a head.

We spent Thanksgiving on the road. I'd just finished a room-service brunch and lazily began to pack. Joe bantered with

Smokey through our adjoining room doorway. Outside, parade floats passed by. Balloon characters floated past our balcony. When Joe stepped out for a better view, Smokey stepped into the room, grabbed my wrist, and pulled me into his room. He had me pinned to the bed with his fingers inside me before I knew what to do. I squirmed free—silently livid—aghast at the brazen move.

❖❖❖

CHRISTMAS HAD ALWAYS BEEN a big deal to me. Shopping, gift wrapping, mall decorations, holiday *muzak*, and light displays; sipping eggnog while listening to Bing Crosby, signing glittery cards with the Grinch or Snow Miser on TV for company. Some people succumbed to depression around the holidays. I succumbed January through October, then became joyful for eight weeks running. For Joe, it was the opposite, and I deferred to his wishes. Instead of celebrating the season that year, we'd monster through it.

That didn't stop Gary, our crazy English dealer, from appearing in our driveway like a manic Father Christmas with a miniature pig named Elvis as a present. Joe was delighted, of course—he loved animals. I was conflicted. "We can barely take care of ourselves!"

Joe doted on Elvis for a week before admitting I was right. We passed the little guy off to my friend Billy Bacon, singer for San Diego swing band, The Forbidden Pigs, who took good care of him. It was Joe and myself I worried about. That we were incapable of raising that sweet little animal… What did that say about us?

By December 23, I'd yet to stop monstering long enough to Christmas shop. Then CLS sent over a driver named Y, a consummate professional and tidy butch dyke, who took swift, efficient charge of my life. She blazed a trail through the mall, weighing in on gifts for half a dozen strangers (my family members), then propped me up at the register as I handed her my wallet to pay for it. When everything was wrapped and mailed, she deposited me at home. I thanked her, apologizing for my sorry state. *Are you kidding? That was the funnest fare I've ever had.* She left and I fell asleep for eighteen hours.

I expected to spend Christmas Eve drinking wine and playing cards with Joe and our friend Sean. Out of the blue, at 8:00 p.m., Joe declared I should have a tree—lights, baubles, the whole shebang.

"Honey, that's sweet, but it's a little late...don't you think?"

"Oh, ye of little faith," he said with a wink.

Once again, CLS made a Christmas tradition happen, enlisting driver Norm as our eleventh-hour tree shopper on a mission. "A tall one," Joe told him, as if ordering pizza. Glancing at our ceiling, "I'm thinking a ten-footer."

Three hours later, I placed ornaments with care while Joe strung lights and Sean steadied the ladder. Stepping back to observe, I was overcome with euphoria, like I'd felt watching Rian's men paint our garage trim. I'd have sold my soul to hold onto that feeling. Instead, the opposite happened.

Mama Told Me Not to Come

MY DRUG USE HAD escalated to a new normal that was anything but. I no longer benefited from periods of forced abstinence in Austin. Extended breaks were nonexistent. In the past, I'd take a week off every month. By the end of 1991, breaks from cocaine averaged forty-eight hours, tops. Two days felt sufficient to reward myself; then I'd be off and running again. Three years had passed since I'd snorted my first line at the penthouse—a momentary indulgence to extend playtime and bond with the man I loved—but now it was a wedge between us. I was on it more often than off. The scales had officially tipped. My "recreational" pastime was no walk in the park. Every stroll a marathon, every hill Kilimanjaro.

To break the cycle, Joe planned a road trip. We'd escape the temptations of LA in a rented RV and travel up the coast in search of organically sourced enjoyment. We'd camp, hike, smell the roses, and count the stars…whatever it took to retrain our brains and reset their blown pleasure gauges. We stocked up at Ralphs with healthy snacks: celery sticks, trail mix, tuna in water, and family-size bags of multigrain Sun Chips. A six-pack of Rolling

Rock found its way into our cart, and since beer was basically harmless, two bottles of Chardonnay joined it. Wine with dinner was sophisticated (even with a tuna sandwich) and if Joe brought a lone liter of Absolut, well, wasn't that the very definition of moderation? I trusted his judgment, and to prove it, placed a bottle of Patron next to it.

The cocaine was Joe's idea. The mushrooms, mine. Quaaludes were a no-brainer, as these were the good shit—the genuine article, all but extinct in modern times. (Leaving them behind would've been the real crime.) We also brought pot, which wasn't my idea (pot was never my idea), but an inclusion I supported as the least toxic substance on board by then. The MDMA I'd been hoarding could go bad any day—or not, I wasn't sure, but erring on the side of caution I brought it anyway. The X was stored in an old prescription bottle with six hits of the General's acid, and since transferring contents seemed needlessly inefficient, I packed the container as is—LSD included. That's when Joe decided to hire a driver, one of his roadies who was capable, experienced, and less cokehead than stoner. We planned to taper off, not quit cold turkey, and couldn't afford to spread our supply any thinner.

On the way out of town, we stopped at Rick's, where I met porn star Jeanna Fine and her young fiancé. Joe and Jeanna had met before. I'd seen the Polaroids tacked up in Rick's studio—innocuous shots of him and Joe with Jeanna and Savannah (another porn star and Jeanna's sometimes girlfriend), fully dressed, and smiling for the camera. I'd seen Jeanna's films on SpectraVision, where her latest releases were always in rotation. She was even more striking in person, both outside and in. Her soft-spoken partner was edgy and handsome, with long dark hair and tattooed skin. As a plate of hog rails made the rounds, I bonded with our new best friends. We hit the road with them aboard, nary a second thought nor toothbrush between them.

Our RV entered the northbound freeway with three sex industry veterans at its table, swapping stories of our insider experiences—my tales of fun and profit from the Texas strip club scene, and their breakdown of the highly competitive porn industry. With Jeanna's exceptional professional success came exceptional pressure to maintain it. Plastic surgery was *de rigueur* in the business, yet her plans for a *fourth* nose job shocked me. She had dazzling teeth, supermodel cheekbones, and a warrior princess jawline—compliments she accepted without false modesty. I was starting to wonder if porn star Jeanna Fine were the most down-to-earth woman in LA, when her fiancé shared his plan to start a production company. "Once Jeanna's contract is up and I quit using speed."

"He'll write the scripts and I'll star in them," Jeanna said with pride.

"That's a great plan, isn't it, Joe?" He was in the front seat, watching the road, not answering. When he spoke, it was to announce our stop in Santa Barbara. At a cute little road motel, the men brought in our luggage while Jeanna and I sat on the bed talking. When she offered to brush my hair, I thrust the brush at her and happily spun around.

"Stop hitting on my girlfriend!"

"Whoa!" I cried, whirling on Joe, in the doorway with fire in his eyes. "What the hell? Jeanna's just being nice."

"Don't defend her!" he exploded. "You're too trusting. Can't you see she's recruiting you for one of her sick porno movies?"

Considering he'd introduced me to those "sick" movies, I found the accusation a mite unfair. Before I could say so, Jeanna stepped in. "C'mon now, Joe. Don't you know I'd never disrespect you?" Her voice was soothing, like an animal trainer's. "You got it all wrong, man. I'm just making friends...nothing weird." She cooed at him, waving her hands around, as if to clear the air between them. Joe was having none of it and continued barking, despite her reassurances.

When I was a girl, my friends and I frequently brushed each other's hair after school. I'd done the same with my mom after dinner, one of the few ways I was able to feel close to her. Also, mere weeks earlier, Lisa had spent half an hour styling my hair into Joe's favorite upswept do while he waited in the other room. Still, he banished our guests from the hotel, calling a car service to drive them to LA. I went to bed with my back to him, afraid to say a word.

###

WE SPENT THE NEXT night camped out in Father Guido Sarducci's driveway. Actor-comedian Don Novello was a good friend of Joe's and the antithesis of the irreverent character he was known for. Don was sophisticated and smart, sensual and stylish, as was his elegantly rustic Bay Area home. Visiting with him and his lady-friend, I sipped wine and made witty conversation, hiding my deep-seated longing for a life that looked more like theirs.

I still felt like a guest on Blairwood Drive. Our home was in constant disarray. Boxes overflowed with stage clothes and tour equipment, arcane electronics, tools, faxes, letters, random paperwork, and a vast array of cords and antennas I wasn't permitted to move, trash, or organize. Whether Joe preferred the chaos or was fundamentally, inextricably attached to it, the mess was but a symptom—a microcosm of the macrocosm of us. We were scattered and in disarray. Until that changed, neither would our house.

When it got late, Don offered his guestroom, but Joe was like a kid with a new tent and opted to sleep in the RV instead. Don grinned. "Sounds fun, sleep well." But it wasn't and we didn't. I tossed and turned and was driven half mad by the driveway's subtle slope and earth's gravitational pull. The next morning, we left for Calistoga, a sweet little town of natural springs and man-made spas, to soak in pools of mineral water and tubs of toxin-sapping mud. We did our treatments side-by-side and worlds apart, lost in our own thoughts. Mine were how to get more bumps out of Joe. His remain unknown. Eventually, I asked for some, knowing I'd just failed us both. Forty-eight hours into our journey of self-care and I'd yet to renounce the worst drug of the bunch. On top of that, he didn't have any. Our cocaine had already run out.

We drove south, hundreds of miles to spend fifteen minutes at Gary's. Then due north to get the hell out of town again, determined not to lose our way this time.

※ ※ ※

AT JOSHUA TREE NATIONAL Park I felt a ray of hope. We scampered up rock formations, took in views, and explored crevices. With strength and balance, we climbed steep faces. We leaped rifts with childlike exuberance. When I needed support, Joe fashioned a walking stick. When he tired, I propped him up in the shade. Thoughts of cocaine were never far off, but for the moment we'd risen above them.

At dusk, we made our way off the rocks. I was bouncy and energetic but kept pace with Joe to extend our closeness. We passed a neighboring campsite where a small group had just settled in. Their boom box played a familiar tune—the unmistakable sound of dueling guitars on "Hotel California." I glanced at Joe to share a laugh then just as quickly stifled it. He'd heard it too, that was clear. His face was grim as he sped past their site, head down, lest they recognize him.

It was easy to forget where Joe had once been, a pinnacle too high to fathom. I was in the fourth grade when "Hotel California" came out, a nine-year-old in braces and headgear. I had no idea how to pull him from this rut, to allow him to soar again. I prayed that I wouldn't weigh him down further. I didn't think it was working.

I found Joe in the RV lining up hog rails. He kept them coming all night. Our driver closed himself off with the front-seat partition while we partied till sunrise. When the hog rails ceased, I tried to sleep, unsuccessfully. Two hours later, I stumbled to the fridge to chase a shot of vodka with half a beer and as much water as I could drink. Joe was engrossed in road maps. Polaroids were everywhere, dozens of shots of a cute couple grinning ear to ear, in hot-pink lipstick and a Santa hat. They looked happy and in love. *Where'd they go?* I thought. The love of my life, ten feet away, had yet to acknowledge my presence. I wormed into his field of vision only to sense it narrow. His face went dark, a partition closed. He willed me not to recognize him.

Preparing to depart, our driver retrieved a note from the windshield. Our neighbors, the Eagles fans, "thanked" us for keeping them awake with our generator. "Should we apologize?" I asked, but no one answered as we pulled away from the site. Exiting the park, I saw two signs. One warned of rattlesnakes on the rocks; the other prohibited generator use at night.

❋❋❋

IN MY HOME GROWING up, a moody, petulant child was persona non grata. Like most kids, I'd learned early on what worked and what didn't, which feelings to mask and behaviors to modify to secure my place in the herd. On my first day of kindergarten, my mom snapped a picture of me in our driveway. I'd concentrated hard on giving her my best smile ever—big and wide and pretty— desperate for her approval, to win her love if only for that day.

She didn't react either way, just put the camera in her purse and walked me to school. A few years later, in a group shot with my sisters and a new friend, I made a silly face while the other girls smiled prettily. Dad snapped the picture and Mom rolled her eyes. "Leave it to Kris to ruin the picture," she'd griped in front of my new friend and her well-to-do parents. I reminded myself to tone it down—one must always smile pretty for the camera.

Inside the RV, winding our way out of Joshua Tree, I projected cheeriness till it hurt. But when my inquiries about the day's itinerary went unanswered, I took a downward spiral from which I could not recover.

Claustrophobia kicked in. I switched seats compulsively, every five minutes, all over the RV. The longer I was ignored, the more diminished and anxious I felt, until I was verging on a meltdown. We stopped at a big box store where I lost sight of Joe, separated so long I panicked. *Why hasn't he sent a search party, blocked the exits and pulled an alarm? Doesn't he miss me? Isn't he worried?* When I found him blithely shopping for supplies, oblivious to my absence (or perhaps grateful for it), I promptly lost my shit, unleashing a tirade in the flashlight aisle for the entire store to witness. Joe barely reacted—his cruelest barb yet—and I retreated to the RV, gobsmacked. Diving into our stash, I took a pinch of this and dose of that until I'd sampled everything in it—cocaine, Quaaludes, mushrooms, and X, washed down with tequila, beer, and two tabs of acid. I even smoked the driver's roach. Anything to divert the rage and loathing I felt, and spare us all its spewing forth.

The men returned and we drove off; I didn't ask where. *I* was master of my destiny now! *I* controlled how I felt! We parked at a woodsy day camp atop a gently sloped pasture surrounded by tree-covered hills. I sat in the sun at a picnic table watching quails peck at the grass. I wasn't angry anymore, just morose and mildly paranoid. When Joe invited me for a walk instead of driving off without me, my relief was all too short-lived.

I'd ingested full doses of numerous substances, all at once, without telling anyone. I hadn't eaten in twenty-four hours. I'd slept ninety minutes, tops. Five minutes into our walk I started feeling like shit. In fifteen, every cell was permeated. I tried to fight it, and lost. I tried to fake it, and failed. My speech became jumbled and thoughts unclear. My body language, too, was disjointed and jerky, and my torso wracked with chills. Joints stiffened and fingers lost dexterity (aside from my thumbs—they refused to move independently). Some muscles went weak, others tensed up. My epidermis was both parched and clammy (such a maddening combination that I'd have peeled it off, if I could have). A breeze on my cheek felt like Velcro tearing. Straw sprouted from hair follicles and sandpaper coated my palms. We came upon a crystalline brook that felt like oil on my skin and sounded like nails on a chalkboard.

I grew increasingly agitated, as trees conspired to drive me insane and Mother Earth prepared to abort me. I retreated to the RV to brace myself, to await the inevitable purge. Joe caught up, looking pensive, but that was all I could discern. Whether he was angry, sad, fearful, or disappointed, I only knew I'd fucked up. We didn't argue, but something between us disconnected. I got on board adrift and alone, emotionally isolated. I have no memory of Joe in the RV from that point on. Only of the driver turning his back to me, preparing to depart. Suddenly, an epiphany—*he hates me*. I heard it like a bullhorn, emanating from his body.

The RV started moving. I stared out the window, sinking into myself and the upholstery. The road became a hairpin, but I held my tongue, afraid my words would be unwelcome—or worse, a distraction. Unable to watch, I ran to the back room to wait out the dangerous curves. There I went from frying pan to fire, descending into psychosis when the door closed.

Apparently, the back bedroom was a portal to hell—*How did I not know?* I wasn't locked in and yet something told me I was trapped. I fell to the bed sobbing, dropping my face in my hands. When the wave passed, I opened my eyes to see a cluster of demons on the bed. Faceless entities of palpable dark energy, there to share a message: *The shame and self-loathing you feel is not an illusion—it's one hundred percent real. You are worthless, useless, faulty, and broken. A grotesque abomination and burden to everyone.*

I'd had bad trips, but not like this. Years earlier, I'd met similar demons while tripping with a sweet young grad student. Entities had taunted me from a distance at first as I cowered on the bed. Suddenly, they'd given chase, and I'd run outside, hearing them laugh at my panic. They'd finally dispersed at sunrise.

The RV crew was a meaner bunch—focused, brazen, and fearless. They delighted in my pain and thrived on hysterics, tears, and hyperventilating. I screamed into a pillow until I was spent. When I looked up, the room was full of them.

I curled in a ball and clawed at my scalp. I pounded my skull with the heel of my fist.

We're not leaving, they chirped.

I want to die, I thought, and the demons laughed and laughed.

❋❋❋

The Ventana at Big Sur had plush, romantic cabins, but their minibars contained no food and there was no room service. The restaurant was closed, and the RV was bare, not a single Sun Chip left. I felt my body turn on itself with a hunger I'd never before felt. I refused to complain or even mention it to Joe. That I was with him and not in a heap on the road humbled me beyond words.

Physically, I was spent. Joe helped me bathe, then wrapped me in a thick robe and led me to the balcony. Our room overlooked a woodsy canyon. The sun had set hours ago. The trees were mere shadows, but the stars brightly shone.

"How many creatures must be out there?" I said.

"Lots," Joe replied. "All kinds."

"Birds and snakes and bunnies," I mused. "All that nesting and hunting... How do they do it?"

He gave me a funny look. "What, live? Survive?"

"I don't know...never mind. I don't know what I mean."

I wanted to tell him I was sorry. I tried to be cheerful and smile pretty when he tucked me into bed. He brushed a strand of hair from my face and kissed my forehead, then settled into a chair next to the bed with a book that went unread.

The Zoo

MY 1992 LAUNCHED WITH LESS promise than previous years. I vowed to turn things around, starting in the Swiss Alps. Joe was taking me skiing.

Though I'd never been to Europe, I'd enjoyed family trips to Mount Shasta, Big Bear, June Lake, and Mammoth, if not entirely for the sport itself. Mom tended to relax on vacation, and her natural athleticism was always a joy to behold. Jumping wakes, dominating a tennis court, or swishing down slopes, she was a vision of strength and grace I could admire from afar, out of the line of fire.

I was a competent skier at best, my limited skills hampered by a constant discomfiting chill. As a thin-skinned girl—in more ways than one—no amount of poly-filled nylon could ease my suffering. Shivering, juggling poles and bulky gloves, I'd press my back to every vertigo-inducing chair lift, wiping a perennial drip with stiff, frozen fingers and dwindling stores of Kleenex (no matter how many I thought to stuff in my pockets each morning). Every minute on every mountain was spent managing my cold, wet nose and icy blue appendages.

Switzerland was different. The Arosa Resort was sunny, temperate, and sheltered from wind, making jeans and a parka adequate coverage. Our rented chalet was situated such that we could shoot out the front door and ski up to the back. On the ride from Zurich, I'd tried to get acquainted with our guide. Hans being Swiss, however, I hadn't gotten far, yet soon came to find his genial reserve comforting. Considering the pathological emotionality of my last vacation, the Swiss way of extreme decorum was refreshing.

I felt already half renewed. Poised atop sweeping views and freshly fallen snow, my head was truly in the clouds. The path shone bright as I prepared to hunker down and ditch my demons—letting them blow clean off my soul and psyche, in a high-altitude, Northern European baptism. With few skiers out, we had room for an exhilarating first run. I hit my stride quickly, feeling strong and fluid halfway down when I heard Joe's muted cry. I stopped and called over, getting a weak ski pole wave in return. I backtracked to where he lay in the snow. *Hurt my knee*, Joe said, so calmly I had to assume the stretcher and four-man rescue team were just a cautionary measure. Not until the doctor cut away Joe's jeans did I realize the extent of injury. His knee swelled up like a melon.

They released him with crutches and instructions for fluid drainage. He encouraged me to keep skiing. I thought the idea absurd. I didn't want to be on top of the world without him.

We grabbed an outdoor table at a mountain café. Joe and Hans drank Irish coffee while I skated around an adjacent frozen pond. When I rejoined them, I felt as partner-less as I'd been on the ice. In truth, Joe had been slipping away all day—from detached to fully disengaged. He shut down my every conversation starter by shrugging and looking away. In front of the punctilious Hans, no less, it was humiliating.

I'd forgotten how Joe got overseas, how the first day of every trip found him brooding, surly, lethargic. I'd yet to miss cocaine. Whether due to the excitement, altitude, or pure mountain air, my first pang didn't arrive until that evening, at a group dinner with Hans's friends. They were lively and fun and I wanted to fit in. Instead, I felt awkward and self-conscious. In the morning, I felt fine again. I strolled as Joe hobbled around the resort village. I people-watched and basked in the setting, pretending Joe's mood wasn't ruining everything. Back at the chalet, he elevated his leg in the living room and asked me to retrieve something from upstairs—a book or his Zippo, probably. Whatever it was remained unfound when I came across something that sent me barreling down the stairs in a decidedly un-Swiss fashion.

"What the fuck are you doing with condoms?"

Joe sighed and slumped forward, bracing himself.

"Answer me, dammit!"

"Would you chill?" he said finally, sounding less defensive than bored. *Bored.*

"Are you fucking kidding me? Who is she? Who did you buy these for?"

"Let it go," he said simply. "Just let—"

"Cocksucker!" *So much for decorum.*

I'd been on the pill since high school. Joe and I didn't use condoms and never had. He had no excuse and his refusal to conjure one compounded the offense. What little he said was insufficiently rueful and I responded by throwing the box at him. The flimsy tri-pack bounced off the table anticlimactically (if you will), as did the half-empty pack of Marlboros I chucked next. Joe must've thought that was the end of it because he got up to hobble away. But between us was a writing desk, where Hans (who'd since disappeared) had just left a full cup of hot spiced wine. Before Joe could pass, I grabbed it.

As someone who drank white almost exclusively and was disinclined to throwing things in general, I found it oddly prescient to have (for the second time in our relationship) a glass of red within reach the very moment words failed me. Not that I wouldn't have thrown Chardonnay, but *clearly* the red was a firm thumbs-up from God, validating my position. I knew my Bible stories, dammit, and this was how He worked—"mysterious ways" and all that.

It was nothing short of miraculous. *Nothing* in that room was unmarred. Splatters went everywhere: walls, ceiling, carpet, couch, curtains, and clothes (all Joe's). As the cup emptied, so did my anger. I ran upstairs and dissolved into sobs. When Joe didn't appear, begging for forgiveness (or calling up the stairwell for it), I decided to salvage what was left of our trip. Taking a cue from Hans, I pretended nothing had happened—*What ugly scene?*—and Joe did the same. We relocated to Zurich, went on a shopping spree, then scored some coke and moved in with Hans for the week. We drank his booze, ate his cheese, and dined on fondue with his boss's family. It was dull and anticlimactic. Also better than being alone.

Back in LA, I called Lisa for a civil, woman-to-woman chat. Why her, I don't know. I was jetlagged and on edge. I needed a target and happened to have her number. At the beep of John Entwistle's answering machine, I unloaded a stream of vitriol so intense it surprised me. From composed and assertive ("to clarify things, with respect") to full-blown crazy and "back off, you cheating whore bitch."

I got no return call. Neither John nor Lisa ever mentioned it to me. Who the condoms were intended for remained a mystery.

❖❖❖

THINGS RETURNED TO NORMAL in February, as much our relationship could be framed in those terms. Joe made a string of sweet gestures. He accompanied me to an extended family gathering and bestowed his childhood clarinet on my sister, who was learning the instrument. He'd let me buy him a custom-made zoot suit that looked as ridiculous on him as he'd (loudly, repeatedly) predicted it would. He traded our Suzuki Samurai (purchased to get me to and from school) for a '73 Mustang convertible.

He even took me to a concert, the kind of arena-size gig Joe hated. After a rushed backstage greeting, we took our seats in the audience and were promptly blown away by Dire Straits. Three songs in, Joe dragged me to the Forum bar, where we stayed through the encore. He didn't say why, but I could guess. To a flailing rock star, Dire Straits's stellar performance must've felt akin to...oh, someone like me catching her boyfriend cheating with a beauty queen.

Playing Farm Aid made up for it. Joe was so honored to be asked by Willie Nelson himself, he cancelled a previous commitment to do it. Afterward was *American Bandstand's 40th Anniversary Special* with Entwistle, Skunk, Bo Diddley, and a host of other biggies. The taping involved a lot of "hurry up and wait," albeit with unintentional comic relief when Dick Clark took a break from barking orders to lose his shit over an AWOL headliner. The last-minute no-show caused scrambling for the crew and delays for the cast. Gregg Allman spent the downtime hunting Joe on a quest for blow. Gregg's girlfriend had already alerted me to the situation, and that Gregg had bailed early from rehab the day before—so together we conspired to keep our boyfriends apart. By showtime, poor Gregg looked downright defeated, having spent all day tracking a phantom Joe who *for some reason* was never where I said he'd be.

Joe and I were alone in his dressing room when Lita Ford burst in, beaming and gushing and rushing at my boyfriend, oblivious to me on the sofa. I stood up, and she froze midstream. I smiled in greeting, but her expression turned cold before she turned heel and left without a word. I raised an eyebrow. "What was that all about, Joe?" But he shrugged as if nothing bizarre had just happened.

I let it go, chalking it up to a one-way crush. Only later did I recall Lita's air of entitlement, entering a private room unannounced. I wondered if Joe was fucking her too. Nina Blackwood had behaved similarly once, albeit with more politeness. The former MTV host had dropped by one day and gone from bubbly to withdrawn in no time. I'd tried to be gracious, but she was clearly uncomfortable and didn't stay long. Who knows why? Joe's female friends were all were suspect, to me, by then.

Joe's male friends never behaved like that. I came home one day to find him and an unknown man rummaging through the boxes in our living room. Joe wanted to show the pale-faced stranger some "cool" bit of gear, and they were looking for it like kids sorting through Christmas gifts. I wondered if they were childhood friends.

"Hey, babe!" He waved me over. "Come meet Harry."

Before I could, Harry rushed up and clasped my hand in both of his. "How wonderful to meet you, Kristi! I've heard so much about you."

"Thanks, uh…nice to meet you, too."

"I'm sorry for barging in. I was in the neighborhood and Joe didn't think you'd mind."

"Of course not, Joe's friends are always welcome. Can I make you boys lunch?"

Harry said he wouldn't dream of putting me out so I went to the kitchen alone. Minutes later, Joe summoned me back. "Do we have something for an upset stomach?" He motioned toward Harry, who wasn't looking so good. I offered to run to the store.

"Harry, would you prefer Alka Seltzer, Pepto Bismol, or something else?"

"Anything's fine. I'm so sorry to trouble you," he replied. When I returned with four separate over-the-counter remedies, Harry went wide-eyed. "Wow, I'm so touched. Thank you!"

After he left, I asked Joe about his health. "Aside from the stomachache, I mean."

"It's serious, actually," Joe said, somber. "Harry's not well. He might not last a year."

Joe's friend Harry Nilsson, the renowned singer-songwriter, did make it another year, then died of a heart attack shortly after that.

✺✺✺

I WANTED TO BE the kind of girlfriend Joe gushed about to everyone he knew and who met everyone's approval. Like Gregg Allman's girlfriend, someone who could have fun and *be* fun, without depending on drugs and alcohol. It happened on rare occasions.

Joe and I attended a David Copperfield show. Midway through his set, the famous illusionist requested an audience volunteer. Arms shot up, mostly women's, as our handsome host scouted the aisles for his prey. I sank into my seat and was chosen anyway. I later learned David Spero, Joe's manager, had prearranged it as a prank.

Copperfield was a consummate showman who added flare to our bit with a flashy hip thrust to kick things off. "Now you try," he said, promptly duly impressed with my execution (of a classic stripper move...I mean, c'mon). He then made it appear as if my bra magically came off, which got a big laugh. After the show, we met Copperfield and his girlfriend backstage. She was pretty and petite and totally Joe's type, as evidenced by his whispered quip: *Let's ask David to swap.* I swatted at him, stifling a laugh. I felt too good to be jealous. I was having fun, overcoming stage fright and shyness without a single drink or line. A few years earlier, that would not have been noteworthy. By 1992, it was a rare victory.

I wasn't a sensation junky, nor did I use drugs just to numb the darker stuff. I needed them to access good stuff, too, baseline levels of pleasure other people achieved through dating, magic shows, and goofing on friends. For me, substance-free fun was elusive. And when I found it—like that day at Copperfield's show—it was both a blessing and curse. It convinced me a joyful life wasn't off the table yet. Also, that I wasn't an addict in need of help.

David Spero had been clean and sober for years. He and Joe had been friends longer than I'd been alive. I respected Spero, but he kept me at arm's length. I assumed he thought I wasn't good enough for Joe. The Copperfield prank felt like a sign of acceptance, if not full-blown approval. Spero was smart and savvy. He herded cats daily, keeping Joe's career on track, no matter how many forces were (inadvertently) derailing it. I wanted him to like me, but when he was around I liked myself less. David was successful. His wife was beautiful, poised, and a skilled equestrian. Though they showed me no unkindness, I was convinced they blamed me for dragging down the very man Spero was charged with promoting.

I had many demons. There was no shortage of devils at my shoulder. Now and then I'd spy an angel in the background, but that was where they stayed. Spero wasn't on my payroll. My addictions made his job harder, but it wasn't his place to step in. And I didn't invite it.

◆◆◆

IN APRIL, WE MET Ringo for dinner at La Toque. As it was a business meeting, I was touched by the inclusion—however, not enough to abstain from monstering. I arrived jittery, wired, and off-kilter but did my best to choke down an appetizer. When entrées arrived, I couldn't stomach another bite. Ringo pretended not to notice (the same man I'd noticed notice *everything*), but I felt compelled to explain anyway, claiming I'd had too big a lunch. Ringo put down his fork and looked into my eyes. "I understand," he said gently. "I've been there myself."

I was both relieved and mortified.

It wasn't my first slip-up with him. One year earlier, Joe had brought Ringo and me to the annual church service on Santa Cruz Island (one of eight Channel Islands off the coast of Santa Barbara, on whose foundation Joe was a board member). Seated in the tiny chapel's front pew, awaiting the proceedings, Ringo whispered to me that he was nervous. "I've never been to a Catholic mass and don't know when to stand or kneel. There's a lot of up and down, right?"

I'd nodded and told him to follow my lead. "Don't worry, I've done this thousands of times. I could do it in my sleep." It was true. And yet I wasn't asleep, I was high as a kite and under the impression pranking the always considerate and admittedly nervous Ringo Starr in the middle of a religious ceremony was a fine idea. During the bishop's homily, as the congregation remained rooted in their seats, I'd whispered at no such appointed time, "Ready...stand!"

Ringo had not so much as flinched. I hadn't fooled him then, and one year later wasn't fooling him or anyone. I was a mess.

✳✳✳

I STARTED KEEPING INTERACTIONS with non-drug users to a minimum. Christine, Vicki, and other old friends were held at bay while I made new ones who were less invested in my well-being.

Annie was an actress whose sexy/smart vibe had yet to land her a bigger role than a real-life fling with Warren Beatty. Trey was a casting director and Annie's gay best friend. Their time in the industry had lent them an irreverent perspective that Joe, especially, got a kick out of. Through their lens he was a character, a disenchanted rebel with nothing to prove. I was his outrageous displaced girlfriend, more Zelda Fitzgerald than rocker chick/train wreck. Success was overrated and a little unhip. *Of course! Why hadn't I seen it?*

One day I lent Trey a book that he'd long wanted to read. He and Annie had spent the day cushioning me like bodyguards, sitting on either side of my seat in the studio audience of *The Dennis Miller Show*, all because Joe's taping happen to occur in the middle of my full-blown monster. I was so grateful, I'd have lent Trey anything he wanted. But Joe went ballistic.

"I told you not to lend out my books!"

"One book, Joe. I lent *one* book. Of which you have *two* copies, by the way."

"Yeah, and they're *both* mine!"

"Learn to share!"

Annie and Trey observed us, three feet away, with blank expressions. They didn't move or say a word.

"Stop embarrassing yourself!" I screamed.

"Don't touch my stuff!" he bellowed.

Joe stormed off and my friends headed out, patting my head as they did so. They came over less often after that, usually when Joe wasn't home. It was just as well. His wildly disproportionate reactions were the new normal.

At La Toque one night, a dozen friends and acquaintances became a silent jury in the kangaroo court of our relationship, when I yanked a stray thread from the brim of Joe's baseball cap thinking he'd prefer it not hang in his face. I was wrong and received a verbal attack while literally cornered in my seat. With a wall behind me, Joe on my left, and six friends seated to my right, my only escape would've been to crawl under the table, and I didn't have the balls (nor cab fare to get home). I stared at my plate while Joe chewed me out, berating me for my thoughtless behavior.

For "obnoxiously" snipping the treasured, two-inch thread he'd "specifically arranged" to hang there. (Yes, he actually said that.) *How dare you?* he screamed. *Idiot!*

No one said anything. There was a long, awkward silence; then someone cleared their throat or commented on the weather, and socializing resumed. I sat up straight—mouth closed, eyes down—tidying my place setting, over and over.

❋❋❋

MY FATHER HAD NEVER been one to give advice, but he had his share of wise sayings. One was that people will always treat others the way they see them *treat themselves*. I wanted to blame Joe for his attacks—and I did—but there was no denying my role in our dysfunction. From the beginning, I'd compromised myself, overlooking slights and offenses that then took root and now dangled their rotten fruit over my head. That tree wasn't going anywhere, and I wasn't safe until I got out from under it.

I still felt like a guest in our home, one year in. Half the rooms were life-sized junk drawers. The remainder were neither stylish nor cozy. Furniture was awkwardly placed or downright uncomfortable. Feng shui was nonexistent. I was no interior designer, but I knew how to put a room together, and I hadn't been allowed to do it. Then Joe turned our sauna room into a sex dungeon—definitely not the direction I would have taken.

He staged a trial run while it was still half finished, infested with construction dust and spiders. I let him strap me into an elaborate sex swing that threatened to come unhinged and take me with it, but I suffered through playtime without complaint. I didn't want to disappoint him, nor be sent to bed and forced jones alone.

My usage was so out of control, I was partying too hard to throw a party.

One night, while still in the sweet spot of a buzz (well before sunrise), I made some calls and invited all our closest friends to a pool party barbecue one week later. Two days before the event, I launched another monster instead of shopping or preparing for guests. The Brothers (having moved to LA) arrived first, assessed the scene, and immediately took over—cleaning the grill, buying supplies, and manning the barbecue. As guests trickled in, I retreated upstairs, unable to greet them or make introductions. Joe was surprisingly sweet about hosting a party he hadn't wanted to throw, while I spent hours holed up in our bedroom. When I finally reentered the living room, I was cajoled to the window ledge by the Brothers calling me from outside. I couldn't say no to them any more than Joe could to Willie Nelson. I sat on the windowsill with a view across the pool, where Angus, Fergus, and Hamish Richardson were serenading me—failed hostess and woman of the house who still felt like a guest. It was a beautiful scene, actually. But instead of sublime euphoria, I felt ashamed and undeserving.

Soon afterward, we received a visit from Charlie and Dilworth, our Kiwi brothers from the Herbs. They'd been in LA on business—a potential record deal, or something—trying to reach us for days. Details of their trip were fuzzy, but I gathered they'd outdone themselves partying and were eager to return to New Zealand the next day. If they'd hoped to find a temporary haven on Blairwood, we sorely disappointed them.

Outrageous as our lifestyle was, some days were crazier than others, and we were neck-deep when our Maori brothers arrived. From the moment they entered, Joe and I talked nonstop, racing around physically and mentally, unfocused, inattentive, and vacuous. Our friends needed to relax, reflect, and bounce their potential deal off Joe, their music industry veteran friend. They deserved the same nurturing they'd once given us, and we failed them. I'd opened the door but no one was home. Midway through their visit, I left the room for a moment and returned to find Dilworth, the mighty ex-rugby player, openly crying.

"You've got to get out of this town before it eats your soul and kills your love," he pleaded.

"Please," Charlie reiterated. "Take care of yourselves. This is no way to live."

As someone who saw prophetic signs in everything from red wine to china patterns, it was like a telegram from God: *You're going the wrong way (stop)—exit now and turn around (stop).* But we didn't stop. We careened onward.

Funeral for a Friend

In April of 1992, Sam Kinison was killed by a drunk driver. Joe was torn up by the news but pulled it together as the word got out and calls came in. One was from Billy, Sam's limo driver and trusted confidant, and also one of ours. It was usually Billy who drove Sam to Vegas, so the tragic turn of events hit him hard and Joe invited him over.

Over the years, Billy had seen us through many a monster, carting us around like errant children in the capable hands of our own Mary Poppins. He'd scooped us in and out of the car for countless meetings, gigs, and airport runs. No matter how trashed we were, Billy delivered us on time and upright, with bystanders none the wiser. He knew when to take orders, when to take charge, and when to chill out and socialize. Many times we invited him inside to play pool or poker. Everyone liked Billy. I considered him a friend, and he and Sam had been even closer.

Billy sat at the bar with his face in his hands, a shell of his exuberant self. Joe consoled him and I poured drinks, wishing I had magical words of comfort to offer. Joe and Sam had had a unique bond; they identified with each other. Billy had, too, as a former child actor, and an adult who was no stranger to substance abuse. Sam had made strides battling those demons. He'd married his girlfriend, Malika, mere days before making her a widow. It was no secret that their relationship had been volatile, but they also truly loved each other.

Joe asked Billy about Malika and someone named Majid, apparently a close friend of Sam's. Malika had been in the car with Sam, Majid in the car behind them. He'd witnessed the accident and helped pull Sam from the wreckage, then looked on helplessly as his friend's spirit left his body. Billy said Malika was in the hospital. "She'll be okay. Maj was living at Sam's and is there now. The house is surrounded by press and it's stressing him out."

"Get him on the phone," Joe said. "Maybe we can help." He rocked side to side, smoking a cigarette, his free hand jammed in his front pocket. The playroom felt like Mission Control suddenly. I loved it when Joe took charge.

Billy confirmed, Majid was penned in by paparazzi with nowhere to go nor a way to get there. "It's not good," Billy said, covering the receiver. "For someone like Maj, especially."

I wondered what "someone like Maj" meant. "Is he holding?" was all Joe asked.

Billy checked then shook his head. "Not even a joint to take the edge off."

"Go get him. He can smoke our pot and hide out here as long as he wants."

I planned to contribute, if only by pouring drinks and cleaning ashtrays while the men bonded in their grief. Then Billy returned with the mysterious Majid and my altruism went out the window.

There was nothing selfless about primal lust. Tongue-tied and trembling weren't terribly helpful, and going weak in the knees made it tough to pour drinks. I stayed behind the bar out of self-preservation, needing a shield from Majid's sexual magnetism.

I observed him from ten feet away, an X-rated montage overtaking my brain: my legs around his waist, his face in my neck, our chests pressed together as I clawed at his back.

My stomach pulled in and hips pushed forward; my entire pelvic region was on autopilot. I felt flushed and my breath quickened. The inappropriateness was staggering—in front of Joe, mourning a friend's death. *I am a horrible person*, I thought, and continued fucking Majid senseless in my head.

❋❋❋

MAJID WAS MORE DISTRAUGHT than Billy, shuffling into the playroom to stop midstream, neither *in* nor *out* of it, but hovering in between (not an uncommon place to find Majid, I'd discover eventually). There were vacant seats galore—two sofas and four barstools—but he seemed to barely register his surroundings. Joe asked innocuous questions in a soothing tone, handling Majid—fittingly, I supposed—like a rescue puppy. Majid replied with vague phrasing and long pauses, less cagey than muddled and mentally far off. Billy had said he was a Vietnam vet, and the word *shell-shocked* came to mind. I wondered if that was what Billy had meant about Majid's reaction to being penned in.

I couldn't take my eyes off of him.

He was handsome and weathered, with high cheekbones, a chiseled jaw, and deep-set eyes framed by lush brows and lashes. I thought he resembled Scott Bakula from *Quantum Leap*, or like the actor's mysterious wayward brother (if he had one), fresh from some wild adventure overseas. He was pirate-like, with salt-and-pepper hair falling in waves from a wide-brimmed, black felt hat. He had a broad chest and a fit physique, what I could gauge of it through his blazer and jeans. But it was his voice that hooked me—smooth and deep, with the faintest of accents that I couldn't place.

I composed myself. "Majid, can I fix you a drink?"

I startled him, and then he did me, locking eyes and sending a jolt through my body. I feared my private thoughts being made transparent, projected like a hologram between us for everyone to see. He looked away, not answering, as if overwhelmed by a query into his wants and needs. I brought him a Heineken and he clasped a hand around it, on autopilot.

"So, where are you from?" I asked, cringing at my banality before plowing deeper in. "I mean, your heritage. Are you Native American?" I really had no idea what I was doing, just that I wanted to know something—*anything*—about him.

Majid looked at me then—really looked this time, peering over his spectacles as the corners of his mouth turned up. It was subtle and brief, but also his first sign of awareness since arriving. I held my breath, seeing a flicker of recognition, as if he understood the crux of my question better than I did. Had I really been so obvious? Joe was standing right next to him.

"No," Majid finally said. "I'm not Native American."

He turned away and I ducked behind the bar, busying myself for all I was worth. The men moved to the sofa to roll a joint. I tossed back a shot of vodka, feeling depraved and ridiculous.

⁕⁕⁕

ON THE DAY OF the funeral, Majid called to confirm we knew where to be and when. I was touched he'd check in on such a painful day, though he'd stayed in contact all week, opening up and expressing gratitude for our kindness. Joe had barely mentioned Sam's death, but I figured that's what the funeral was for. To grieve with Sam's friends and loved ones, without me in the way.

Majid gasped. "What do you mean you're not coming? You must! Joe needs you there!"

"Oh...okay," I stammered. "I'll go, then. Of course I will." Until that moment, I honestly had no idea that supporting a partner by being *at his side* was what one *did* as a girlfriend.

I'd never been good at comforting people. I picked up their emotions as easily as the smell of fresh baked bread, yet was helpless to ease the pain I frequently sensed. I'd been taught that fear, loneliness, and insecurity should not be coddled. Mine had been ignored or shamed; thus, I was at a loss in soothing those things in others. My cluelessness embarrassed me—How could I be so stupid? I told Joe I'd go with him, and he looked so relieved I had to wonder why he hadn't asked me to himself.

The more pressing issue was that we were two days into a monster with a funeral to attend. The good news: I wasn't too spacey, strung-out, or anxious yet. The bad: I'd just eaten a handful of high-quality mushrooms and was about to start tripping my ass off.

We needed to hurry. I was clad, at that moment, in a DayGlo, rhinestone stripper bikini and pink, peekaboo stilettos. My skin was slick with almond oil. Joe was wearing a blue Speedo and NASA baseball cap—that's it. His hair was matted and his face covered in stubble.

"Here's the drill," I told him. "I need a shower, a boom box, and a timer set for one hour." I'd never given Joe orders before and was stunned to see him fall in line.

"Anything else?"

"You need to shower, shave, and put on a suit. Pack enough bumps to get us both through the day and *don't eat any mushrooms.* You can tomorrow, but not today."

"Yeah, sure...no problem."

"I'm serious, Joe. It's too late for me but you *cannot* trip today."

"I won't," he said. "Don't worry."

While I showered, Joe brought in a boom box and hit play on my Rank and File cassette. Then he snuck into the hallway cabinet drawer and helped himself to some mushrooms. I sensed it like a drop in air pressure, just as we were to leave. The vibe in our bedroom took a noticeable shift. "Joseph!" I wailed. "You promised!"

"Aw, c'mon." He waved me off. "I'm fine. It'll be good."

I zipped up my boots and led him to the limo. It would not be good.

⁕⁕⁕

I WAS RELIEVED TO see both Billy and Norm in our driveway. If ever we needed to be bookended by a two-man entourage, now was it. I would've preferred Smokey and Sean (the former was out of town, the latter in rehab), yet Norm and Billy were capable of escorting us in and out of the chapel, blocking the press, and managing other threats to our vulnerable psyches. If Joe (or I) got overemotional, one of them would swoop in and extricate us. Tripping in public was unwise, but I was cautiously optimistic. Joe was quiet and calm, and I felt relatively clear and centered.

At some point en route, I made full disclosure to Billy. He had a right to know what he was up against (and I would've expected the same in his position). When he asked if I had a hit to spare, I didn't hesitate to give him a few stems to chew on later. At Forrest Lawn, Norm and Billy got us inside without incident. Majid led us to a pew so near the front as to be dangerously conspicuous. *We'll keep to ourselves and be fine*, I thought, but things went south from there.

I sensed Joe deteriorating by his despondent expression and collapsed posture. I held his hand and stroked his arm, asking in a whisper if he was okay. He didn't respond but clenched his jaw and started fidgeting wildly. I could almost feel the darkness inside radiating off his body. Having had my share of nightmare trips, I knew exactly how helpless he was against his. I propped him up throughout the service as the jerking grew more pronounced. If it weren't for the string of bittersweet tributes being given at the podium, we would've surely attracted attention. At one point, I had to forcefully yank down Joe's arm as he gestured crazily at Richard Belzer *mid-speech* to convey his desire to get up and speak. Belzer didn't seem to notice and the service ended without incident.

In the parking lot, Joe refused to let Billy back in the car. No longer mute and unresponsive, he railed against our stalwart driver for no apparent reason. Billy, smartly, disengaged and caught a ride elsewhere. Norm ducked into the driver's seat, but I demanded that Joe explain his behavior.

"*Get in the car!*" he snapped.

Once we'd entered the freeway he unloaded on me. "How could you betray me like that?"

"What are you talking about?"

"You are my fucking girlfriend and I do not permit you to share drugs with a chauffeur!"

"*That's* what this is about? Are you nuts? Billy's our *friend*, remember?"

"Your job is to take care of me, no one else, *get it?*"

"Look," I sighed. "Let's not do this now. Let's calm down and discuss it later. It's an emotional day and I'm sure you don't—"

"Screw you! I'm not emotional! You're selfish and stupid and I'm tired of it."

"Joe, please...let's not fight." I touched his shoulder but he swatted my hand away. Things were escalating quickly, even for Joe. I took a cue from Billy and ran for cover. I moved to the seat across from Joe, stared out the window, and waited for it to be over.

It would be a while. "Billy used you like a doormat. How do you think that makes me feel?!"

"Please stop. You're making something out of nothing. Just because you're having a bad trip, don't make me have one."

"Act like a doormat and I'll treat you like one."

Whenever Joe made that leap, from mildly absurd to full-blown illogical, I knew I was in trouble. I wasn't just tripping anymore, I was peaking, and I went from centered to desperate in no time at all. I was so highly suggestible that the enclosing darkness was unstoppable. I pleaded and argued, but nothing worked, and when I asked Norm to pull over, Joe demanded he drive on. Until we reached our destination—Gary Belz's home studio in Encino—I was an open target.

One year earlier, right after moving in together, we'd had an exceptionally nasty fight during which Joe had chased me through the house. I'd begged him to stop, running from room to room, hoping he'd come to his senses before one of us got hurt. He'd cornered me near the bedroom windows—four of which opened, two with a crank and two with a push. When he still refused to back off, I snapped. *You're suffocating me! You're making it so I can't breathe!* I spun to my left, planted my palms on two panes of one window, and, without thinking, threw all my weight behind them and pushed. Unfortunately, that window required a crank to open, so it didn't move on its hinges. Instead, my hands went straight through the glass. Leftover shards encircled my arms at the elbows, one of which had cut a deep, two-inch gash in my right forearm. Joe calmed down instantly. He grabbed a first aid kit, sat me on the bed, and dressed my wound with great tenderness. When Angelina arrived for work, she took one look under the bandage and rushed me to an emergency clinic for stitches. Since then, we had a new house rule: *Whenever an argument gets out of hand, we separate to neutral corners of the house.* In a split-level ranch, that was easy enough. In the back of a limo? I was shit out of luck.

My only hope was that he'd tire of the drama. He got meaner and louder instead. Totally out of control, he didn't know what he was doing—certainly that it was wrong, but how susceptible I was? I don't think he knew. Though I tried to tell him, repeatedly.

"I'm *begging you* to stop."

"Beg all you want. Beg like a dog."

"Don't you see? This is going to end so badly—just stop, honey, please!"

"Fuck you. You're a whore."

With that, the writing was on the wall. In a confined space with no escape, I was unable to keep myself calm. Bit by bit, I lost control, shaking from head to toe. Every muscle tensed. My back was petrified stone. "Don't make me have a bad trip. You *cannot* do that to me. *Please, please, please stop.*"

He didn't stop.

"I can't get out! Don't you see? I'm losing my mind right now. Please, listen to me. I'm telling you, I'll lose control. I will, so help me, *I will unless you stop.*"

He didn't stop.

To this day, I have never lost my shit on another person like I did on him right then, launching off my seat like a rocket across the limo. Closing the distance before he had time to flinch, I landed half on the seat and half in his lap, poised over him and swinging both fists at his head.

He never fought back or resisted at all. He turned his face and shielded his head. Maybe he thought he deserved a beating. I didn't know and didn't care. I didn't quit until I was spent, completely out of breath. I clambered to my seat and neither of us moved. When I raised my eyes, Joe looked gutted, like a lump of discarded clothing. Like the man inside had spontaneously combusted.

Norm announced our ETA over the intercom sounding more shaken than either of us. I realized he'd heard the whole thing.

⚜⚜⚜

Gary Belz's LA home housed a state-of-the-art recording studio. The day of Sam's funeral, Steve Cropper and other musicians awaited Joe for some project I knew nothing about. I just wanted him out of the car.

I'd never felt so cold toward him, so completely and utterly detached. As we made our way up Gary's long driveway, Joe came back to life—the old Joe, the sweet and vulnerable man I'd loved through more than one lifetime—begging me to pretend that everything was fine. Like nothing life-altering had just happened.

"I know it's a lot to ask, and I'll make it up to you, I swear, but I need this favor right now." He said he'd be mortified if anyone at Gary's found out, but that was hardly *my* problem. I didn't even intend to get out. When Norm dropped Joe off, I'd go home, maybe all the way to Texas—I was that *done*. We needed to be separated—nothing could be more obvious—except he wouldn't hear of it and begged me to stay with him at Gary's. He wouldn't take no for an answer, probably sensing how close he was to losing me. I agreed, to avoid a scene.

"You'll pretend everything's fine? Kill me tomorrow, but fake it today?"

"Whatever you say." As if Norm wouldn't tell all of CLS as soon as he drove away. Not that Norm had any more insight into what had really taken place than I suspected Joe did.

I had finally clued in to at least one finer point in my role as girlfriend. I'd stepped up as a stabilizing force, provided guidance and a solid shoulder to lean on. I'd pulled it together, onward through the fog on this trippy, challenging day, stupidly feeling proud of myself, right before Joe wiped his feet on me again. Could I not be a good girlfriend to him *and* a friend to Billy? Or was Billy just an excuse for Joe to sabotage our relationship the moment I fulfilled my role in it?

I don't claim to know what went on in Joe's head. His pointed, sustained maleficence that day was not who I knew him to be, and yet my ex-girlfriend Eileen could've said the same of me. Twice in my life I'd been that vicious. Once, berating Eileen *specifically* to sabotage our relationship—to yank off the Band-Aid *but quick*. The other incident sickens me to this day. Testing the loyalty of our family dog (who really did love me best), I'd called him to me, then pushed him away, repeatedly, half a dozen times—*bad dog, I hate you, go away*. Then, *c'mere, Obi! G'boy! Such a good doggie!* I'd needed to know he'd always return, no matter how ugly and unlovable I could be. He did, of course, though more cautiously each time. More confused with every dagger-sharp rebuke.

What Joe was trying to prove that day, I couldn't say. I didn't have many answers for him, anyway. My inner ratio of self-love to blind loyalty fluctuated daily. Eileen had walked out never to return, even to collect her belongings. She'd moved in with Stella, another Sugar's stripper, and became her girlfriend days later. Obi loved me till the end, but dogs are forgiving and resilient. And look where it got him: neglected, abandoned, and put to sleep while I'd been partying half a world away in Australia.

Still, I gave Joe my word and let him help me out of the limo. Then I skirted past him and straight up to Gary. "Get me away from that motherfucker this instant before I kill him."

I had met Gary only once or twice before. Longtime friends with Joe and Isaac Tigrett, he seemed like a good man. He had a guru in India and an uncommon inner peace about him. Gary also had a special place in my heart for having named a Peabody duck after me, but all he knew about me was that I suddenly wanted to kill the man who'd asked him to do it.

Gary didn't bat an eye. I may as well have asked him for a soda. Joe, however, crumbled, the pain of my betrayal written all over his face. He deflated before my eyes, and still I *did not care*. I followed Gary's wife Shelly to their guesthouse, so nonchalant a hostess I had to wonder if the Hatfields and McCoys dropped by her place regularly. (I made a mental note to look into this Indian guru thing.) Shelly insisted I stay as long as needed. "Make yourself at home, take a nap or a bath…whatever you need, don't worry about a thing."

When she left, my bad trip ended—*whoosh*. The comedown was instantaneous. I lay back on the bed's plush white comforter, feeling my head clear and heart open. Cold dispassion from earlier was gone. I felt normal, wholly reconnected. My love for Joe came flooding back, as did the fear of losing him. Well, shit. *Now what?*

Then an angel appeared. I didn't see her any more than I'd "seen" demons in the RV, but she was as tangible and present as Shelly had been ten minutes earlier. She had a message for me: *Everything will be okay. Tell Joe you love him, then go home and clean the house from top to bottom. You'll be fine then. I promise.*

Whether divine apparition or delusional hallucination, I knew she spoke the truth. Elated, I flew off the bed, fixed my hair, and marched into the studio. I spied Joe in back, eyeing my approach like a man facing a noose. He told me later that he'd been convinced it was over and that I'd come to say I was leaving him for good. Instead, I hugged him. "I love you. I'm going home to clean the house. When you finish, hurry back and everything will be fine, I promise."

He looked at me like I was nuts, but I'd never felt more sane. When Norm dropped me off, I took one look around and called Angelina for help. By 9:00 p.m. the place was immaculate, but Joe barely noticed. He walked through the door, flung his arms around me, and wept in my arms—an occurrence as rare as angelic apparitions. "I can't believe you're here," he croaked.

"Of course I am... I said I'd be, didn't I?"

"I thought you'd be gone. I'd die if that happened, Kristi. Losing you would kill me."

"I will never leave you," I said. A mix of emotions welled up in me too: shame and remorse for hurting him again, but also something new—a tangible sense of leverage. The power balance had shifted. Less of the reliable doormat I'd been, I was now a moving target.

Gold Dust Woman

JOE SPENT THE SUMMER of 1992 revisiting the Ringo experience in his second All-Starr Band. I spent the summer getting reacquainted with crack.

It started with Lisa. With the best intentions, Joe encouraged me to spend time with her. He had every reason to think I might benefit. Lisa had been navigating the rock-and-roll lifestyle longer than I had (not to mention, for a time, the same rocker). She thrived in her role as girlfriend and muse, whereas I was still finding my footing. I liked Lisa, and I admired her self-assurance, but underlying my fondness was a lingering jealousy. It kept our friendship superficial.

I had more in common with Malika Kinison, whom Majid brought to the house some weeks after Sam's funeral. Before they arrived, I confirmed with a mutual acquaintance that Malika was indeed smart, strong, and outspoken, as I suspected. He then shared an interesting tidbit. "She can tell whether you're a good or bad person by touching you."

"That sounds weird. Touch me how, exactly? Is she psychic?"

"'All I know is, she'll find an excuse to touch you, then either relax and stay, or leave immediately."

When I answered the door that night, Malika grabbed my hand before I knew what hit me and held it a few beats longer than normal. Whether she was "reading" me or naturally outgoing, I couldn't say. I was just happy she and Majid stayed, though Joe didn't feel the same.

Since the funeral, he'd been reserved around Majid, who was a complex character with a lot churning beneath the surface. Sam had been his best friend and employer, and his death set Majid adrift—a place not unfamiliar to him. At age eight, Majid had been sent by his family in Jordan to an American orphanage. Ten years later he'd gone to Vietnam, eager to repay the country that had taken him in. He returned changed, somewhat broken, and had since lived on the fringe, though with no shortage of women to care for him. I knew the type. I'd *been* that type, and I liked to think I wasn't anymore. So, while my heart went out to Majid, the rest of me was off limits. A man without roots had nothing to lose. As reckless as I could be, I was not completely stupid.

Though a loner, Majid had loved Sam like a brother and been protective of him. I thought Joe could use a friend like that, and that I could befriend Malika in the process. That didn't happen. Shortly after they arrived, Joe went to bed early. "I'm fine," he said when I checked on him. "Just too tired to be good company."

I returned to our guests, which is what he would've done. It felt wrong when I did it, yet also like a taste of the independence I needed. I splurged on cocaine (using my new credit card's cash advances), making four runs to our dealer in all and feeling like the ultimate woman-of-the-house hostess.

Eighteen hours later, Maj and Malika were still hanging out and Joe was still ensconced upstairs. I apologized for his antisocialness, but Malika said Sam had been like that, too. "Success is stressful for guys like Joe and Sam. They end up feeling responsible for entertaining everyone. He doesn't have to with us, but he may not realize that."

"I wish I could make him understand. He could kick back while we entertain *him*."

"I bet we can," she said. When I asked how, Malika grinned. "Pillow fight! It works every time."

Her confidence was infectious. The next thing I knew, we were in the guestroom, snipping holes in two (rather expensive) pillows. While Majid waited downstairs, she and I tiptoed to the master bedroom. Sliding open the rice paper doors, we burst in and leaped on the bed, pummeling each other with the jerry-rigged pillows. We squealed and giggled on either side of Joe as he slowly regained consciousness and took in the ruckus. He looked from Malika to me, as downy stuffing settled on every surface, including his head, face, and eyelashes. Then he bellowed and we raced out faster than we'd entered.

Flying down the hall on Malika's heels, it occurred to me our little stunt had less eased Joe's stress than fueled it. When I pointed this out, she shrugged, unruffled to the end.

❦❦❦

I LONGED TO BE so dauntless, to walk through the world with Malika's moxie and Lisa's magnetism, instead of shrinking from rebuke and rejection. I often felt exposed, less for what I *did* than what I *was*. Joe's fury told me I was defective and inadequate—or that's what I heard, anyway.

I was once chastised in kindergarten by an overworked, stressed-out teacher. With one look at the massive lather I'd worked up at the corner sink, she'd snapped. *Kristin! I specifically told you not to use so much soap!* (It was true, she'd told the whole class that very morning.) *That's the point*, I wanted to say. I'd made that huge froth using just one drop, hoping to impress her with my hand-washing/soap-conserving ability. *See how ingenious I am? How smart and deserving of love?* But I couldn't explain it, roiling and frozen by her public scolding. I hung my head and rinsed my hands, vowing to never try again. Never excel, experiment, or attempt to impress another grown-up, ever. I was four years old and I already hated myself.

I didn't stop striving, of course, but the slightest criticism wounded me. Dad wasn't a critical person, but Mom had only to make one exasperated sigh to send me reeling. Not only were her standards high but her values didn't align with mine. She hated my clothes and hair, humor, politics, causes, and what little she knew of my belief system. She hated the way I stuck out, especially at church where she wanted to make a good impression. By the time I left home, we'd given up trying to connect.

After my meth debacle, I couldn't really connect with anyone...until Joe. With him I was attuned for the first time ever. I felt safe to open up, for a while. But old patterns don't just disappear. Learned helplessness is real and powerful, and I slowly succumbed to it again. Drugs and alcohol blew open the rare portal, but one rogue wave—a harsh word or look from someone who mattered—would slam it shut again. The pillow fight had been my attempt to connect through playfulness. Being playful made me feel vulnerable—*leave it to Kris to ruin the picture*—so Joe's lambasting had done damage. Feeling like I couldn't win made me ashamed and angry. I stuffed those feelings down because no one loves an angry woman. I'd learned that lesson by kindergarten.

❖❖❖

ONE DAY, LISA CAME by to hang out. When it was time to go, she needed a ride and Joe volunteered me. After a couple of stops, we arrived at a nondescript apartment in the Valley. I met her roommate Felicia, a pretty, petite brunette. Unlike Lisa, who was dark-eyed and olive-skinned, Felicia was fair and finely boned, bubbly, with an approachable kind of beauty, whereas Lisa was mysterious and smoldering. The girls were polar opposites, with one commonality.

I thought it odd to draw the curtains on such a lovely spring day, until Lisa dumped the product of our errands on her coffee table: Bic lighters and crack cocaine. Without a word, the girls proceeded to stuff rocks into the charred ends of two glass straws, then fire them up to smoke. One of them offered me a hit.

"No thanks," I chirped, guzzling a beer instead. I hadn't been in the same room with crack in six years and was grateful not to feel a craving. I was also aghast at their amateur tactics. *What a waste of perfectly good drugs.*

The man I'd smoked crack with in Austin had set a high bar. Freddie had used precise techniques and expensive paraphernalia: three-piece pipes with dual stems, rubber stoppers, stacked screens, and variable butane torches. On Felicia's table was a keepsake box full of nearly dead Bic lighters. This was not the girls' first rodeo, and I felt duty-bound to tutor them.

"Give me that," I said, reaching for Felicia's pipette. Without inserting a rock, I demonstrated how to tilt the glass, heat it, rotate it, and inhale with careful, practiced technique. Receiving blank looks, I gave up and handed it back. "It's been fun, girls, but I gotta go."

The next time Lisa came over, she spent so much time smoking in our bathroom I was tempted to betray her confidence. I waited for Joe to notice—the chemical smell alone!—but he didn't. I considered telling Lisa what Marcy Horky had told me—*frankly, I'm worried about you*—but I didn't have the balls. The closest I got was joking that her pee breaks were disrupting our pool game. Lisa laughed and continued on, oblivious.

Days later, I dumped out half a gram on a plate taken from the dishwasher that was still damp, ruining the only blow I had.

Unless…? I'd seen cocaine cooked into crack many times, yet hadn't paid close enough attention to memorize the process. Also, Freddie had purposely concealed the recipe from me.

I called Lisa and got Felicia on the phone. "I've never cooked it either," she said. "Want me to come over and help you figure it out?" I declined and hung up instead.

The All-Starr rehearsals were in full swing. I needed to clean up my act, not mess around with crack. What the hell was I thinking?

❖❖❖

I ACCOMPANIED JOE TO the final rehearsal, seeing many familiar faces: Ringo and Barb, Hillary Gerard, Nils Lofgren, Timothy B. Schmit, and Zak Starkey. New members included the Guess Who's Burton Cummings, saxophonist Tim Cappello, and prog rocker Todd Rundgren (whose presence ensured Joe would no longer be the worst-dressed band member). I met Ringo's tour manager Arlie (Richard Manuel's widow, the Band's original singer). She made me feel welcome and cleared a spot on the couch where I could sit and watch the men play.

Right away, I noticed their new guitarist, a rough-and-tumble guy in his late forties, with ginger hair and tousled looks. He seemed vaguely familiar, though I was certain we'd never met. When he started playing, I knew why. I'd danced to those exact guitar sounds hundreds of times at Sugar's. It was *Dave fucking Edmunds!*

I had no one to share my excitement with. Sandy Helm and Liz Danko weren't there this time, which saddened me. Then the wife of a new band member walked in—a beautiful, blond, buxom rocker chick, straight out of an MTV video. She was so striking as to be intimidating, but the feeling didn't last because Cici Edmunds was as sweet as she was stunning. What's more, she and Dave had just bought a house in our neighborhood, walking distance from Blairwood.

There was a buzz in the air and adventure on the horizon. My drug use and Joe's moods were as unpredictable as ever, but when our upswings coincided, life was good. All I had to do was not fuck it up, to resist the urge to self-sabotage.

✢✢✢

WHEN I FIRST MADE the leap from snorting coke to smoking crack, Joe voiced concern and then went quiet, rocking side to side, brow furrowed and lips pursed. Did he fear being hypocritical? Did he feel at all responsible for my dependency and perforated septum? I hoped he grappled with those questions. For all my talk of personal freedom, I sometimes blamed him for both. Other times I blamed myself. Either way, I rationalized smoking crack as a break for my beleaguered septum. That's what I told my boyfriend and myself, which at the time sounded perfectly logical. I remember that clearly—the insanity looked sane to me. Above all, I was certain of two things: first, that I had crack under control (I didn't), and second, that I'd never seen Joe look quite so helpless as he did while watching me do it.

I don't recall exactly how it started, but probably the night Lisa and Felicia came over together. One thing led to another and I fell into it with them. I didn't hide it from Joe, who was in a buoyant mood, surrounded by three young attractive women. I don't recall where I scored more when the girls left or how I came to possess an entire cigar-tube-full. I do remember Joe's expression as I went through it, rock by rock. Next to me in bed, he eyed the size of my stash, timidly inquiring how long I thought it might last. Sensing he felt shut out and scared to death, I offered to cease and desist right then. *I'll save it for tomorrow or next week...say the word, babe*, but he didn't.

I don't recall acquiring my first or second pipe, only that, one fine morning at 8:45 a.m., I took a limo to a head shop for a third. Why, I don't know…in case of an earthquake, I guess. I believed in preparedness. Waiting for the store to open, I cranked the radio and stood through the sunroof dancing my ass off. When the shop opened, I rushed inside, chatty and ecstatic. The clerk scowled in return. I brushed him off, pitying the peasant. How could anyone punch a timecard when there was so much good crack to be smoked?

I have one other clear memory. An afternoon when Joe was out of town (on Ringo's tour, which launched concurrently with my crack smoking), I was with Lisa and a friend of hers, driving all over LA and failing to score. We were strung out and broke, and I was frustrated that their dealer refused to front us any. Then, a wondrous moment, as Lisa's friend remembered an apartment where she'd recently spilled some rocks. It was a long shot, she said, but also all we had. Gaining entry through an unlatched patio door, we found it vacant except for the crack hailstorm that covered the living room carpet.

Imprinted in my memory is a sense of camaraderie, sitting in a circle smoking rocks off the floor, like friends eating s'mores, laughing gaily around a campfire.

✸✸✸

MY CHOPPY MEMORIES OF crack are entwined with equally vague images of the tour. There was drinking and drugging and the usual late-night silliness, costarring Zak, Joe's new, temporary sidekick. The band traveled partly by private plane, and though I don't recall being on it, I have a bunch of photos that suggest I was. If I was touched by Ringo's magic, I do not recall that either. I remember going out of my way to watch Burton and Dave perform, but overall the show didn't hold my attention.

One highlight was Radio City Music Hall, where I hung out with Cici amidst the usual backstage frenzy. We found an alcove with a private bathroom and while waiting our turn, Cici mentioned seeing Howard Stern among the celebrity guests. I relayed my experience, adding, "He's a groundbreaker, but also a cunning little shit I don't trust any farther than I can throw him."

Just then, the bathroom door opened and out walked Howard. "Gotcha!" he yelled, pointing at me in mock fury. "I heard every word! Shame on you...shame, shame, *shame*." Cici doubled over laughing as I stammered an apology. Howard waved it off. "Forget it," he grinned. "Happens all the time, actually."

Post-gig, the band was in high spirits. They'd had fun and sounded tight. Joe and I celebrated with bumps in our room, and suddenly I was monstering. The next day Joe suggested a Madison Avenue shopping spree, but I was too strung out to risk being seen in that condition. Joe left and returned with a gift—an Issey Miyake party dress in iridescent green-black taffeta. The size and color were ideal, but the fashionable look didn't suit me. It belonged on someone with real poise and femininity.

I flew home to recoup, rejoining the band in Kansas City. The previous night Joe had called me in LA, upbeat but lonely, saying he missed me terribly. I arrived at the hotel rested and refreshed, but instead of being given a room key, I was told to have a seat. Hotel security needed to talk to me.

"Security?" I said, trying to mirror the desk clerk's buttery tone.

"Well," he replied carefully. "It seems there's an issue with Mr. Walsh's...furnishings."

"I don't understand," I said, images of chainsaws and airborne TV sets filling my head.

The clerk leaned in conspiratorially. "I don't know the whole story," he whispered, with barely concealed delight, *"but there may have been a glue gun involved."*

A glue gun had been involved—an industrial-strength one. Also, a desk chair, a coffee table, and an ashtray complete with a *lit* cigarette inside. Those and other items had been stuck to Joe's ceiling, most of them surprisingly successfully. The weight of the TV, however, proved too much, and shortly after it hit the floor, security showed up. Joe and his minions—one Zak Starkey and a Mr. Burton Cummings—managed to bluff their way out of an inspection. It wasn't until a housekeeper stumbled upon the scene (which by then included Burton actively vomiting into Joe's suitcase) that security returned, demanding entry.

I waited in the lobby while Ringo's team pleaded for leniency. Once it was determined the culprits could stay another night, I was reunited with my mate, who looked as sheepish as I'd ever seen him. I thought the incident both immature and hilarious, and politely suggested he channel his energy more productively in the future. I should've taken my own advice.

❦

I BROKE OFF THE affairs with Smokey and Terry Reid to divert my energy toward something, if not more productive, then within my control. Terry and Smokey were married men who'd seen me when it was convenient for them. I hadn't started two affairs to *increase* my frustration and insecurity. Besides, the real thrills had been dwindling from the beginning. The passions I shared with Smokey and Terry proved no less fleeting than too many others in my life had been.

Crack highs were the very definition of fleeting, but at least I had a say in their *how* and *when*. (Though *how much* was another story, I didn't know it then.) With time to kill and credit cards to burn, I could have crack on *my* schedule, available when *I* snapped my fingers. It was hardly guilt-free, but less so than cheating, I had to believe.

Goodbyes with Terry took an interesting turn when his disappointment and open longing seduced me more than any of the moves he'd made previously. The sudden chemistry caught me off guard, and had I not been craving a hit, I'd have indulged in "one last go" with him. Instead, I cut the cord and he left without arguing, only a look of concern for the vice that had replaced him.

Breaking off with Smokey was the more complicated feat—more than expected, actually. At a window table at the Great Greek restaurant, he gloated about finally having real time to spend with me—a rarity, in that Joe was traveling while Smokey (for reasons I don't recall) was neither with him nor in Detroit—the two places he'd normally be. Smokey expected to spend all evening with me, our first chance to have sex without rushing. I told him it was over before his first bite of salad, my terrible timing par for the course.

Little about my affairs had been the way I'd hoped. Why should ending them go any better? It was too late for Smokey and me to even have one last go. After a year of sneaking around—to the day, he wistfully informed me—I no longer felt uplifted in his arms, but dirty. I thought ending it would be a favor to us both—that he'd feel relieved or have seen it coming. Instead, he was hurt and got sentimental on me. I tried to be kind, but inside I fumed, appalled at the notion I should feel bad for him, when throughout our affair *his* scarcity had left me wanting.

❋❋❋

IN JULY, THE ALL-STARRS spent three weeks in Europe and though Joe wanted to take me, he didn't. He said the band would make a dozen border crossings, and as he was still flagged from the caffeine bust in Hawaii, if I traveled with him, I'd be subjected to extra searches too, potentially delaying the band. "Besides," he said, "we have the rest of our lives to do Europe together."

I believed him. Joe's career would get back on track, and I'd bore with cocaine in all forms. We'd buckle down to write his biography, a true team, like Jeanna Fine and her fiancé. Until then, I'd saturate self-doubt in dopamine, a feel-good flood of biblical proportions.

In picking a partner in crime, my options were limited and Felicia was easy—also clingy, which had its pros and cons. Joe ruled the roost at home—where he led, I followed. When he was a clown, I applauded. Felicia idolized me. We had had our own sick chemistry.

For starters, we smoked crack like a Vegas act. We were the big-game illusionists meets comedic improv contortionists of freebasing. For the first time, I understood the impetus behind Joe and Rick's fart noise and prank call recordings, though my videos with Felicia were the funnier shtick. Our best was a workout class—the aerobics of crack. *Out with the good air, in with the bad*, I intoned, demonstrating with exaggerated exhales while Felicia made Vanna White gestures at my diaphragm. We'd wrap it up by taking massive hits and dancing around the room like idiots.

I'd finally taught Felicia to freebase properly—Olympic-level techniques meant to maximize every toxic molecule. A dubious talent to be sure, it nonetheless impressed her dealer. Max made a long, slow whistle at my performance. "Never seen anything like it," he said, and I beamed like I'd won an Oscar. We had Max deliver twice, but since I knew Joe would blow a gasket, I made Felicia drive us to Max's after that. His girlfriend was young—fifteen at most— with a slack-toned moon face and minimal reading skills. When she ruined a batch of cooktop pudding, Max scolded her in a way that made me want to leave. I couldn't get home fast enough.

I didn't equate my lifestyle with theirs. I lived in Studio City and hung out in VIP rooms and limousines. Max trolled Hollywood selling to addicts (I imagined) and was as different from me as Austin speed freaks. I started wanting distance from Felicia, too. Initially, she would go home between binges; then one day she just stopped leaving. If I hinted at it, she'd score more crack to distract me. One day I woke with a pipe in my mouth, because (as Felicia explained) she didn't like getting high alone and thought waking me up that way would be funny. When Joe was due home, Felicia finally got the boot. I cleaned house, erased our videos, and stashed my gear under the bathroom sink.

I went to LAX with Cici, Dave being on Joe's same flight. Between my friendship with her and Joe's return, my heart was full enough to burst. Our foursome piled into the limo and I handed Joe the eight ball (three and half grams) I'd brought from Gary's. For the rest of the day, Joe and I floated on air. It felt like starting over, like re-falling in love.

He apparently thought so too, because at 11:00 p.m. he set aside my pool cue, took my hands, and dropped to one knee. Gazing up into my eyes, he said, "Will you marry me?"

I squealed. "Yes! Of course I will!" I pulled him to his feet for a kiss, then said, "I had no idea. When did you—I mean, why...?" I didn't know what to say. I never saw it coming.

"Being apart three weeks made me realize I can't live without you. I want you with me forever. On the flight home, it hit me, *I have to propose*. Lock Kristi down and make it official."

It was the fulfillment of a premonition from four years earlier, yet the moment felt oddly flat. I'd been smoking crack for weeks and snorting hog rails for hours. Maybe that was it. All I knew was that the voice in my head that had once said with conviction *This is the man you're meant to marry,* now whispered numbly, *Is this even real? Is this really happening?*

Crawling from the Wreckage

August 1, 1992

 The night after Joe proposed we celebrated at the Bistro Garden. Our corner table was as wobbly and unbalanced as I was. We sat as close as we could and wrote on the tablecloth, in Sharpie, eleven promises and vows. When I went to the ladies' room, Joe wrote "12" on a napkin and laid it atop a ring box (a temporary "fill-in" ring—fake diamonds, still pretty).

 Laughter, kisses, tequila shots at the bar. Joe raised his glass and yelled, "We're getting married!" The owner and staff patted his back and said congratulations.

 We've been monstering since (days now). More in love than ever.

❋❋❋

I'D BEEN HONEST WITH Joe about my activities while he was in Europe. He'd taken it in stride, and even allowed me to switch from snorting to smoking later that night. We were on a roll—

celebrating his homecoming and our engagement, both. In twenty-four hours we'd done enough blow for forty-eight, making my segue to crack feel, if not "natural," at least practical. I called Max for a delivery, after which Joe said, "Nothing against the guy, but let's not use him again. The fewer people who know our business, the better."

Most of our friends looked down their coke-encrusted noses on crack. I had a hole in my septum partly caused by a bad batch of blow from one of those very insiders. Hardly the only casualty in our circle, I knew of at least one, and suspected two more, with septal perforations. Not because it was openly discussed (it wasn't), but from a telltale whistle I heard when they inhaled. Though faint, it was unmistakably pitched, and every time it sounded I wondered if they noticed, either in their own breathing, or in mine.

Alternating blow with crack gave my nasal tissue a break, the drawback being that once the smoking started I couldn't just roll it back. To switch from blow to crack was easy, but the reverse caused jonesing. So when Joe suggested dinner out, I hesitated. "Down the street to the Bistro Garden," he said. "We'll be gone ninety minutes."

"I'll be climbing the walls before your entrée is served." (For obvious reasons I didn't plan to eat, myself.)

"Oh," he said. "I hadn't thought of that." The man hadn't eaten a decent meal since Europe, and I suggested he go without me. "No way. Only if you come too."

"How? I'll need three or four hits in that time frame."

Joe had an idea. He put a piece of notebook paper on the bar, then rolled an unlit cigarette softly between his fingers until a third of its contents fell out onto it. Then he inserted a small crack rock in the hollowed-out paper, mixed in some of the displaced tobacco, then kept mixing in little rocks with tobacco until the cigarette was full again. He dosed three Marlboros that way. All I had to do was light up at dinner every twenty minutes, for a maintenance drip, basically. I did a test run before heading out, smoking in my normal fashion, until burning embers reached one of the little rocks, when I got an extra whoosh of crack smoke in my lungs—not enough to rush, but enough to stave off a jones.

His ingenuity impressed me. "But won't the smell give me away?"

"It's barely noticeable," Joe assured me.

We didn't count on the inconsistency of those rocks—some bigger than others, or that what had been barely noticeable at home would be cartoonishly absurd at the restaurant. Thick, smelly plumes of bright white smoke wafted from my cigarette, engulfing our table like an out-of-control magic trick. I looked to Joe, alarmed, preparing to stub out the culprit. He scanned the room, but it was late on a weeknight, with hardly anyone there to notice. Nearby, at the bar, a group of servers waited to close out for the night. They could hardly help noticing the bizarre display, and we got a raised eyebrow or two—that was all. I asked Joe what to do and he shrugged. "It's LA... No one cares what we're up to."

Maybe that was true, but I cared. I hated what I'd gotten up to.

One of the vows on our tablecloth was that I would quit crack before we got married. I'd signed off with a flourish, excited by the prospect. Meanwhile, I couldn't even *pause* to celebrate our engagement. I'd ended my affairs. The love of my life had just proposed. If this wasn't a fresh start, what was? But it didn't feel like it.

❋❋❋

I DO NOT RECALL how I finally learned to cook my own crack, but from that day on I eschewed powdered blow whenever possible in favor of a home-cooked batch.

Back in Austin, Freddie had cooked big batches at the stove using a pot of water, tongs, and a test tube. I needed only a spoon, a Zippo, and ten minutes at my vanity-cum-chem lab. My batches were small yet potent, and for the next two weeks I left the house only to resupply. My sudden uptick in business worried Gary, but instead of a scolding, he extended a sailing invitation. I loved sailing so much I agreed to leave my pipe behind. Then Captain Gary informed me of a policy—*no coke on the boat*—in his booming, British voice.

"At *all*? Not even lines?"

"Which part of 'no coke' don't you get, little girl?"

"I'm just clarifying, Gary, don't get pissy."

"I'm not being pissy, you! Now, c'mon, let's have fun in the sun. It'll be good for you."

I appreciated what Gary was trying to do, but I was too far gone to get onboard. A cold-turkey crash landing, miles from shore, would not be good for me or anyone else on his boat. I couldn't be bothered to grab a life preserver until I was officially drowning.

In 1986, at the peak of my meth use, my partner in crime—a suspected murderer and two-decade-long addict—begged me to *go home and get some sleep already*. I'd just offered him a full syringe, which he flatly rejected before banishing me from his home. Distraught, I peeled out in the middle of the night, tweaking too hard to remember headlights or which side of the road to drive on. My friends (my real friends) had been worried for weeks, but until that night I'd been convinced I was fine, right up to a very narrowly missed head-on collision.

My track record for self-appraisement left much to be desired. I slipped in and out of denial with the speed of a strobe light.

###

As MY CRACK HABIT spiraled, so did Joe's tolerance for it.

Post-Europe, the All-Starrs had one week off, then a week on the road, followed by a string of local shows. During that time, Joe played almost every night and spent most of every day trying to distract me from the pipe. He'd suggest hot tub dips and backyard photo shoots, anything to make me put it down for twenty minutes. I participated in spurts, like Lisa shooting pool that night. When Joe complained about my behavior, I told him to lighten up and quit being a jerk.

I liked the Polaroids, having never been thinner or, to my mind, looked better. I'd always been trim, but in LA, *skinny* was lauded. I had dropped from a size four to a size two that summer. I planned to wow them backstage at the Greek— if I could put down the pipe long enough to get there. The Bistro Garden incident had scared me off smoking away from home. I also wanted to abide by Joe's wishes and Ringo's rules, but there were bigger forces in play—inertia, for starters. The day of the gig, I may as well have been shot out of a cannon for how unstoppable I was.

Instead of going with Joe to the venue (which would've required more "pee breaks" than ever), I planned to drive myself later, despite that after four years of limos, I didn't know my way around LA sober, much less high. I made it, albeit not without incident when the Mustang's roof got stuck at half-mast. I'd tried to lower it while flying down the freeway, and the malfunction made for a less-than-aerodynamic ride, and, for all I knew, an illegal one.

I pulled over to fix it, wearing the stretchy, white, tank dress Vicki had given me in St. Louis, on the date that launched my and Joe's relationship. It was his favorite, and I'd worn it in the hopes of seeing that awed look he made whenever I did. I arrived backstage streaked in grime and sweat from throwing my body weight against the car's ragtop to collapse it. I ducked into Joe's bathroom to freshen up and smoke a few hits. During the show, I snuck back for more but that time couldn't get a good hit. Whenever I'd start to rush, a surge of anxiety rose up to block it. After five or six tries I gave up, having just enough clarity to see what an asshole I was.

The revelation acted like an antidote. Something in me found the strength to stash my pipe for the night. I eked by on bumps until I felt within the realm of normal, then went to find Cici. She was in the wings watching Dave do his thing, and the line of her adoring gaze gave me flashbacks to myself in better days—loving Joe and being loved back, pre-crack. I retreated to his dressing room and curled up in a ball on the couch. When he found me after the show, he hugged me and said I looked nice. Not the awe I'd hoped for, but better than I deserved.

"I have to make my goodbyes before we leave," Joe said.

I followed him to the hallway, overflowing with guests. "I'll wait here," I said. "Holding up the wall until you return."

He grinned and it gave me peace. *He still loves me*, I thought. *We're not dead yet.* As the crowd dispersed, I felt my tension dissipate with it. Then Bonnie Raitt tried to slut-shame me and a smidge of it came back.

I'd never met the woman. All I knew about Bonnie was that she played a mean slide and that she and Joe were, or had been, friends. To hear him tell it, she'd tried to kiss him one night and he'd shoved her aside in surprise. Apparently she hadn't liked that much. (*She was pissed!* Joe had told me, relaying the story. I'd shaken my head at him. *Well, yeah. You should probably stop doing that.*)

Backstage at the Greek, I was lost in my own world, fighting yawns and shifting my weight, when a group of women passed by. I barely noticed, too tired to raise my eyes or stand up straight, until a catty remark made my head snap up. It was all in the tone—I wasn't sure what had been said, but knew I'd been insulted. I looked to my left, at a cluster women by the exit door. Bonnie led the pack, blocking them from leaving until she finished what she'd started. Holding my gaze, as her mortified friends looked every which way, she went on, "Seriously, my husband would *never* let me out in public like that." Then she left, followed by three red-faced, cringing friends.

Again, I could only shake my head. *I have a crack pipe stuffed in my purse, you crazy bitch. My demons are a mite bigger than your petty diva bullshit.* Even by LA standards, it was absurd. I called Cici over and filled her in. She sighed and rolled her eyes. "Bonnie's like that sometimes. Just ignore it."

Joe reappeared. "Ready for home?" he said, putting an arm around my shoulders.

I pushed off the wall. "You have no idea." I'd spent enough of my life traveling alone, lost in circles or broken down on the side of the road. To the depths of my soul I wanted nothing more than to quit crack forever and return to the loving, happy couple we'd once been.

❖❖❖

THERE WERE FOUR WEEKS left on tour and an early stop was Austin. I proudly pointed out landmarks as the bus wound through traffic. After the show, it was straight to Dallas with no time to see friends, but I was content to be with Joe in the life raft of Ringo's band.

Minutes after settling into our room at the Four Seasons, I noticed a stone missing from my opal-and-diamond bracelet— Joe's Valentine's Day gift to me that year. Combing the carpet on my knees, I decided to have a word with God. *One more chance, Lord, please. And I'll never be careless again.* Seconds later I found the gem—a sign, I was sure of it.

I returned to simple pleasures—spooning, snuggling, and socializing. Having regained a little weight, I received compliments all around, and after two weeks of sleep and solid meals, I was feeling almost normal.

In New York City, in the Royalton lobby, we bumped into Jack Nicholson and Pete Townshend. Pete greeted Joe like a long-lost brother, then gave me a hug as well. "How wonderful to meet

Joe's lady!" he exclaimed, as Jack nodded in my direction. The men and their dates made room in their booth, then re-launched the sing-along we'd interrupted. After a rousing rendition of "Rocky Raccoon" and idle conversation, we headed to the elevator. Jack followed, heading to his room too. That's when Joe decided to share our big news.

"I'm taking the leap again, Jack. I've asked this one to marry me, and she said yes."

Jack gave me a once-over before turning to Joe. "Well, my friend," he said, raising both eyebrows. "Good luck with that."

The cynicism was not unique to Jack. I sensed it from Geno, Rick the Bass Player, and others, despite their supportive comments. Those who were more excited for us were acquaintances who didn't know me well.

Back in LA, we went to an Elton John concert where I soon lost sight of Joe backstage. I was deep in conversation when he reappeared, urging me to "come meet someone special." Suddenly I was standing before Lionel Richie, dazed by his beatific smile. "Lionel is licensed to perform marriages," Joe said. "He's agreed to do ours, on one condition."

Lionel extended his hand. "I told Joe I had to meet you first."

I grabbed it and held on. "Such a pleasure to meet you!"

"She's from Texas," Joe said and Lionel chuckled.

"Austin, if that makes a difference. I'm just so honored you'd consider this."

"I know all I need to," Lionel said. "I'd be happy to do it." (He probably should've gotten to know me better.)

✦✦✦

As soon as we got home, I was off and running. Joe scored a stash and I cooked my share into crack. Blow was anticlimactic by then,

pedestrian by comparison. I told myself I could handle it after
so much time off, but if anything, I was worse. Three days later,
we hit the road, and this time my problem came with us.

When we first got to Denver, everything seemed fine. I did
lines, and drank tequila with a girlfriend of Rick's who lived in
the area. Had I gone straight to bed when she left, it would've
been a perfect evening. Instead, I locked myself in the bathroom.
Using gear smuggled in my luggage—a pinch of baking soda and
a glass stem stuffed with Brillo, plus the blow I'd finagled earlier
from Joe—I cooked up three small rocks. It wasn't a monster I was
after, but a nightcap. Like three fingers of cognac by the fire—
that's how I'd envisioned it. Deluded myself, rather.

Unable to get a good hit with that pitifully short stem,
I MacGyver'd something more intricate using a small Advil bottle.
The result was an improvement but far from ideal. With one rock
left, I did my best to seal the makeshift pipe's air leaks ruining my
hit (with what, I don't recall, maybe candle wax or ChapStick).
By the half hour mark, Joe was growing impatient and I was
regretting the whole endeavor. I was also too invested to quit.
I prepped the final hit just as Joe pounded the door, demanding
I open it. His anger heightened my resolve to take control of the
next few minutes, since I'd surely have none afterward.

"I've had all I can take, dammit. Put down that shit and get
out here!"

"One sec!" I yelled back, then flicked my Bic and inhaled.

Bingo! I knew immediately it was the hit I'd been after and
used all my best tricks to push it down and hold it in, counting the
seconds as the drug worked its magic.

Joe continued pounding. "Open this door or I will break it down!"

I'd never heard him so angry (which was saying a lot),
approaching his breaking point at the precise moment my lungs
were ready to burst too. What happened next was the most
spectacularly ill-timed clash of wills I could've orchestrated,

stemming from a simple desire to kill two birds with one stone. Joe wanted me to finish and exit. I wanted to exit and finish *with a bang*. Our desires were so closely aligned, I figured that as long as I exited everything would be fine. If I made him laugh in the process, all the better to avoid an argument.

With only a few seconds to plan, it's fair to say I didn't think things through. I don't know why I thought he'd find it funny, the way I flung open the door and exhaled all that crack smoke in his face.

He didn't think it was funny. Two seconds, maybe three passed as the beginning of an amazing rush came over me and Joe's expression morphed from shock to rage. He attacked me, grabbing my upper arms and hurling with such force my feet left the ground and I landed in the next room. *This is not* at all *how I meant it to go*, I thought. Before I could ponder it further, he'd flung me halfway back again. I scrambled to my feet. He caught up and overpowered me, and then he took a swing. He'd never been violent with me before, and the shock of it made me go limp. My brain and body detached, one aching to defend myself, the other refusing it.

I shut down internally, my default response. Unable to fight back or flee, I froze, like I did most times—save one: a fight with my mother at fifteen years old, when she'd slapped me, triggered by my (admittedly ill-timed) sarcasm. I'd hit back without thinking, I'd felt so violated. My personal space was all I had, and dammit, I would defend it. We'd hit the floor swinging, and though our tussle ended in a draw, to me it was a win—the first time I'd stood up for myself.

That night with Joe in Denver, something similar happened. I thought, *sure, I fucked up, but no hitting allowed, man*. It wasn't instantaneous. I had to summon the courage, but I felt proud for taking a stance and swinging back.

It didn't go well for me. Joe doubled his efforts, slamming me so hard into a wall that I was disoriented. He wasn't done, but I was. I gathered my wits and protected my head. It ended quickly when he shoved me to the floor and walked away. I lay in a ball, catching my breath. When he didn't come back, I jumped up and screamed obscenities at him. He ignored me and picked up the phone.

"It's Joe. Come to my room before I kill my girlfriend."

The statement was eerily similar to one I'd made to Gary Belz after Sam Kinison's funeral. My comment had humbled Joe, but his made me defiant. Ringo's head of security arrived, a quiet man with kind eyes and a thick moustache. He sat me down and relayed my options, straight from Ringo himself. "First thing in the morning, he'll put you on a flight to Arizona where his rehab center has a room reserved. Or if you prefer, he'll fly you home."

"You think *I* need rehab? *What about him?*" I screeched. The men looked at me blankly. There was nothing to discuss.

Joe had a tour to finish. I didn't have an entire band counting on me. I didn't have a job at all, or anything keeping me from accepting the offer other than denial about needing it in the first place. Immersed in the insanity as long as I'd been, I had zero clarity or discernment. I felt like I'd been breaking the same rules as everyone else in Joe's circle, but while his level-ten crimes went unpunished, I was banished for going to eleven. The whole thing seemed unfair, but it was the banishment that scared me. Rehab was another planet and they were sending me *alone.* "Fly me to LA," I said, panicked. "I want to go home."

A flight was booked to coincide with the band's itinerary. I had to ride to the airport and traverse the terminal with them. I kept to myself, off to the side, eyes on the ground. I had no clue how much the others knew until Zak rushed over, concerned. "Are you okay?" he whispered. "What's happened? No one will tell me."

I wanted to hug him. Without breaking stride, I whispered, "It doesn't matter, just know it wasn't all my fault." As if that made a difference.

Zak and the band went on to their gate. Ringo's security made sure I boarded my plane. At LAX, a driver held a sign with my name. Joe wanted to be sure I got home safely. I directed the driver to Gary's, then I went home and smoked crack for two days. When it was gone, I threw out all my gear: pipes, Brillo, everything.

◆◆◆

I'D BEEN OFF CRACK for a week, eating, sleeping, and trying to move forward. Outwardly I was doing well and didn't understand Joe's cold withdrawal. Our lifestyle had been so wild for so long, I couldn't see the line I'd crossed. I swore to stay off crack. Wasn't that enough? *Can't we just talk...about that or anything else?* No, he pulled away and clammed up.

I automatically turned to Smokey, who pretended things were normal, but in a phony way—looking near me, not at me, and biding time speaking superficially. I'd seen him that way with others, and I'd been that way myself. But we had never been like that to each other.

I'd been cast from the kingdom, bested by Joe's drugs and Smokey's desire. Unable to keep up, hold my own, or roll over on command, I'd failed them both—my two best friends.

I'd also failed Ringo. In the heat of the moment, I'd thought rehab an overreaction, that Ringo was a hardline recovery geek who didn't really "get" casual crack using. Later, I wondered if I'd made a mistake, but when I imagined returning from rehab to live clean and sober in Joe's house, sleeping every night while he, Rick, and Geno partied on downstairs—I knew I'd done the right thing. Ringo and Barb had done rehab together; surely they could grasp my dilemma. If one of us went, Joe and I were doomed. I'd stuck by him at Hazelden, but he'd said nothing about Arizona. I would be abandoned in the desert while he toured the country in search of a new girlfriend.

I hadn't gone to rehab, but I was losing Joe anyway. We coexisted at Blairwood in silence. For whatever reason,

I had no desire for crack. I wanted to believe it was gone forever. I wanted Joe to notice my good behavior and trust me again.

After two weeks of silence, I was tidying up at the bar and came across a note with some unfinished song lyrics. They'd been written on a legal pad, torn off, crumpled up, and then smoothed flat again. The note said little more than that he loved me very *very* much. And that he'd started a song about me. He'd written one verse.

> *I don't understand you*
> *I don't really need to*
> *But darling you're my*
> *Salt and pepper*

It was our relationship in a nutshell—pained, loving, trashed, and salvaged, full of potential, yet stuck. I wanted to explain myself—the back and forth, the salt and pepper—but I didn't understand it either.

We eventually settled into our routine—outwardly, at least—so that by the time Barb reached out, I was cloaked in pseudo-security. In the bedroom on a balmy, late-summer afternoon, a breeze drifted in through the open window. I listened to Barb carry the conversation. My mind wandered to the familiar view of the Valley and its attendant yellow-brown overlay. I wondered for the hundredth time how toxic that cloud was, grateful, as always, to reside above it.

Barb's story of addiction touched yet baffled me. I passed the receiver from ear to ear, comparing the wreckage of her past to that of my present and—as hers sounded worse—decided they had nothing in common. When she asked if there was anything *I* wanted to share, I glanced around the Zen-like room, at my Jerry's Famous tuna melt and the book I was reading, a memoir by a man who'd walked around the world. "Not really, Barb," I said. "But thanks for asking."

Soon afterward, Arlie Manuel stopped by in person, sharing, as Barbara had, painful, private stories of addiction. She spoke of her husband's suicide, something called "speedballs" (a mix of cocaine and heroin), and a prison stint during which she'd found peace through meditation. Intrigued by her experience, I asked for the speedball recipe. Arlie sighed, though not unkindly. "Maybe you're not quite ready."

She meant ready for recovery, and she wasn't wrong about that. I thought that because I wasn't in prison and had only experienced rare bouts of violence, I wasn't so bad off I needed something so drastic. Despite all evidence to the contrary, I figured if I wasn't craving it right *then*, I'd be fine from then on.

It's too Junky in Here

IN THE FALL OF 1992, I turned twenty-five years old. Joe was out of town and sent roses. Annie, Trey, and Sean surprised me with a gift, cake, and balloons. We shot pool and used the hot tub, and I had fun without booze or coke. When Joe got home, we monstered. I kept pace snorting lines, but our standard pastime felt different. I was bored.

We spent November on tour promoting *Songs for a Dying Planet*. The only track I liked was "I Know," an exquisitely wispy ballad that was a little too haunting to listen to. Also, I was hurt (if unsurprised) to see Smokey's name in the liner notes and not mine. It was time to cede the fantasy of myself as any kind of muse. The verdict was in; that ship had sailed.

Zak was a welcome addition to the band, but if I were being honest about the after-hours antics, I would've said I was sick of them. Prank calls, devil horns, and improv skits weren't new—and therein lay the problem. The tenth time Joe dressed up in his "Butt Crack McClonskey" character, I wanted to scream *grow up*, *already!* But I'd never embarrass him that way, despite not being afforded the same courtesy.

His mood swings were scary enough at home, where I (usually) could leave the room. Not so in airplanes, bars, and restaurants, where I was as likely a target as unsuspecting wait staff and flight attendants. They never knew what hit them, berated for banal things, like requesting he put up his tray table for landing. As soon as it started, I'd turn away—*better them than me*—though I spoke up one time for a young Midwestern barmaid. In the process of taking our drink order, the poor girl got crucified. Joe's venom came out of nowhere, demanding obscure brands of beer the tiny bar clearly didn't have. The Speros pretended it wasn't happening, employing my go-to tactic. I might've followed suit were it not for Ellen's presence. She seemed so classy to me. I thought if I couldn't reach her level, I could prove I knew the difference.

"Dammit, Joseph, knock it off! They have five American beers and Heineken. *Fucking pick one.*" Unfazed, he let up long enough for the shell-shocked server to scamper away and send someone else over with our drinks.

Most of our circle was on Joe's payroll, with little incentive to call out his abominable behavior. Whether they registered my pain or pitied me silently, I never expected more from them than *better her than me.* Joe's business manager had reason to be vocal, albeit about something else entirely. After the tour, we returned home to an answering machine full of messages from him. The next time he called, I put Joe on. After ten minutes of "Uh-huh, yeah… uh-huh," he hung up and whirled on me. "Why did you tell him I was here?"

"He said it was urgent. Call me crazy, *but I thought it might be urgent.*"

It *was* urgent. For starters, we learned that a $3,000 monthly tab at Tony's Liquor was unsupportable (also, apparently, "bizarre"). There were other reprimands, but the point was that we were broke, or close to it. Suddenly I realized Joe had known all along.

✦✦✦

I'D LIVED SIMPLY MOST of my life and could certainly do it again. I started researching local strip clubs in secret, thinking it couldn't hurt to be prepared. Cici Edmunds was a makeup artist, contributing to her and Dave's household income. Next to her I was a slacker, and I wanted to do better. Kind and wise beyond her years, Cici's insights had helped me better understand my relationship issues, and have more forgiveness and compassion than I would have otherwise.

Because I treasured her friendship, I should've anticipated what came next, but when Joe decided to sabotage it, I was shocked and furious. During a game of pool, completely out of the blue, Joe accused Dave of flirting with me—ridiculous for many reasons, including that Cici was standing right there. I yelled myself hoarse, while Dave and Cici said not a word, just slowly, sadly collected their things and left.

Joe had pushed away everyone I'd befriended: Jeanna, Annie, Trey, Billy, Malika, Majid, and finally Cici and Dave. Meanwhile, I'd let slide every discourtesy from Kevin, JD, Warren, Lita, Bonnie, Jack Nicolson, and Todd Rundgren. I'd never complained about Joe's friend's tainted cocaine that had destroyed my septum. On Thanksgiving, I sat at Geno's table watching him, Joe, and Rick pass around a plate of coke, along with the same old, tired jokes. I caught myself fake laughing three times in a row.

What am I doing here? I thought. Then, *Where else is there to go?* I didn't have the answer, but I started keeping an eye out.

The bond I'd felt with his friends was one of the first things to fade. Then other aspects of our life together began to wane. For years I'd accommodated Joe's kink, adjusting my desires and expectations to meet his every whim. I'd never turned down a single request, in that vein. I was nothing if not adaptable—like many women of my generation, socialized to believe our value was measured in sexual access and emotional labor. Well, that way of being was over. I didn't quit having sex, I just went through the motions instead, responding with appropriate movements and noises while rolling my eyes behind the blindfold.

I blamed Joe and I hated him. I also loved him, or thought I did. My feelings were confusing and I asked advice from an acquaintance. Jimmy at Tony's Deli was the owner's son, and though no older than me, he was thoughtful, candid, and experienced with women. When he delivered my lunch one day, I invited him in for a game of pool, racked the table, and unloaded. "How do you make relationships work? How do you compromise? How do you make someone grow up or redirect a sex life?"

His answer was to the point. "Communication is key. And if you're this unhappy, you should talk to Joe about it." He paused. "But don't expect him to change. Women always do that and it never works."

If one of us didn't change, Joe and I were through—that I knew. I wondered if couple's therapy would help, but before I could broach it, I overheard Joe disparage one of his roadies for going. Doug had just gotten engaged and Joe was sharing the news with Rick. "They're going for premarital counseling. That idiot is actually looking forward to it."

Rick snickered. "If you need therapy *before* the wedding, your divorce is a given."

"No shit," Joe laughed. "Like, hurry up and dump her now, before alimony kicks in."

✦✦✦

IN DECEMBER, JOE PLAYED a gig with Glenn Frey at a venue in LA. Lucy arrived for a rare visit with her dad, so I left them in his dressing room to roam backstage. Among the usual strangers and celebrities, I spotted Arlie waving at me. She approached with a friend in tow, an actress I'd seen on TV: an auburn-haired beauty with bright green eyes and an aura of serenity. The actress gazed at me steadily as Arlie asked about my health and other things.

I didn't mind the interrogation because I wanted to share some things, if not the exact things they were asking. I had plenty of problems, but booze and drugs were low on my list. Arlie and her friend saw it differently, and while I respected their opinion, I was no candidate for recovery. I wanted solution without sacrifice, change without risk. An authentic relationship without working for it. To moderate, not abstain—*that's* what I wanted.

They spoke of having "been there" as if the parallels were obvious. But I was a mystery to myself, a composite of traits and experiences labeled good or bad based on how high I was. Dropping out of college was both a relief *and* a shame. Kinky sex was fun *and* frustrating. Cocaine was my best friend *and* worst enemy. How could I hit "my bottom" when I didn't know which way was up? As for my relationship, maybe I *was* only as sick as my secrets, but my secrets were Joe's, too…so ugly, tangled, and toxic, we dare not discuss them between *ourselves*.

I rationalized my silence as loyalty. I defaulted to self-preservation. I wanted what they had without doing what they'd done to get it. I also wanted Arlie's friendship, and in a circular bit of logic I had convinced myself she'd never befriend an addict. "Seriously, guys. *I'm fine*." And with that, our connection ended.

The light went out in Arlie's eyes. I felt it like a power grid. "Okay," she said, stepping back. "Good luck to you, then." I felt their absence like a vacuum.

❀❀❀

I CAME FROM A long line of bootstrap-pulling, secret-keeping, emotion-stuffing Northern Europeans. We didn't discuss feelings or personal failings. Anger, fear, confusion, self-doubt...what of 'em, kid? Suck it up and go milk the cows. My parents' parents hailed from North Dakota and Minnesota farmland, the coldest areas of the country. Endurance was their way of life. My father and his five siblings shared a single outhouse. Dad delivered newspapers as a kid, the route, uphill both ways.

I would make my ancestors proud. With willpower and inner strength, *I shall moderate my intake*. Whatever it took, I'd learn to use drugs *right*.

###

ONE NIGHT, DURING A rare, relaxed evening at home, I heard the buzz of our front gate. Joe was busy on his ham radio or in the garage studio, and since our policy of late was to discourage uninvited guests, I ignored it. Two buzzes later, I put down my book and went to the intercom.

"Who is this and what do you want?"

"It's Mark from Trader Jim's. I have an appointment with Mr. Walsh."

"I don't think he's expecting anyone."

"Tell him it's Mark from Trader Jim's. I have the tea he ordered."

"*Tea?* Is this a joke?"

Silence, then, "We met at [famous actor's] party last week. I'm delivering Joe's tea."

The guy was clearly nuts. Who the hell delivers tea door-to-door at 9:00 p.m.?

Joe appeared. "Who is it?"

"Something about a tea delivery."

"Weird," he said, then he spoke into the intercom. "Hey, how ya doin'?"

"Hi, Joe. It's Mark from Trader Jim's and I have your tea."

"C'mon in," he said, opening the gate.

"Joseph!"

"What?"

"What do you mean, 'what'? Who the hell is Mark from Trader Jim's?"

"Dunno, never heard of him."

Turned out he had, exactly as Mark had claimed—at a party where a famous actor had encouraged Joe to place an order with his prestigious underground pot dealer.

Downstairs, at the bar, Mark popped open his briefcase to reveal eight or ten individual packages, vacuum-sealed and labeled like a selection of teas. I hadn't known such varieties existed. Years earlier, in my teens, I'd smoked something called redbud sensimilla and danced around the living room with a man I barely knew, carrying on like the best of friends. It had felt more like MDMA than pot, which usually made me self-conscious. I wondered if Mark had any of that redbud stuff but for some reason didn't ask.

While Joe deliberated, I skimmed label descriptions—PERFECT FOR A RELAXING, INTROSPECTIVE EVENING and TO LIVEN ANY SOCIAL GATHERING—then chose one based on name alone, like a newbie at the horse track: SNOOPY's REVENGE. How could I go wrong with a beloved cartoon dog?

Easily, it turned out. A few light tokes of Snoopy's Revenge brought on the worst paranoia I'd ever had. Like a bad acid trip, hallucinatory and weighted with certainty that everything in my life is wrong and will never be right again. I didn't want to believe it, but when our nightstands, dresser, and walls came to life and chimed in—confirming the doomsday prediction in cold, cruel voices while speaking perfect English—what choice did I have?

I turned to Joe. "I'm not doing so hot."

"Me neither," he admitted. "This is…something else."

"It's bad, right?"

"It's not good," he said.

"I'm scared," I whimpered.

"It'll be okay. I won't let anything happen to you. Try to ride it out."

I knew he'd fix it for me, if he could. I loved him for that, but it wasn't enough. The walls and furniture piped down in time, but a sense of despair lingered, and soon afterward I went to Gary's alone. Behind Joe's back, I MacGyver'd a pipe and didn't put it down for ten months.

✦✦✦

My memories of the first half of 1993 are spotty. I recall moments, not infrequent, of intense love and joy, followed by explosive arguments. The roller coaster we'd been on suddenly compressed to the sharp angles of an accordion—up, down, up, down, rocket skyward, plummet to earth. Our transitions came out of nowhere. We defied the laws of physics.

Initially, I hid in my bathroom to cook up and smoke. Having thrown out my old pipes, I made new ones from cashew jars—squat glass urns with wide cork toppers, collected over the years from so many Plaza hotel minibars. For stems, I broke one of Joe's antique seltzer bottles. The subtle glint of its interior glass straw had tantalized me for months. One day, I got sloppy and used Joe's study to clean my pipe at his late father's desk. I poured the rinse onto a plate of glass, then lit it to burn off the alcohol. The resin left behind could be scraped up and smoked, often for the best hit of the bunch. Joe was clueless about such things—resin hits and the like—so the sight of me starting a bonfire in his study both confused and terrified him.

"What the hell are you doing?!"

"What? Oh…just prepping the resin, why?"

"Because you're going to burn down the house!"

He banished me from the study and forbade me from setting fires anywhere under our roof. I saw his point and apologized, but he wasn't through. Racing upstairs, he ransacked my bathroom, turning up two sooty spoons as evidence of my ongoing betrayal.

"Look," he finally sighed. "If you insist on smoking that shit, stop hiding out like a crackhead. Do it openly, no more locked doors." Grateful, I offered to do a sexy photo shoot (between crack hits, of course), prancing and posing throughout the house while he followed, more distraught than aroused. I should've felt guilty, but didn't. It was wrong, yet also freeing.

I was out of my mind. The sweet, cerebral stripper and earnest student Joe had fallen in love with was gone. A psychotic crackhead had taken her place, and he was afraid to take his eyes off her. I remember one afternoon smoking rock after rock while Joe lay on the sofa with an arm across his eyes. My hits were good and strong that day, my stash abundant, and yet I missed my playmate. In a burst of sanity, I decided that as soon as I ran out, I'd quit that shit for good. The thought made me happy.

Just then, Zak walked in the room.

Joe was vigilant about securing the house, keeping the doors locked and gate closed, but had forgotten both that day. Zak had let himself in and was quietly looking from me to Joe and back again. I stashed my pipe where I stood, behind the bar, too late to be slick about it. Joe glanced up at Zak, sighed, and shielded his eyes again.

"Hey, guys. Everything okay?"

"Yeah, yeah. Sure, sure," I said, in a high-pitched voice. "But, uh…we're kind of in the middle of something." My comment made zero sense in that setting.

"Okay, well…I'll come back another time, then." He shuffled out, giving me a sad look.

Zak had not led a sheltered life. He'd been surrounded by musicians and drug use since he could walk. He was nobody's fool, and he cared deeply about his friends. I felt bad for worrying him, but I reminded myself I'd be quitting soon. I'd make it up to him then.

I told myself the same thing, a week later, about Rian, our friend and contractor. He was playing chess with Joe at the bar while I alternated between hits in my bathroom and visiting them downstairs. Joe must've filled Rian in at some point, because when I joined them next, his expression was drastically different. Later he pulled me aside, telling me about a pal of his who'd gone to the ER with a tiny piece of Brillo stuck in his throat. Rian's cautionary tale both touched and annoyed me. I don't know when the disconnect occurred, but I could bounce from self-loathing to self-righteousness in a blink, and sometimes I didn't bounce back. I didn't like being underestimated.

Around that time, Joe agreed to let me redecorate one room—a hallway—and I threw myself into it, consulting with Rian on paint brands and brushstroke techniques. I sensed he thought I was in over my head, but he wished me well and left. (After viewing the finished project, he exclaimed, "Kristi, this is professional-quality painting!") I hung an antique wedding kimono on the wall and placed bamboo tables on either side, with Japanese art and other knick-knacks. I felt real pride, walking through that hall a dozen times a day. I'd envisioned something and created it! No big deal to a guy like Joe, but I was hurt that he didn't mention it. He had bigger things on his mind. I wanted praise for my hallway. He wanted me not to die.

###

ONE NIGHT I STOPPED breathing. The saga began when Felicia showed up, fresh from rehab, bright-eyed and gushing about sobriety. I was happy for her, despite the craving her presence triggered. The sight of me triggered her, as well, and within minutes we left to score. I didn't return for two days.

Our escapades are a blank to me, other than repeated calls home to reassure Joe—*A few more hours, that's all. We're almost done*—like a mantra into the phone. I don't know where I went or how I got home, but I can still see Joe in our driveway, equal parts relieved and enraged. He carried me to bed, exhausted and grateful, swearing that I was done for good. I fell asleep, giddy at the notion of waking to a drug-free life. Instead, I woke to Joe shaking me and screaming my name. *Breathe, Kristi, breathe!*

"Where am I? What's wrong?"

"You scared the hell out of me!"

"Sorry, sorry…I'm okay now, don't worry," I mumbled, then fell asleep and did it again. He shouted and shook me, then peppered me with questions to check my brain activity. "Bill Clinton is president. *Jesus, Joe.* Let me sleep."

The next time I dozed off, an angel appeared. A beautiful, loving female presence who whispered soothing, reassuring words to me, right before Joe slapped me awake again.

"Wait, wait…I'm okay. You can stop." Joe was crouched over me, straddling my legs, trying to pull me into a seated position. Too weak to push him off, I begged him to calm down. "She said I won't die," I repeated. "She said to tell you I'll be okay."

"What are you talking about? Who said that? Felicia? How would she know?"

"No, silly, the angel. She was just here. Didn't you see her?"

Judging by his reaction, he hadn't. What's more, a celestial apparition coinciding with the cessation of my breathing did not comfort Joe in the slightest. He dragged me into the hallway, to pace until I was fully awake. Then he made me drink a glass of fresh squeezed beet-and-spinach juice before allowing me to sleep. He got none himself, that night, watching my chest rise and fall till sunrise.

I had always loved waking up to Joe's love notes (rare as they were, by then). The one I found next had a different tone. *I'M PUTTING MY FOOT DOWN*, it read, each letter etched so deeply into an old file folder that its imprint went straight through the cardboard. *YOU'RE GOIING TO STOP DOING CRACK WHETHER YOU WANT TO OR NOT. (CHECKMATE, FELICIA.)* It went on to state that he loved me, whether I hated him or not, and as for our marriage plans: *STOP CRACK—WE'LL SET A DATE.*

###

I NEEDED A BREAK from LA, and Joe needed one from me. It was decided that I would visit Austin. Before I left, he gave me another note, in a softer tone.

Kristin—I warned you when this adventure began that LA was tough. Remember? We have more to learn or we don't stand a chance. I have to take care of myself a lot more responsibly. You're so loving and dedicated, you make it almost too easy...I take way too much for granted.

Working against us, he said, was our age difference, my insecurity (which he saw as his fault as much as mine), and the fact that he used to be wealthy with a bad habit of spoiling the people he loved. I was comforted to hear he thought we'd caught it in time. He professed desire to be a better man and a commitment clean up his own mess—*instead of assuming that you're around to do it.* My job, apparently, was to get my "balls back"—*I must have my woman tough. You are. That's why I picked you.* Though he hated me being on the pipe, he admitted to being a bad influence—*always have been.* He ended with instructions to keep my chin up and knees together. *Methinks we'll make it with some hard work. I do love you. Always have/always will, Joseph*

###

YEARS EARLIER, I'D BOUGHT Joe a variety of rubber ink stamps, phrases like TOP SECRET and CONFIDENTIAL, plus one custom-made of his favorite catchphrase: HOW YA DOIN'? He'd used all three in the margins of that somber missive. It made me laugh even as I cried.

I stayed at DK's and worked at Sugar's, where he was now the general manager. I reconnected with friends and traces of my old self—the independence and spark I'd once had. I earned some cash and drank some tequila, with barely a thought to cocaine— well, some, but that's all they were: thoughts. Though DK was likely intended to keep an eye on me for Joe, I slipped out for a date with Charles. It was good to see my artist friend, always so encouraging. He asked about my life and gave great advice in addition to the passionate sex I'd been craving.

I drove back to DK's feeling torn. I liked the person I was in Austin, but my soul mate was in LA, and I felt incomplete without him. When Joe asked me to come home, I jumped at the chance and he showered me with affection. He had a new favorite game, imitating a dog food commercial, sniffing around my neck like a hyperactive puppy, then shouting, "It's bacon!" It was goofy as hell and every time he did it I fell in love all over again. I could barely believe we were still together. I had no idea he felt the same.

One night, I got a phone call from Texas. I took it in Joe's office, leaving him in the playroom with our guests, though he eavesdropped from the hallway. The call was from one of my sisters, announcing her upcoming wedding, with lots of squealing on both ends. After our guests left, Joe asked if I was planning to dump him. He'd thought the call was a ruse, that my sister had just agreed to let me move in with her, giving me the green light to leave him.

I gasped. "Are you crazy? I don't want to break up! And do you really think I'd squeal about something like that?"

"I don't know. No, I guess not. Never mind."

✦✦✦

ALL MY YEARS WITH Joe, I never understood how much he loved me. Even as a kid, I couldn't fathom anyone feeling that way about me. Like a new color in the rainbow, I couldn't wrap my head around it. He used the word "forever" a lot, but I assumed I had no right to expect him to put it on paper, despite his marriage proposal. We had made only vague plans—a backyard ceremony for close friends and family. I wanted Timothy to sing "Love Will Keep Us Alive" and Joe said that sounded nice. Unbeknownst to me, he'd asked Jim Fox from the James Gang (who was in the gem business) to search the world for its most perfect diamond.

Due to a scheduling conflict, Joe couldn't make the wedding in Texas, but the weeks before I left were blissfully romantic. When my car arrived for LAX, Joe walked me out and put something in my hand—a one-carat diamond, sparkling like crazy in the sun.

"Have it set right away," he said. "Then catch the bouquet. *You're* getting married next."

I shrieked and threw my arms around him. *He'd meant it.* I held the proof in my hand and took it straight to a jeweler when I landed. The elderly proprietor checked and rechecked it. "Thirty years in the diamond business," she said. "I ain't never seen one this flawless."

The morning of the wedding I called Joe at home and heard the familiar clicking of our bedroom extension. That particular phone was old and cheap and made a distinctive sound when the receiver was lifted. I knew the bedroom phone had been answered. What I didn't know was who the woman was who answered it.

"Who is this?" I demanded.

Silence, as she put Joe on. "Don't freak out, honey—"

"*Who is she?*"

"My ex Stefany, but nothing happened, I swear. I can explain!"

He told a believable story. They'd spent all evening catching up, then crashed in our bed because the guest bed was covered in junk. I wanted to believe him, but it was a lot to ask, and he knew it, so from the moment I deplaned he kissed my ass like never before. Stefany, too, felt bad for worrying me. I'd learned to pick my battles, and this one seemed pointless. I shrugged it off and invited Stefany to stay for the evening. When we ran out of wine around midnight, I offered to run to the store, but Joe insisted I take off my engagement ring first. "Whenever you go out alone at night," he cautioned, "leave the ring behind in my safe."

I took it off for the first and last time. I never saw it again. Before sunrise we were fighting—about what I don't recall, only that it lasted a very long time. Forever, in a way.

❉❉❉

I STARTED SMOKING CRACK again—a lot of it. Joe did a tour with Glenn Frey, and though I'm told I was there for most of it, I don't recall a single show. I remember a few nights spent at home, racking up debt smoking crack and feeling awful about it. There was epic paranoia, also Feds in trees whispering about me. I heard them from inside (really) while crawling down the hallway on my belly. I had a crack pipe in one hand and a loaded gun in the other. I kept my finger on the safety, but whether it was on or off, I don't remember.

There had always been guns in the house, so many we lost count. One time, Joe went through airport security with a gun in his carry-on. We discovered it in the limo *after* reaching our destination. Most of his guns were big and terrifying and I refused to touch them. I preferred my .22 pistol, given to me years earlier by a Sugar's customer after an attempted burglary at my apartment. Joe insisted I learn to use his Uzi.

"It's better for home protection," he said. "Especially in an ambush."

"Thanks for the visual," I said. "So you know, I can't cock it. I'm not strong enough."

"Trust me, if someone's coming at you, adrenaline will kick in."

"But I won't be able to control it!"

"Won't matter, honey," Joe laughed. "Think about it."

I didn't want to think about it. I smoked crack so I didn't have to think. When Joe came home on a tour break, we weren't laughing anymore. We were on our last legs and what I did next was a mercy killing. Why else would I tell him about Weasel?

It had happened after a show in Detroit weeks earlier. Joe had continued on with the band while I'd stayed to catch a flight home in the morning. Too wired to sleep, I called Weasel for company (who was living there, having quit Sugar's the previous year). We talked in my room, then made out a little before Weasel pulled the brakes. He said he respected Joe and me, and wanted us to make it as a couple. So did I, in theory.

It was late spring, 1993, five years and change from our fateful first meeting. Joe and I were in the playroom shooting pool, pretending not to be miserable, pretending we didn't each have one foot out the door already, awaiting any excuse to pivot. To reveal my affairs within his innermost sphere was unnecessary, total overkill. The confession of one trifling transgression—with a favorite past lover from my passionate pre-Joe youth—would do.

Joe sank the eight ball, but instead of racking them up, I was unable to continue. The angel on my right said, *you can make it work, don't hurt him*. The devil on my left, *you don't deserve him, keep digging*.

"Joe," I said, clearing my throat. "I have to tell you something."

❋❋❋

THAT NIGHT I MOVED into the Sportsmen's Lodge on Ventura. The next day, I called a number I'd had stored for weeks in my purse. It had a Las Vegas area code scribbled inside a casino matchbook. It picked up on the second ring.

"I'm on my own for a while," I said. "In a hotel room getting space. I don't know for how long, exactly, but wondered if you'd like to visit."

"I'm on my way," Majid said.

It was a seven-hour drive. He was at my door in eight.

Can't Find
My Way Home

I DIDN'T KNOW WHAT to expect when Majid arrived. He'd never flirted or been suggestive in the slightest, not even on the phone when I invited him to visit. I'd shown my hand the day we met, then pulled back for fourteen months, keeping it close to my chest.

Turned out, he'd done the same, hiding his attraction right up to his arrival at the Sportsmen's. We exchanged hellos and a pleasantry or two—*glad you could come; thanks for inviting me*—and that was that. The space between our bodies slammed shut before the door did. Pinned to the wall, with his lips crushing mine and one of my legs flung around his trim, taut waist, I felt gloriously weightless, like I'd been yanked aboard the last helicopter in a war zone. The pounding in my chest was the rhythm of a rotor, its deafening roar the sound of one word over and over...*this, this, this, this, this*. This.

Our physical chemistry was off the charts, but the attraction was more than that. Majid and I identified with each other.

I brushed aside the implications of being so drawn to someone like him—a lost and lonely drifter and PTSD-afflicted veteran—my predilection for wounded men well established by then. From Joe and Terry Reid to past punk boys and meth-heads, I had a type and haunted was part of it. On the surface, Maj and I had little in common, but the same undercurrent that coursed through me coursed through him.

Much of his appeal was obvious. He was masculine, mysterious, sensual, and gorgeous, something women stopped him on the street to profess. He was naturally charming, casually elegant, and surprisingly guileless. He'd never be called boyish or innocent, but there was a sweetness about him. When Majid opened his heart, he opened large. He was easy to be with; we were on a level playing field. Joe had always been in the game, whereas Maj and I spent our lives on the bench. Give Joe the ball, he'd run with it—maybe score, maybe get sacked, but the fact was, he could play. I was a fumble waiting to happen. Joe never understood that about me. I think he'd thought I was a ringer, and that together we'd go all the way. I was destined to disappoint him.

Unable to save myself, I couldn't save him...any more than Majid could've saved Sam. We bonded in our failures, and Majid's empathy validated me. I knew people would think of him as downgrading, but what other direction would I go?

❋❋❋

MAJID SYMPATHIZED WITH MY troubles, taking a neutral stance. He suspected I still loved Joe and cautioned me not to act rash. I wasn't making hard decisions yet. I was in a holding pattern, circling two equally unappealing destinations—stay in a bad relationship or leave the love of my life. Did it matter where I landed? I'd run out of fuel and crash where I crashed. Until then, the Sportsmen's was home.

Everything I needed was tacked to the bill: room service for breakfast, lunch at the pool, cocktails in the bar, and gift shop cigarettes by the carton. The restaurant specialized in wild game, and though I didn't eat meat, watching Majid tear into a plate of ribs or quail—sucking their juices and licking sauce from his fingers—was like a crazy hot new genre of porn. It was visceral and primal and made me squirm in my seat. Guilt? I had it, along with memories of Joe's affairs and years of sexual frustration. I paid for our drugs, at least. Majid's dealers were cheaper than Gary (everyone was cheaper than Gary) and the Sportsmen's lobby ATM became the next best thing to a crack-dispensing machine.

It's not that I didn't grasp how things worked. I knew my day of reckoning would come and that it would hurt (I had no idea how badly), but those weeks at the Sportsmen's were my last hurrah. At worst, they increased my future circle of hell from a ten to an eleven. I was going anyway…*may as well go with a bang*. Good food, great sex, lazy days at the pool, and crazy nights high on crack. It was self-medication disguised as hedonism, because there wasn't one day, one hour, one minute that shame and remorse weren't pushing on the gate, looking for a weak spot to exploit and flood my fragile brain. Pain management and pleasure-seeking look a lot alike to outsiders—insiders too, for the record.

One night we smoked through our stash quickly. Having already maxed out my cash advance limit, I needed something tangible to barter with. All my valuables were gifts from Joe, and though I considered my jewelry sacrosanct, the furs certainly weren't. I gave Majid the cheaper of two. He returned with an evening's worth of crack.

Majid's dealer had a strict "no fronts, no barters" rule, so I was curious what he'd said about the coat. "Not a word," Maj replied, which unsettled me. I'd crossed a line from a good person displaying atrocious behavior to a bad person not worth raising an eyebrow over.

❖❖❖

ONE DAY, I AWOKE to find Majid collecting his things. "You're leaving?" I asked groggily.

"I just realized tomorrow is the Fourth of July."

"And?"

"Fireworks," he mumbled, scanning the floor for his shoes. He found them, slipped his feet inside, and retrieved his sunglasses from a front pocket.

I sat up. "Majid, what are you talking about?"

"PTSD," he explained. "If I clear out of town I won't hear them go off. I get flashbacks from fireworks and war movies and stuff."

"Oh," I said, unsure how to respond.

He kissed me goodbye and left. The next day I reached out to Joe to ask if I could visit Rocky at the house. Angelina had been caring for my cat while Joe was on tour, but I missed Rocky and the home we shared. Joe understood and allowed me inside. He said I could relieve Angelina, if I had no guests and didn't stay overnight.

When Majid returned to LA, he was dying to see me. I was at Blairwood and reluctant to leave, so I said okay. "Two hours, that's it. Then I'm going to bed."

We sat on the couch watching sitcoms. When the third one ended, Majid flipped through channels and landed on a war movie. "Keep going," I instructed.

"In a few minutes," he replied, eyes glued to the screen.

"Won't this trigger your PTSD?" I asked, but he seemed not to hear me. "Seriously, this seems like a bad idea." When he grunted dismissively, I gave up. "Well, I've seen *Apocalypse Now* eight times, so I'm going bed."

"Mind if I let myself out at the next commercial?"

"All right...I guess."

Three hours later, I awoke to the sound of screaming. I raced downstairs and found Majid on the couch, his horrified wails reduced to throaty whimpering as he tossed about, eyes squeezed shut, wrestling with an invisible opponent. I shook him awake and helped him up, then waited quietly till got his bearings. He finally assured me he was okay, but he did it while looking straight through me.

❀❀❀

I RETURNED TO MY room at the Sportsmen's to spend more time with Majid. Then Joe came home and checked me out of the hotel, saying he wanted me at the house. I packed my things and did what he said. Not knowing what I wanted, I stuck with what I had.

We were cordial and careful with each other and did not monster at all. A fight erupted anyway, Joe's fuse shorter than ever. He set upon me like a prairie fire, with miles of parched landscape to burn. I don't recall what started it, only that it was absurd. The glee he took in thwarting all logic was maddening, and this time it broke me quickly. I ran from him in tears, palms clamped to my temples. Joe chased me, ranting like a madman.

I cannot go through this again, I thought. Then a light bulb moment: *Really, I cannot.*

I wasn't cornered at La Toque without cab fare, nor hurtling through the clouds strapped to an airplane chair. I had free will and four wheels, which I used to peel out of the driveway as my stupefied boyfriend stared after me. Majid was staying nearby in a buddy's spare room, furnished with a mattress and little else, yet he puffed up like a king in a castle when I entered. That's why I'd gone there; I was Majid's queen and he was in love with me. Women threw themselves at him, but I was all he could see. That he thought I hung the moon was intoxicating.

Later that night, passing me the crack pipe, he asked me to marry him and I said yes. When he insisted on sharing the news with a relative (an aunt, I believe)—to lock me in before we slept—I let him. When I awoke, reality hit. I tried to slip out unnoticed, but Majid popped up like a kid at Christmas. "Ready to drive to Vegas?"

That had been our plan: a twenty-four-hour engagement (or however long Nevada required before giving us a marriage license). *That's* how off the deep end I'd been.

"Majid, baby…" I started, as his face fell a thousand floors. "*I can't*. Don't you see? I'm still technically engaged. I can't marry you till I break up with Joe."

"But we called my family…" he croaked.

I couldn't get out of there fast enough.

###

OVER THE NEXT FEW days, Joe was subdued and thoughtful. He inquired into my whereabouts that night, and I conjured up some vague excuse for being out till morning. I was only a little surprised that he didn't pursue it. Our problems were bigger than one night or one fight, and I assumed he knew it himself. We settled into an unspoken truce.

Seeing Majid on the sly was complicated by his couch-surfing status. One night, I sprung for a room at a cheap motel on Ventura, not far from Blairwood Drive. When the clerk asked how many hours I needed it for, I stared blankly until it clicked. "Eight, I guess—*no*, six," I replied. I wanted out of that dump by sunrise.

"I had no idea hookers worked in Studio City," I remarked as we entered the room.

"You mean the hourly rate?" Maj asked. "That's for people who come to smoke crack."

"You're out of your mind," I laughed, certain sex was the more popular pastime. Seconds later I noticed a shadow in the bathroom light fixture and pulled out a Chore Boy Brillo pad—a forgotten bit of paraphernalia from a previous guest.

"Told ya," Majid said. I didn't know whether to laugh or cry.

Had I stood on the sidewalk outside the motel and looked southwest, half a mile up the hill, I'd have seen Joe's ham radio antenna through the trees in our yard—that's how close we were to my fairy tale.

I couldn't get a good hit that night. Rock after rock, I did not rush once.

∗∗∗

MAJ WANTED TO MOVE to Vegas, where there were jobs and affordable houses. He presented his unused VA loan benefits to me as a gift, for a home as much mine as his.

I was noncommittal. I loved his company and was thrilled by our sex, but of long-term compatibility I was dubious. He sensed it and built a case for himself with celebrity friend references. We met Dabney Coleman for dinner at Dan Tana's and had drinks at the St. James with Richard Belzer. At a barbecue in Sherman Oaks, I met actor Bill Forsythe from *Raising Arizona* and *The Untouchables* TV show. We gathered in the kitchen, where Maj extolled the virtues of Vegas and I countered with praise for Austin (where I thought I might move instead). Wrapping up my case, I noticed Bill studying me. I knew that look and the feeling was mutual, though I tried to play it cool. I asked where he planned to go when filming wrapped in Chicago. His reply was a sly grin and a not-so-vague speculation about Austin.

It was a meaningless flirtation that triggered a minor epiphany. Bill Forsythe had a presence. He had an overtly sexual energy I found intensely compelling. But more than that, he was inspiring. He sparked me in a way neither Majid nor Joe did. Bill was accomplished, creative, sophisticated, and driven. Bill Forsythe was a force to be reckoned with. Not only did I want to be with a man like that, I wanted to *be* that, myself.

A part of me still hoped I'd make something of myself, and that part was disinclined to align with Majid. I'd been assuming my options were limited, yet suddenly things felt different. Something inside me was alive and kicking. I never saw Bill Forsythe again, but the exchange stuck with me. It was the moment I realized that Majid was temporary.

###

IN JULY, I FLEW to Chicago to meet Joe, who was there for John Mellencamp's Concert for the Heartland. I waited at the hotel while he checked in at the venue, which apparently didn't go well. Joe was rebuked by Mellencamp and denied access to catering. He'd traveled all day, on his own dime and an empty stomach, only to be forced to order a pizza delivery backstage.

Joe kept his cool until arriving at the hotel, where he unloaded on me. He burst in the room hurling accusations so outrageous, even seen-it-all Spero was taken aback. I'd gone to Chicago hoping to reconnect, stupidly thinking we had something to salvage. Joe stormed out, demanding Spero book him a separate room. I left the next day for Austin.

I moved into an extended-stay hotel next door to Sugar's. My plan: to work, work, work until I was standing on my own two feet. Find the strong, self-reliant woman hopefully still inside me, then pay down the current version's credit cards. If all went well, I could send for my things, settle back in Austin, and enroll at ACC.

I only wished I hadn't invited Majid, but he'd been persistent, and I was weak.

Suddenly, I had a firsthand glimpse of the untenable position I'd put Joe in for years. I was working my ass off, stressed to the max, while Majid grew restless at the hotel. Stuck in a commercial area without transportation, he spent most days at the pool getting stoned with one of the wealthy owners of Sugar's. Yet somehow, I was the bad guy for not taking him to Mezzaluna after my tenth-in-a-row grueling shift.

"Dinner plus cab fare is, like, a hundred bucks, Maj. Just walk to Schlotzsky's."

"I've eaten there four times this week. A man can't live on sandwiches alone."

"What do you want me to do about it? This is a work trip, Majid, not a vacation!"

"One night out, that's all I ask! Indulge a little. What's the big deal?"

He didn't understand how dangerous that sounded. I'd never indulged in "a little" of anything, and yet I knew how he felt: bored and neglected, just as I had in New Zealand. God gave me Majid as penance. I nixed Mezzaluna's, but enlisted a friend the next day to take us to Lake Travis, then the Oasis for margaritas at sunset. Majid was happy and chatty. I was stressed about the missed income and my friend's open disapproval of my new boyfriend.

Majid continued pushing Vegas on me. I found his optimism endearing but naïve. I knew better what we were up against and refused to depend on someone less proven than myself. Maj was convinced I was the key to turning his life around. He thought love was transformative. I thought love was bullshit.

I was the only woman he'd ever loved—only *person* other than Sam. His previous relationships were superficial. His past girlfriends, he said, tiresome. He rarely mentioned family but Maj had many friends, all excited to meet the woman who'd stolen his heart. When he talked me up like that, I'd feel my chest inflate, from collapsed to resuscitated. Were we compatible long-term? *Who gives a shit?* For now, I could breathe again.

❈❈❈

JOE CALLED THE HOTEL one day, his voice grave. "I'm so sorry to tell you this. It's Rocky. He's...gone."

"What?! What the fuck are you talking about?" I shrieked, gripping the receiver.

"Rocky's dead, honey. He got sick and I took him to the vet but it was too late."

I was trembling all over, trying to speak but unable. Joe stayed silent until I choked something out—*No, please, he can't be... how, when...?*

"Angelina found him on the kitchen floor. She thought he was dead but picked him up and he was alive, still fighting...." Joe's voice broke and it did me in. I cracked right in half. In the middle of a bland hotel room, thousands of miles from my true family—Joe and Rocky, now minus one—an unrecognizable sound came out of me, primal and gut-wrenching. I wailed like an animal torn from the herd. I dropped the receiver and hit my knees sobbing. When I could, I put the phone to my ear again.

"I'll take care of everything," Joe said. "Come on home, if you want."

Majid sat, frozen, waiting to hear which of my parents or siblings had been killed. That it was my cat elicited a baffled look. "I just hope you react like that when *I* kick the bucket."

I didn't reply. He wouldn't have liked my answer.

Rocky had been the runt of the litter, a nervous, vulnerable ball of fur entrusted to an inadequate caretaker. He'd caught a virus the previous year that weakened his liver. I hadn't been warned it could kill him. Nor had I asked the right questions. Back in Austin I'd drilled Rocky's vet about everything from hairballs to feline vitamins. It had been years since I'd paid attention. If there were signs Rocky was unwell, it was no wonder I'd missed them.

He'd been the last gasp of purity in my toxic world, a symbol of the light and love I could not see in myself. I corrupted or ruined everything I held dear, and now I'd extinguished a *life*. I thought of Rocky, alone in the dark, slowly dying in an empty house, wondering where his momma was and why she'd abandoned him. Why she'd abandoned us both.

❀❀❀

IN MY ABSENCE, JOE had Rocky cremated. We buried his ashes in the grass between the pool and the barbecue patio, the spot of our once future vegetable garden.

We dealt with sorrow and awkwardness by monstering—our way of feeling close. A pseudo, superficial intimacy and our last common ground. I took advantage of Joe's generosity and cooked my share into crack. One thing led to another, then everything went to shit. Feeling nudged out by the pipe, he tried to get me out of the house. He suggested roleplaying at the Sportsmen's, as strangers who meet in a bar. He'd "pick me up" and whisk me off to a hotel room for some sexy fun. He left first and I promised to follow after a shower and change of clothes. *I'll be right there,* I promised. *Twenty minutes, dressed to kill.*

I felt neither horny nor playful, but it was the right thing to do. I had to prove I could take crack or leave crack, and yet that turned out not to be true. As much as I'd struggled in the past, this was my worst failure yet. Joe was waiting, at that moment, praying the girl he loved was still here. Meanwhile, I had "one last hit" at least twenty times. Ninety minutes later, our worst blowout ever.

"You're out of here!" he screamed, bursting in the house. "You don't deserve to live here if you can't quit that fucking shit. I want my woman back—I love *her* but I *hate* you. You've ruined us and I refuse to watch you kill yourself. You blew it. Pack your shit and get out!"

It was true and I didn't argue. I agreed—*you're right, I have a problem*—but he was too mad to listen. I wanted to explain that

I hadn't shown up because I was chained to the pipe, a slave to it. That trying to quit crack was like trying to quit breathing—my body wouldn't do it. Instead, I went upstairs to pack my stash, toiletries, and some clothes. Joe followed, then in the bedroom he pushed a pile of homemade sex tapes out of reach.

I reacted. "Are you serious? You think I want those? That I might do something unscrupulous?" I was addicted to crack, but I had my integrity. *Jesus.* The issue then, though, was how disorganized he could be. I'd come across half a dozen of Lisa's sex tapes at the penthouse, and no way was I letting that happen to me. "But I'm not leaving them here, either!"

"Fine!" he screamed, and started chucking them at the wall and stomping on the remnants until they were destroyed. At first, I begged him to calm down, but then his rage triggered my own. We chased each other through the house, though it was mostly me on the run. There was a standoff in the garage studio when Joe cornered me between a tool bench and glass brick wall, built with fiber optics inside to create a beautiful, scrolling rainbow. That wall was my favorite feature in the house. Also the last thing on my mind as I grabbed a nearby golf club and swung it at Joe's head.

I swung high on purpose; Joe's head was perfectly fine. The glass wall wasn't. After a stunned silence observing the damage, we were off again. Downstairs in the playroom, in the midst of our full-on screaming match, Smokey appeared. He grabbed me, pinning my arms at my sides. One minute I was yelling at Joe from five or six feet away, the next I was immobilized by a man twice my size and weight.

My entire life, nothing made me snap like constraint. Aggression shut me down, but being penned in made me insane. It broke my brain and broke my heart. The two men I loved most in the world considered me a hostile force. I knew Joe felt betrayed, but I did, too, betrayed by the life we lived. The one he'd introduced me to.

Smokey had seen drugs kill John Belushi. Joe had seen drugs kill many. Couldn't they see what was happening to me? I needed protection from myself. Instead, Smokey protected Joe by wrestling my hundred-pound frame to the carpet. "I'm sick of this bullshit," he growled. "It's all I ever get from you."

"That's not *all* you got, motherfucker," I spat back, too incensed to worry what Joe might think. I already suspected Smokey had been less than discreet about our affair (I later discovered he'd bragged about it), but if Joe had a clue, I was unaware. Did it matter? Affairs were de rigueur. Psychotic crack addiction was kind of an issue.

That was the end of life as I knew it on Blairwood. I was banished to another hotel, the Beverly Garland, four short miles and a million light-years away from the remnants of my fairy tale. At first, I was too high to care, but then the drugs ran out. Overcome with remorse and despair, I contemplated suicide. I had no razor or pills, and my pistol was back at the house. I probably wouldn't have used it. At that moment, it was a comforting fantasy. Distracting myself from pain, with an imaginary escape route.

❖❖❖

THE BREAKUP WAS NOT yet official, but we were on our last legs. We'd had five whole years together, four of them pretty good. I moved back into the Sportsmen's until we could figure out what to do. I needed time to plot my next move and prepare for the shock that was to come. I had a lot of thinking to do. I was going to need drugs.

I also needed more of my stuff from the house, but as hard as I banged on the door, Joe refused to acknowledge my presence. Through the window I saw Joe, Rick, and someone else (possibly

Terry) rehearsing, not twenty feet away. "Quit being jerks. All my stuff is in there!"

Undeterred, I went to the backyard, slipped through the unlocked sauna room door, and climbed the ladder to a trapdoor in the ceiling. Installed during dungeon renovations, it gave access directly to the house. I threw it open. *Bam!*—the deafening sound of hardwood slamming hardwood propelled by the weight of that twelve-inch-thick trapdoor/floor. All three men froze in shock, two of them quite confused to see a person emerge from a hole in the living room they hadn't known was there. No one tried to stop me from marching upstairs. I packed what I could carry and walked out without a word.

I offered Gary my gun in exchange for some coke and he reluctantly agreed, after I thrice promised to unload it first (which I promptly forgot to do). He didn't come to my room or even park his car. He stopped under the hotel awning for a handoff through the window, his message loud and clear: Gary was done with me. The stories were officially circulating.

Alone in my room, I monstered for two days, dismantling light fixtures, outlets, and wall hangings in a paranoid search for bugging devices. Majid moved in. We used his dealer and my credit cards. I signed for everything at the hotel, including huge tips for the staff. If they smelled or noticed anything weird, they kept it to themselves. When I ran out of booze, one call to the bar and a bottle of Glenlivet appeared at my door. I kept Everclear on the desk for cleaning resin from my pipe. Sometimes I drank from the bottle. Sometimes I gulped Everclear like water.

We took a break from crack to eat mushrooms instead, driving around Malibu in a rented convertible. When the drugs hit, I started laughing and couldn't stop. I laughed so long and hard that Majid pulled over and parked. In the hills above the coast, with the gray-blue ocean below, I stood on the dirt shoulder, doubled over in tears. Majid's look of concern made me laugh even harder.

We spent a day in artsy-earthy Ojai, window-shopping for things we couldn't afford, drinking margaritas made with limes plucked from a tree over the open-air bar. We fantasized about moving there, hitting up one of Majid's industry friends. He knew a director with a guest cottage where I could write screenplays while he networked. I was reminded of New Zealand's Butterfly Bay, where Joe and I had daydreamed about leaving LA. Maj drove the convertible to Vegas with the sun on our shoulders, my feet on the dash getting tan. I flirted with passing truckers, feeling freer than I ever had. At Caesars Palace, Majid introduced me to a charming Evel Knievel and manic Buddy Hackett whose mile-a-minute one-liners made me want to hold his head to my breast and/or slip him a Valium.

Back in LA, we took a limo to my aunt and uncle's, where my parents were visiting. Dad inquired as to Majid's "intentions." He said *to marry your daughter* and my whole family cringed (myself included). I got us out of there, but not before sneaking baking soda from the pantry. We cooked up in the limo and smoked crack all the way back to the Sportsmen's.

❀❀❀

I CALLED SMOKEY, DESPERATE to see Joe. They were in Florida. I begged—literally begged—and was allowed to fly out. Allowed to get the last of my delusions dashed in person. When they spoke to me at all, it was with suspicion and contempt. I returned to LA humiliated, then two weeks later asked to see him again. We had a short, cordial visit at Blairwood that gave me hope we might stay friends. A short time later, I got a call from an acquaintance in Texas, a twenty-two-year-old, waifish blonde I'd introduced Joe to. She'd just returned from spending the weekend with him. He'd invited her, out of the blue, and though she'd gone, she'd also brought a friend to chaperone. "Nothing happened," she assured me. "I just wanted you to know."

In September, Joe hit the road again, leaving me a house key in case I needed anything. I used it to start packing. He called a few times, surprisingly friendly. One day he said, "If you're there when I get home...that would be okay." I assumed it was pity. Maybe he'd met another woman and forgotten how much he hated me. I didn't mention the moving boxes stacked in the entryway. I told myself it was the mature thing to do—detangle our belongings, begin the process of closure. And yet, I must've hoped it would shock his system, because I didn't warn him at all. I let him enter the house to be greeted by the full force of it.

I got what I wanted. He walked in smiling, excited to see me, then his face went from confused to crestfallen. I found out later, he'd harbored a sliver of hope for our reconciliation.

I'd never understood how much he loved me or how much power I had to hurt him.

Change It

MY FIRST TWO WEEKS in Vegas were a mix of cold, hard reality and blissful ignorance. The latter was drug-induced. The former was, too.

Majid's best friend there was Sid, a longhaired, sleepy-eyed thirty-something who dealt coke out of his mom's house, where he lived. I liked Sid's low-drama, no-bullshit vibe. I was a stranger in a strange town, in need of a place to crash until I got my bearings, and a place to smoke crack until I crashed. Sid opened his (mom's) home to us and was generous with his stash, but houseguests were one thing, crackheads another, and we wore out our welcome fast. I got us a cheap motel room that sapped my last credit card.

I wasn't an experienced couch surfer and did not intend to learn. I wanted our own apartment and for Majid to land one of those great jobs he'd gone on about. His hopes were pinned on a valet parking gig, apparently quite lucrative according to a well-connected friend. But when Majid called, the news wasn't good. A supervisor had been fired, there was a personnel shift... something like that, but a dead end nonetheless. Calls to other friends had similar results.

I was a practical girl, accustomed to men who got things done. Joe's career was in decline, but at least he'd had one. The men in my life tended to be proactive and ambitious: my father, Brad, Abe, and my closest high school friends—Marc, Mike, and Daryl. The punk boys I'd dated were twenty-something men, working on graduate degrees and/or playing in bands. Even meth dealers I'd dealt with had had a certain (delusional) imperious vision. I started to wonder if I was being conned. Majid accused me of being unreasonable—*me*, who funded every motel room and tank of gas. We argued and I drove off, spending the night in the Mustang, scrunched below the window line so Circus Circus security guards wouldn't run me off the lot.

It wasn't the first time I'd spent a night like that. Less than eight years earlier, at a low point with meth, I'd had to hunker down in my Dodge Colt wagon, vowing never to be there again. Majid promised to try harder. I pushed him to job hunt the regular way—submitting forms, lining up interviews, that sort of thing—but that path was blocked, too. A background check turned up a criminal record—the plague, as far as casinos were concerned.

"What were you busted for?"

"I wasn't, my brother was. That's my twin's rap sheet. He uses my identity whenever he gets arrested. He's done it for years." (I was skeptical at first—until I met him and he copped to it without a hint of remorse.) Maj felt bad about his lack of prospects, but (I thought) also relieved. When I'd dropped out of college for the third and last time, I'd felt much the same.

I drew a line in the sand: Majid was free to reclaim his drifter life without me in it. That day, he found a temporary pad with a friend on Flamingo Road, west of the strip. An upscale apartment with a spare guest bath. I jumped on it, desperate for space to shower and primp. I had my own applications in process.

❦❦❦

Majid's "friend" turned out to be an ex-girlfriend, and a jilted one, at that. To hear him talk, they'd had a casual thing, but based on her chilly greeting, I guessed Mindy felt differently. Pulling Maj aside, I learned she'd been in love with him when he'd dumped her two months ago *for me*.

"Jesus, Maj!" I was mortified. Months later, Mindy and I would laugh about it, but that day she acted like I didn't exist. She sat in the kitchen drinking wine with friends, a group of fit, tan, beautiful strippers—my soon-to-be competition.

Mindy did well, if her home was any indication. The complex itself was recently built, with pink stucco, gurgling streams, and tidy desert landscaping. Mindy's unit could've been their showroom, with a trendy black-and-red color scheme, potted palms, and framed Nagel prints. I imagined myself in a similar place (with better artwork, of course) and was hopefully positioning myself to get it. The strip club scene in LA had not impressed me. It managed to feel both seedy and snobby at the same time (like much of LA, really), but Vegas was for the everyman, or so it seemed. A place where screw-ups like me could start fresh. I locked myself in the bathroom preparing to do exactly that at Olympic Garden, the best strip club in Vegas.

❁❁❁

I was hired at OG without an audition (on the recommendation of a Sugar's friend who worked there on occasion), then spent each shift watching their dancers rake it in while I eked out a sum that could only be called embarrassing. At a lower-end club I would've been a big fish in a small pond, but I was too proud to go that route. Instead, I staked my claim at one of the big three, sticking it out at OG with the doggedness of an addict.

My first regular was more talker than spender but also better company than the video poker machine I'd sat at (without playing) for three days running. He came every day for a two-hour chat and one lap dance—earning me an income on par with minimum wage. Later, the connection would pay off in a way I couldn't predict, but until then he was just a guy who happened to be the first mobster I'd met.

He was the brawn of the outfit, quite clearly not the brains—a low-level guy with "highly respected" bosses, whatever that meant. Unlike me, he'd settled comfortably on the bottom rung, claiming not to mind its meager pay. He liked his work and, when I denounced violence, assured me those he hurt always had it coming. I chose to believe him without further details; I didn't request them and he didn't offer. He asked me out a number of times, which was both flattering and offensive. I said I was in a relationship, not bothering to hide my unhappiness.

"Anything I can do to help?"

"No, thanks," I replied hurriedly. "It's fine, really."

I'd just acquired a cheap suite at the Frontier (thanks to a surprise credit increase on my MasterCard). It was spacious and tasteful, and best of all, it had a phone where Majid could be reached 24/7. Prior to that, his friends had acted as an answering service, taking messages on job leads and passing them on whenever they got around to it. I hoped the Frontier would be the break Majid needed to turn things around—if not for us, then for himself.

"Once he's on his feet, I'll decide what to do about our relationship."

"You'll break up," my customer said. "You're too good for him and you know it."

"That's sweet of you to say, but I can't pull the rug out yet. He's under too much stress… It wouldn't be right."

"Sounds to me like you've got the stress and he's got it made."

I patted the mobster's arm and changed the subject.

I looked pretty and put-together in a cocktail dress and my best jewelry. Barely one week earlier, I'd slept in my car, yards from a row of Dumpsters. I had to give Majid time. What if believing in him made the difference? What if I *was* key to his success? Didn't all men need that?

What if he would always hold me back?

We went apartment hunting for the hell of it. (In truth, I hoped it would motivate Majid.) I fell in love with a luxury complex in the foothills outside of town. It had a high-end finish-out and spectacular view of the strip. Ultra-exclusive, leagues beyond Mindy's, it was the place I was destined to live. I padded my income on the application (rationalizing that I'd soon earn something close to it) but was rejected due to my independent contractor status. I begged for an exception, but the manager was unmoved. Strippers made good money, but didn't get W2s.

"We need to be closer in, anyway," Majid said. "I can't live this far out."

Maybe you can't, I thought. *I* had a car and no problem with the forty-mile round-trip. I didn't share that, because Majid's temper had recently surfaced, triggered by my discontentment and unrest. He (rightfully) perceived those feelings as a threat to our relationship. I tried to keep them under wraps.

Days after moving into the Frontier, I returned from work to find Majid lazing around, half buzzed from drinking with friends. Instead of airing my real beef, I complained about the stiff competition at work. My attempt to guilt-trip him backfired when Majid concurred my performance thus far sucked. "You should be making more money, so why aren't you? Aren't you any good?"

I snapped, "Who do you think you are talking to me like that?"

Without a word, he reached out and knocked me to the floor. In one swift motion, he grabbed a fistful of my hair, then dragged me the full length of our suite. I kicked and screamed and finally wormed free, then ran to the phone and called security. Majid didn't try to stop me.

Two guards showed up with a single question. "Whose room is this?"

"Mine," I shouted. "It's in my name, *not his.*"

They escorted Majid out and I collapsed on the sofa, overcome with relief. A bellman arrived to collect Majid's things, which they'd store until he cooled off and returned for them. He'd not been arrested, just barred from the hotel, and I was safe now, not to worry. Nice as the bellman was, I was horribly embarrassed. I let the story slip only to my regular at OG, knowing he wouldn't judge me. He was sympathetic and a little angry, which I thought was very sweet. A few days later, Majid called to apologize and shared a shocking turn of events. Returning for his belongings, he'd been led to a storage room where two security guards beat the crap out of him. "It was nuts," Majid said. "They jumped me for no reason! For the life of me I don't know why."

"That *is* nuts," I agreed, trying to sound incredulous—not hard, as my heart was racing.

Whether my mobster customer had had a hand in Majid's comeuppance, I'll never know. I'd be lying if I said I lost sleep over it. I did, however, quit OG and go to work at the Crazy Horse Too. It was a good move. One week later I had earned enough to secure an apartment on par with Mindy's. Her complex was full, but their sister property wasn't, and the manager couldn't care less that I was a stripper.

Dialing my old home number, I felt the excitement fade. I had to tell Joe where to send my furniture, yet all I wanted to hear was, "I miss you, come home." Neither happened. I got the answering machine, then a callback from Smokey. He sent my stuff right away, so fast it hurt my feelings. Later I spoke with Majid, and before the week was out, he'd moved in.

He told me he'd lived a lifetime with me in our four months together. That I'd taught him to believe in himself and strive for his goals. That without knowing me he would not have known love. I'd failed Joe and I'd failed myself. Being Majid's muse was what I had left. In my attempt to revive a sexy, sassy stripper identity, holding my own at the Horse took everything I had. Majid's relentless adoration boosted my ego and self-confidence. As a Vegas stripper, in one of the city's best clubs, that bit of extra mojo translated to cold, hard cash. My survival depended on it. That's what I told myself.

❦❦❦

THE CRAZY HORSE TOO was a top-tier club that drew more business than its competitors. If things held steady, my monthly nut was covered, with a smidge leftover to pay down credit cards. At that rate, I'd be debt-free by the time social security kicked in, but I refused to complain. I had a job, a car, and a two-bedroom apartment in the fastest-growing city in the country. Life wasn't great, but it was better.

In October, I celebrated my twenty-sixth birthday. Had I been alone, I might've had wine and called friends in Texas. With Majid at my disposal, I sent him on a drug run. I sent him on a few of them. Finally, tapped out and jonesing hard, I searched for something to pawn.

"It's over, let it go," Majid said, pouring us some Jack. "Drink this and try to relax."

"I'm not done yet!" I snapped and stormed into the bedroom, emerging with a bracelet in hand. Majid shook his head, wanting nothing to do with it, so I ordered him to drive me instead. The streets were deserted at 5:00 a.m. as we pulled up to an all-night pawn window. Majid stayed in the car while I strode up and handed over my opal-and-diamond bracelet.

"Five bucks?" I wailed at his offer. "This is a *thousand-dollar* bracelet." My protestations elicited a smug shrug. I could pawn it for five or sell it outright for fifteen—*take it or leave it*, his look said. For fifteen bucks Majid procured a single rock that may or may not have had cocaine in it. The rush it provided was so brief and thin, there was a good chance I imagined it.

Crack withdrawal was a brutal thing, and on that day it was especially torturous. Combined with the shame of losing Joe's bracelet, I simply couldn't take it. Desperate to lighten the untenable load, I sliced blindly at the lowest-hanging baggage.

"Maj?"

"Mm-hmm?"

"I have to tell you something."

"What's that?"

"We need to break up." I felt better just for saying it. "I'm sorry. I need space. I—I think you should move out...today, if possible."

We were on the floor facing each other. He was propped against my once-white sofa, and I, the love seat across from it. Daylight seeped through mini-blinds over an east-facing window, enough to illuminate the look on Majid's face, one I didn't recognize.

I gave him the "it's not you, it's me" spiel, hoping to soften, if not retract, my statement. As indecisive as I could be, when I finally took a stand I threw myself behind it. Ten years earlier, I'd become a vegetarian after reading two articles on the meat industry. It was a Wednesday in November and, though I hadn't realized it then, the day before Mom's big holiday dinner. I'd had no choice but to refuse the main dish (because a vow was a vow, and also, that poor bird had been tortured). A decade later, I still didn't eat meat. And I wasn't taking Majid back...even after he stopped beating me.

The man was a veteran with PTSD, strung out on whiskey and crack, stripped of a home and the woman he loved—*snap*, just like that. I was lucky he didn't break me in half. I was hit, throttled, slammed into a wall, and bounced off an end table, but that was all. I didn't fight or go limp. Mostly, I braced myself, and as soon as I got the chance, I ran. Slamming the guestroom door, I locked myself in. It was empty but for one item: a phone, which I used to call my most loyal friend. Christine reacted to the chaotic scene—I was crying while Majid yelled and banged on the door—by hanging up and calling the Las Vegas police from her home in LA.

I didn't think it would help. Back in Austin, when I'd been mugged, the police had refused to take my report. Hearing that my attacker was also my former meth dealer, they'd pocketed their notebooks and told me to go home. Why should Vegas cops be any different? But they were, and at my door minutes later. When I exited the guestroom, Majid slipped inside, hissing at me to get rid of them.

"It's okay," I lied through a crack in the door. "He left. I'm fine now. You can go."

"The thing is, ma'am," the younger cop said, not unkindly, "on domestic violence calls we don't need permission to enter or make an arrest, so why not make this easy and step aside?"

I did as I was told. The older cop headed straight for my bedroom, while his partner stopped to offer me a tissue. I looked at it, confused, and he motioned toward my chin and cheek. "Have you seen your face?" I took it, swiped away blood, then pressed it to my split lip, hanging back while the officers did their thing. With only a thousand square feet to search, they quickly closed in, the older cop positioned at the guestroom's bathroom entrance, the younger one at the door nearest me. "Nod, if he's in there," he whispered.

I looked into the eyes of the man who would protect me, and I nodded.

They found Majid in the closet and cuffed him. He didn't speak or resist as they led him away. He didn't look at me once. Only the young cop did, on the walkway outside, turning back to me in the doorway. He caught my eye and set his mouth, then made a small, soft nod of goodbye. If he'd been wearing a hat, he would've tipped it. He was unbelievably kind.

I closed the door and sat on the couch, trying not to break down, and failing. I'd made such a mess of things, I was afraid to be alone. In desperation I called my parents.

Within minutes I was booked on the next flight out. Minutes later, there was an elderly couple at my door—friends of my father's to drive me to the airport. They didn't ask questions, as if it were totally normal to help a complete stranger and full-grown woman pack a bag and navigate the terminal. On my layover in Phoenix, I sipped water at the bar while a man two seats over gawked at my face. The bartender distracted him with sports talk, then placed a tequila shot in front of me, knowing full well I had no money. I drank it and thanked her, and without a word she stepped up and refilled it.

＊＊＊

I DIDN'T KNOW WHAT to expect from my parents. We weren't close, but their disappointment in me was no secret. I'd been raised with strict rules about curfews, good grades, and keeping my legs together. Coping skills weren't on the curriculum. I was given a list of sins that pissed off God, yet no real guidance on managing life. Fear of hell, on its own, should steer a girl clear of sex and drugs. Self-respect was too convoluted a route.

I'd learned life was about what *not* to do, to refrain, abstain, and restrict. That self-sacrifice built self-worth. Self-expression was not encouraged. I was sixteen the day Mom saw my new punk haircut, threw her hands up, and cried, *"Why are you doing this to me?"* When I'd organized a small—miniscule, really—No Nukes protest, she cursed me for making her look bad to her politically conservative coworkers.

She was a child of the fifties and had been raised to conform. My nonconformist attitude rubbed her wrong. I embodied everything she'd rejected in her youth—audacity, irreverence, and critical thinking. She'd given birth to her shadow self—the type of freethinking heretic her Catholic Church denounced. She wanted to ensure my spot in heaven, but my independent streak was a liability God might hold against me *and* the woman who'd raised me.

I was an extremely strong-willed person. I inherited that trait from her. But in a battle of wills between a child and an adult, the adult will always win. I may have gotten on her last nerve, but in the process I'd lost my confidence and personhood. And once that damage was done, that I would lead a life of dependency should not have surprised anyone. But to see the truth of my failings would be to face the truth of their parenting, and it was easier to blame Satan. I began to regret getting on that plane. In my haste to be comforted, I'd left myself wide open.

But they surprised me. In fact, barely a word passed between us. Dad went to the office like always. None of us knew what to say. Mostly, I caught up on sleep. When I emerged from the basement, my parents said I was welcome to stay indefinitely. It was kind of them, but I left anyway. I'd found the clarity I needed. Cocaine had done a number on me, but I was still young and healthy. I had an opportunity for a fresh start in Vegas, and the idea excited me.

When I got home I discovered my pearls were missing—their blue velvet box on the dresser empty and accusing. I didn't know who'd taken them, maybe Majid or the maintenance man who'd fixed the sink while I was in Texas. I was to blame, regardless. I'd left them out. I didn't deserve them.

❖❖❖

I SAW VEGAS AS a soulless, neon dust bowl, built on greed and misfortune. A tacky tourist destination in need of a music scene, and yet I identified with its scrappy population. Austinites were cool and Angelinos polished, but Vegas was for getting down to business. It was not hip, creative, progressive, or health-conscious, but neither was I, were I honest about it. Austin was home, but Vegas had my back. By my count: one mobster, a bellman, two cops, and a couple of Dad's elderly friends. Also, Majid's pals, who'd refused to post his bail upon learning the nature of his charges. My Texas friends loved me, but they had expected me to marry my prince. In Vegas, no one expected anything. They couldn't have cared less.

Earlier that summer, I'd spent a day with Majid and an artist friend of his painting on spare canvases. Hours into it, I'd produced a single blue-and-beige landscape, a simple flat background. We'd joked about my creative block, but looking back, I realized it was a self-portrait—a blank slate awaiting substance. On the flight home from Texas, I'd been giddy about starting over. Suddenly, I felt lost and uncertain.

Too bruised still to work, I moped around the apartment. An acquaintance from Austin called, in town with her husband. Did I want to join them at the Dunes implosion? I didn't, but she was persuasive. We met at the Sahara and were soon separated, which didn't bother me any. I was as far from sociable as was possible to be, and having a hard time talking—literally, as if over the course of the evening my voice box had fallen into a deep sleep.

With traffic blocked, the strip was one long drunken throng, part maze, part obstacle course. My goal was to make it four blocks to the Dunes, point A to point B, without succumbing to claustrophobia. Twelve years earlier, at age fourteen, after sneaking out to my first concert, I almost got crushed by a packed house of hardcore English Beat fans. Bigger, stronger bodies had pressed on me from all sides, so tightly they suspended me, arms pinned and feet dangling. Unable to push anyone away or expand my lungs to breathe, much less scream, I started to panic internally. Just then, a muscular security guard spied me. He launched himself over half a dozen concertgoers and plucked me out to safety. Since then, I avoided densely packed crowds.

The mob on the strip was a hundred times larger, but loosely packed with some room to maneuver. I stepped off the curb, my first solid perch in weeks, and plowed ahead, worming through bodies, angled sideways. Leading with my shoulder, I zigzagged through, dodging elbows, backpacks, and three-foot-long slushy daiquiris. I lost direction midway and anxiety set in. I stopped, took a breath, and looked straight up. The sky was starless and relatively dull, which calmed and comforted me. When I got my bearings I moved on, feeling the crowd amp up. The clock was ticking and I knew I was close. A space opened up and I broke into a run, the energy of the crowd seeming to spit me out, past the perimeter and onto a patch of dirt. I looked up and my jaw dropped; before me was the Dunes.

I'd landed exactly where I'd meant to.

A rent-a-cop allowed me to catch my breath—*take as long as you need, kiddo.* I rejoined the crowd to await the countdown, gazing at the Dunes. A once-gleaming jewel in the Vegas crown, the magnetic hub had not aged well. In need of repairs cosmetic and structural, she was deemed obsolete, unstable, and too much trouble to keep around. An obstacle to progress, her number was up. The sign was lit, but the building was dark. I wondered if anything of value were left inside, and felt sad that there might be, sadder still that there might not.

The countdown began and I grew envious. *What a way to go,* I thought.

When the first round of charges went off, I felt them in my body, catapulting despair and a headful of morbid imagery. A series of staccato explosions came at me in waves. Bursts of energy pummeled my chest, like an invisible fist that reached inside and pulled out *a laughing fit.* Like on mushrooms in Malibu, I was overcome with hysterics, involuntary and magnificent.

As the building surrendered to a vast cloud of dust, the crowd behind me roared and whooped. I barely heard them, holding my sides, gasping for breath, and laughing until I cried.

Hotel California

MY LIFE WAS A demolition site where the dust had yet to settle. I couldn't see past the haze, but one thing was clear: I'd let the best thing to ever happen to me slip through my fingers. With Joe, my life had shape, if not structure and stability. Without him, I was rubble.

I had to win him back and pay off ten grand in debt, and neither was possible while smoking crack. My resolve was firm, and though I slipped up twice, as of 1994 I never smoked it again. I snorted coke once in a while, and when I did, would keep on till it was gone, but it wasn't a daily or even weekly thing, by then. Out of sight, out of mind—no truer words were said. The real challenge was my drinking. Booze had always been my first love, and living in Vegas primed that pump. It was available 24/7, free in casinos, and free to me at work where it literally flowed from the tap. I did my best to rein it in, and when I failed, I would call Sid, who'd bring bumps to the club to perk me up. If he was busy, I'd call Gavin, a friend of his, who'd share his stash in the hopes of getting in my pants. I let him on occasion, as much for the company as his coke. Going home alone didn't always appeal to me.

Nothing would get me to take Majid back, though I didn't hold a grudge. I was no saint, after all, no stranger to blind rage and loss of control. I'd handed down one beating in life and taken five myself, all told. Aside from Joe's attack in Denver (plus my first, in high school, by an Amazonian punk rock chick whose boyfriend I'd fucked, believing them broken up), I usually felt released afterward, with a sense of closure and freedom. I saw those who turned to violence as having a hopeless inner weakness. One that severed our connection and any sense of obligation I had to that person. What remained was a sense of superiority, overlaid with compassion and/or pity. With Joe and my mom, things were more complicated than that. But with Majid and my meth dealer, lingering emotional ties became the fastest Band-Aid yank ever.

My attraction to Majid was dead and gone, but I'd occasionally meet him for drinks. His new girlfriend was a pretty blonde bartender with a biker edge that I found alternately silly and intimidating. She was aware Majid was using her—he'd made no secret of his stalwart love for me—and though she'd be aloof in my presence, she gave him hell for it later, at home. That Majid was punished for pining for me gave me a certain, secret glee. That's the main reason I'd meet him at the pub she managed. Also, as a reminder of the life I no longer wanted to lead.

###

I LIKED WORKING AS a stripper in Vegas. Moreso than Texas, the outfits were skimpy and flashy, and the new style of platform shoes was more comfortable than old-school stilettos. One day, fresh from buying my first pair, I cut through Caesars Palace and heard a voice in my head near the roulette tables. *Play twenty-six*, it said, growing insistent. *Play twenty-six, play twenty-six!* I wasn't a gambler and couldn't afford to become one, but when disembodied voices spoke, I listened. I picked a table and lay everything I had left on twenty-six—five measly dollars. When the marble landed, my hand flew to my mouth. I'd won. It was a sign; I was sure of it.

My mojo was back, and Joe would be next.

He finally agreed to see me sometime around the holidays, and we spent an awkward evening shooting pool at the house. I felt more like a guest than ever (for obvious reasons), but I tried to be patient. Our next visit was less awkward. In February, I saw him again.

We were at the Sportsmen's because the house was trashed. I didn't ask questions; I was just happy to be with him, placing candles around our hotel room for ambiance. The coffee table was a makeshift bar with vodka, beer, and wine, plus a pile of cocaine in the middle. I'd just gotten started, though Joe looked like he'd been up for days. I'd heard rumors he'd been out of control in my absence, and his appearance didn't belie them. He seemed haggard and detached, but mostly sad. The eye contact he was so big on was elusive. Whatever the cause, reconciliation would fix it.

"We're *destined*," I told him, going on and on about the good old days, the fun we'd had and the plans we'd made. I listed my regrets and apologies, with heartfelt promises he'd heard already. I used everything in my arsenal, from nostalgia to outright pleading, wearing him down until I heard those magical words: "Okay, I guess we can try again."

"Really? You mean it? We're *officially* boyfriend and girlfriend?"

"Officially, yeah…sure."

I hugged him with enough excitement for both of us.

Almost immediately, the phone started ringing. Call after call, for hours on end. Apparently a business matter of some urgency. I went to primp in the bathroom, emerging just as he slammed down the phone. My plan to consummate our rekindled bond was on hold, and the reason for it beat all. It seemed mine wasn't the only reunion plot that night, and when I heard the whole story I fell back laughing.

I'd just been cock-blocked by Don Henley, Glenn Frey, and the gang. *Are you fucking kidding me?*

It was no joke. Calls from the Eagles camp came in all night, with a singular message—*we want you back, on one condition*—and Joe was having none of it. As he went from annoyed to infuriated, I put on a robe and sat down. "Spill it," I said. "What are you so mad about?"

"They're trying to send me to rehab! The band gets back together *only* if I get clean."

Whoa.

Joe was on a tear, on and off the phone, barking objections and chain-smoking, disgruntled as hell.

"You're doing it, right?" I finally asked. Angry or not, he wasn't stupid.

"Yeah," he snapped. "But when the tour is over, I'm throwing the biggest party LA's ever had." I laughed and he laughed with me. It was our most—perhaps only—connected moment of the night.

It seemed like a great thing, a surprise ending out of the movies. He'd straighten up and fly right, get his career on track, and then we could party again…in moderation, obviously. They were coming for him right away. He went to Blairwood to pack a bag, leaving me alone at the Sportsmen's. "Can I call you there? How long will you be?"

"Don't worry," he said. "I'll arrange for you to visit. I need you now more than ever."

❀❀❀

TRUE TO HIS WORD, he arranged weekly visits at a Marina Del Rey hotel near Exodus rehab center.

"How's it been?" I asked when I saw him.

He shrugged. "Not bad."

The newly sober Joe was a man of few words. He'd been quiet at Hazelden, but this bordered on mute. I was dying to know what he was feeling and thinking, but I didn't pry. His therapists were surely doing that already. Besides, I knew how moody he could be coming off drugs. I walked on eggshells for a while, but he never blew up. He didn't do much of anything other than watch TV. I began to take it personally.

"You sure everything is okay? I haven't done something to upset you?"

"Don't be silly. Now c'mere; *Seinfeld* is on."

I joined him on the bed to spoon and watch sitcoms. If I couldn't get inside his head, I'd curl around his body. I kept hoping it would lead to sex, but it wasn't happening.

"Not even a quickie?"

"Maybe later."

"That's what you said earlier…." He shot me a look and I shut up. Then, "Is it me? If it is just say—"

"It's not you, okay? It's not uncommon to lose your sex drive temporarily in sobriety."

"Really?"

"I swear it. They told me so at Exodus."

I told him I understood. But in the absence of cocaine there was nothing blocking *my* sex drive. I didn't miss the coke, but I missed sex like crazy. I also missed the man I used to have it with. Joe just seemed so different…I hoped that was temporary, too.

He had very little energy. Enough for TV, card games, and what appeared to be his sole new hobby: clothes shopping. He was putting on weight and needed new stuff, all of which looked just like Don Henley's. I liked the new style but not his short haircut (of course I lied and said it looked great). I didn't really care about his hair. I missed the man underneath, his silly jokes, seductive looks, bouncy walk, and boundless affection. Joe no longer sniffed around my neck screaming *bacon*, or made that strangely sexy *woof* when I dressed up. I liked his new way of speaking—softly, with thoughtful pauses—but his deflated posture worried me. His thumbs were always tucked into his fists and he'd lost his boyish spirit.

In the end, I decided that that stuff wasn't mine to miss. A life was on the line—this sobriety thing was big. Everything had changed, and my needs didn't matter—only his. I wanted to be supportive, if only someone could show me how. Instead, I felt a chill from Smokey and Dallas Taylor (a drummer and interventionist with some unknown role in Joe's recovery). I didn't mention it to Joe, afraid of adding to his stress. They were helping him stay sober, after all. I wanted that as much as anyone. I'd wanted that since Hazelden.

After one of our visits, on a return flight to Vegas, I sat next to film director Peter Bogdanovich. He asked all about my life and what it was like to be a stripper. He said he thought I was fascinating and wished the flight were longer. He encouraged me to write—not about Joe, but about myself. Instead, I pondered how to support my boyfriend, how to contribute to his success rather than my own.

The following week, Joe asked me a favor. He'd be going home soon and wanted his records organized. When I'd lived at Blairwood, every week I'd tidy his collection, returning his records to their sleeves, then placing them on the shelves in alphabetical order. In the six months he'd lived as a bachelor, hundreds had been strewn and left on the floor. It took me longer to organize his collection than when I'd moved in, and this time without coke to enliven the process. Still, I loved being helpful. *Joe needs me more than ever now.* He'd said so himself.

\#\#\#

FOR MOST OF JOE's rehab, I was careful not to drink in front of him. One day, he gave me the okay to have wine with lunch.

"You sure?"

"I swear."

I had one with every meal thereafter. Sometimes two. Also on flights in from Vegas and sometimes at the hotel bar, waiting for Smokey to arrive with Joe. I'd been terribly remorseful the day they'd caught me after one too many, drunkenly ranting at the bartender. But I wasn't scolded. Joe and Smokey waved me off like an errant child, too stupid to know better.

The reality of my behavior came to me in spurts, then faded just as quickly. I'd tolerated so much worse from him over the years. Back at Hazelden, I'd spoken my truth to Dr. Oh through anguished tears. *He drinks too much and it embarrasses me.* I knew how gut-wrenching confrontation could be, but I was not afforded the same courtesy. There were new rules in play—hell, the whole game had changed, and no one bothered to tell me. Joe was fighting his own demons, with no time to manage mine. For Smokey, it was easier to let me dig my own grave than to lead me to safety.

At home, in Vegas, there was no one to speak up, and yet I quit calling Sid and Gavin. I quit cocaine entirely, and then I doubled down on my drinking. It happened so fast it scared me, so I turned to the resident expert, peppering Joe with questions. *Is it hard to abstain? Why not moderate? Where does willpower fit in? What does therapy have to do with it and what are AA meetings all about?* Every response was some version of "It's complicated" or "It's hard to explain." Finally I asked him point-blank, "Do *you* think I need help?"

He said I had to answer that for myself.

If that was the kind of wishy-washy shit they dished out at Exodus, *I'd pass.* Not that it mattered, because rehab was time-consuming and expensive. I had a lease to fulfill and credit cards to pay off. The responsible thing was to work. At the club, where booze flowed like water.

When Joe's rehab stint was over, I started meeting him at the house. Visits were calm, quiet, and mildly affectionate, though not intimate in the slightest. We didn't discuss anything of substance and he remained achingly emotionally distant. I told myself everything was fine, but I had a hard time believing it. One day I broke down and asked him.

"You never want sex. We barely talk. Why am I even here?"

For a moment, the old Joe reappeared, my soul mate and best friend. He pulled me close and spoke with emotion. "You're my family, Kristi. I'm going through a lot right now and it's scary. That's why I want you here. That's why I need you right now."

I heard "want" and "need" but ignored "right now." I pretended he'd never said it.

He was busy with the Eagles, preparing to tour. I did not join him at rehearsals, but when Felder came by the house one day, his presence noticeably lifted Joe's spirits. Like Timothy, whom I'd known for years, Felder was genuine, warm, and friendly. As for the other two members, I had only secondhand stories of petty conflicts and arguments that made Henley and Frey sound like the two most childish men in LA. Joe said the band was a democracy with two kings and called them *the Egos* behind their backs. The level of dysfunction in that band made my relationship with Joe seem downright healthy.

###

THE TOUR LAUNCHED IN May, with a soft opening in April—a private concert for media and industry folk at Warner Brothers Studios. I was excited to attend until Smokey greeted me in LA with more disdain than I'd felt from anyone, ever. His body language and vocal tone conveyed the immense burden of my presence. Then, after three years of handling my travel arrangements, he suddenly acted like getting me to the gig was a massive, even *offensive*, inconvenience. The attitude was cutting, but rather than bleed out in front of him, I pretended not to notice. I let Smokey stick me in a cab like a stranger.

At the venue, I went straight to Joe's trailer, one of five in a cozy circle like a camp of stagecoach wagons. Outside them, a handful of guests milled about, a contrast to the usual backstage mayhem. Joe was more nervous than I'd ever seen him, and I quietly racked my brains for something inspirational. Then Felder arrived and nailed it. Breezy as could be, like heading to a ballgame, he stuck his head in and smiled. "Ready, buddy?" Receiving a pained look in reply, Felder's grin only widened. He motioned at an invisible something in the vicinity of Joe's nose, then whispered seriously, "Hey man, I think you're showing."

Joe chuckled, breaking the tension. He stood up with resolve.

It was a private joke between them, the same one from the Hotel California video. The idea of coke residue on his nostrils—onstage and caught on film—had cracked Joe up, which can be seen in the live footage. This time, fresh from rehab and sober as a judge, it was even more ridiculous. I don't know what Joe heard in Felder's joke, but what I heard was: *You can do this, buddy, remember? Let's have fun...like we did before.*

❁❁❁

THE AUDIENCE WAS SMALL but pumped and I felt out of place among them. I stood in back, behind the last row of seats, observing from a distance. The performances were flawless and Felder's flamenco-styled intro was truly brilliant, but I was an Austinite at heart and that level of polish just wasn't my thing. I dug raw passion and spontaneity, funky tangents and freewheeling jams. That wasn't the road Joe traveled now. Raw and freewheeling were no longer in his best interest.

As proud as I was to see him up there, I sensed an untenable dichotomy. What it said about us remained to be seen—to me, anyway, if no one else. The writing was on the wall, but I couldn't bring myself to read it. And Joe, bless his heart, wouldn't make me.

If I Needed You

THE HELL FREEZES OVER Tour ran through September without a break. I met up with Joe about once a month, the gap between us wider each time, an unscalable distance. Like any dependency, it was a one-sided attachment to something that was never coming back.

The tour seemed just as spiritless. The concerts I saw did nothing for me. There were no group dinners or socializing. From what I could tell, the guys barely spoke to each other. Once, three band members ended up in the same elevator, then proceeded to pretend the others weren't there. They ignored each other through the lobby, and outside, where they climbed inside separate transport vans. It was the antithesis of a Ringo tour. A twenty-minute bus ride with the All-Starrs was more uplifting than an entire Eagles concert. I'd take a Kiwi minivan pub tour over their big-budget spectacle, any day.

Still, I was thrilled for Joe's renewed success and couldn't help hoping some forward momentum and positive energy would seep into our relationship. Why couldn't we start fresh like his band (minus the strangers-on-an-elevator business)? But we didn't. When the tour stopped in Vegas, I met Joe at Treasure Island and suggested a drive through Red Rock Canyon or up Mount Charleston. He seemed annoyed to be asked, opting for a long nap instead. Two weeks later, we met in Dallas for a show at Texas Stadium. I took my parents and sister, then right before it started I got stuck in a crowded passageway to the concession stands. Claustrophobia kicked in—my worst attack yet. My throat tightened and all I could do was whimper for help. A tall stranger noticed and took charge, barking at everyone to clear a path for me, but it was one in a series of panicked moments that had become my new, *new* normal.

I felt stuck. Invisible and short on air. I lived in a bubble of anxiety. My once moderate fear of heights grew so strong that one look at the Stratosphere triggered vertigo while *standing on the sidewalk*. Eventually, a simple mental image of that freakishly tall building would make me nauseated and lightheaded.

When I told Joe about getting stuck and having a claustrophobia attack, he sighed, annoyed again. Wounded, I ordered a bottle of wine from room service. The next morning, distracted and hungover, I left a very pricey pair of d'Orsay pumps behind (never to be seen again). On our next visit, Joe asked me to hold his custom-made earpiece, which promptly disappeared (eventually recovered from the floorboard of his transport van, where I'd dropped it). Again, I wasn't scolded, but Smokey and Joe exchanged a look that said everything.

❖❖❖

DURING A BREAK IN the tour, our visits returned to Blairwood. Joe's mood improved and I took advantage of it, wheedling a reluctant promise from him to move me back in "eventually."

The house looked better than ever, but I was crushed to discover he'd let his ex-wife redecorate, having refused me the same for so long. Instead of acting hurt, I joked about it, then Joe surprised me by saying he should've been open to my suggestions

back then. It made me so happy I baked him a pie—my first ever—
and in the process I left two knife marks in his new kitchen table.
Realizing what I'd done, I burst into tears. I knew in my heart
we were just a charade. That despite my best efforts, I never be
anything more than a bull in Joe's china shop.

In the evenings he attended AA meetings while I stayed behind,
reading or watching TV. I kept pestering him to explain AA to me, but
he was either unable or unwilling, so I finally asked him to take me.
"I don't think it's a good idea," he said, and that was that. I never brought
it up again. The next time he went to a meeting, I raced to Tony's for a
bottle of wine, then drank the whole thing before he returned an hour
later. I did it every time, then would bury the bottles deep in his kitchen
trash. As if that's all it would take to hide my condition.

When Isaac Tigrett lent Joe the use of his private, antique
railroad car, I spent the first night on board with him, an offer
Joe promptly regretted when I got sloppy drunk. Stuck together
all night in that small—albeit beautiful and luxurious—space, it
could not have been any clearer: the time had come to disengage.

❀❀❀

LATE ONE EVENING, WHILE driving up Laurel Canyon, he suddenly
presented me with a mea culpa. No lengthier than his offhand regret
over the redecorating thing, it was still the most heartfelt apology he'd
ever given me. After some hemming and hawing and struggling with
words, he gave up and said, "I want you to know how sorry I am."

It came out of nowhere, on the way to dinner, and I looked at
him, perplexed. "For what?"

He paused, struggling again. "Everything...all of it. All the
ways I hurt you." He looked like he was about to cry.

"It's okay, babe," I said softly. "Don't you know I forgave all
that long ago?"

I wasn't lying. We'd hurt each other equally. It was a wash, in my mind, and as we drove on in silence I felt something clear between us. Wholly unaware he'd cleared the way for our breakup.

The first sign to hit me—like, really slap me across the face—was his refusal to cover my monthly brow-and-lash tint, a fifty-dollar expense. Since I had no cash on me that night, I was forced to grovel for a loan, within hearing distance of my mortified aesthetician. More than the fact of our wildly disparate incomes, pettiness like that was unlike him. Years later, I wondered if he'd done it on a lawyer's advice, cutting off that final financial tie as a preemptive strike against palimony—a word that wasn't even in my vocabulary.

Weeks later, another awkward visit when he went mute on me. We had lunch, saw a movie, and then hung out at the house—six or eight hours, during which he said not a single word. I could see him chewing on something he couldn't spit out. I knew what was up...of course I did. But neither of us would say it.

※ ※ ※

OUR VISITS DWINDLED FURTHER in 1995, but on one of our few visits he very much wanted see me. It was the day he found out Denise was pregnant.

I was packing at home in Vegas, about to catch my flight, when he called unexpectedly. "I have to tell you something." His voice sounded different, distraught for one, but authentic and vulnerable—like the old Joe I knew and loved.

"Go on."

"I met someone in rehab last year, and, well...she's pregnant. I just found out."

Surprisingly calm, I asked him a short string of questions. Did he love her? *No.* Were they in a relationship? *No.* Did he plan to pursue one? *No.* Did he still want me to come? *Yes!*

"I need you," he said, just like he had before going to rehab.

When he was stressed or scared, he needed me. When *I* was, it annoyed him. I recognized the unfairness, but being needed by him was everything. Boarding the plane, I asked a flight attendant how soon she might start drink service. "I just found out my boyfriend got someone pregnant." I had to laugh at how ridiculous I sounded. "Anyway, I could really use a drink."

"I'll do you one better," she said, and one minute later, she slipped two mini vodkas into my hand. "I feel you, honey," she whispered. "Good luck with that."

Joe did his best to comfort me, claiming sex with Denise had "just happened."

It wasn't his wayward penis I worried about. "You're really not in love?"

"I swear, she's just a friend. You'd like her, actually...."

"Don't," I said. "Just don't."

But I did like Denise, who kindly offered to speak on the phone and assure me, exactly as Joe had, that they weren't dating or in love. They were just having a baby. The one I'd been asked to have repeatedly. The one he no longer wanted.

Ironically, Denise's pregnancy brought Joe and I closer together, but it didn't last. Back on tour, we met up in Minneapolis. I didn't see him again until the band returned to Vegas. I watched the Hard Rock show with Don Henley's fiancée, Sharon. I had a beer in hand, and she, a cigarette, and we joked about how delighted our men would be to smell booze and smoke on us afterward. When it was over, I watched her and Don leave holding hands and smiling happily. My goodbyes with Joe couldn't have been more rushed. He didn't kiss me or return my hug before Smokey whisked him off. I stood alone in a crowded hallway.

For the next two months, I had a tough time reaching him, succeeding on rare occasions. I consoled myself by drinking daily, desperate to cushion the blow that was coming. The few times I got

Joe on the phone I was sentimental and morose. The more desperate I sounded, the colder he got, until one day in June. The conversation was stilted, strained, and terse, but what had gone *unsaid* too long roared like a freight train between us. I don't know where I found the courage to say what I did, but one of us had to, and I couldn't bear waiting on him. I was the queen of inaction, incapable of the next right move, so I opened the door to let him walk through.

"Joseph," I said, taking a breath to calm my voice. "Please, just say it." My eyes flooded with tears as I finished in a rush. *"I need to hear you say it.* You owe me that much."

Apparently, he agreed. "I don't love you anymore," he said. Then, as if the words hurt him, too, "Oh, Kristi, I'm sorry...I am so very sorry."

A dam broke and I cried and cried, clamping the receiver to my ear, the last, fragile connection to the man I was once meant to marry. "I'm so sorry, baby," he repeated, with more love than I'd heard in months. "I'll fly up tomorrow, I promise. I'll say goodbye in person."

***

HE CAME AS PROMISED and spent a few hours with me, driving through Red Rock Canyon and strolling through Caesars Palace. Over a late lunch at the Palm restaurant, as our time together grew short, I made a mad scramble to stop the inevitable free fall that was long past stopping. I'd talked all day about how well I was doing, paying down debt (a half-truth) and moderating my drinking (a total falsehood). He'd listened without comment or changing the subject. Then he gave a straightforward answer to the question he'd surely been dreading.

"Can't we try again? Are you sure there's no chance?"

"No," he said firmly. "There isn't."

I wept. I couldn't help it. Then I asked a final question. An absurd one, perhaps, in retrospect, and yet—if I were ever to make sense of it all, to someday move on—a necessary one. I must know my fatal flaw, the part I'd played in our downfall. *What had I done to make it all go wrong?*

"You made it too easy for me," he replied, and I choked on my Perrier.

I didn't ask him to elaborate. I knew what he was saying. I hadn't made him a better man; I'd sunk to his level instead. The statement was not inaccurate, but a slap in the face nonetheless.

"It's no one's fault," Joe insisted. "It's really not." I nodded, blaming myself, and suspecting he did, too. I was an out-of-control alcoholic, alone, confused, and in debt. He was a clean-and-sober success washing his hands of my predicament. He didn't offer help, and I didn't think to ask.

At my apartment, we shared a long hug in the parking lot, and then Joe got in a cab. I watched the back of his head get smaller until the car pulled onto the street, turned, and disappeared.

###

THE CURTAIN CAME DOWN with a thud. Everything by which I'd defined myself, for seven years, was gone. What came over me then was a terror so massive, claustrophobia felt like Disneyland by comparison. A primal panic so intense my mind nearly split in half. And in the millisecond between sanity and psychosis, a voice in my head spit out a desperate defense. Like a fighter pilot with no time to think, I pulled the lever and jettisoned.

Facing a future without Joe, I chose no future at all. *Life without him is a fate worse than death, so I'll continue on my current path for a quick end to this mess.* A calm came over me as I walked to my apartment. I had an escape plan. I'd even calculated a rough ETA by the time I turned the doorknob. Bad as my drinking already was, with a little extra effort, I'd be dead in twenty-four months.

Without You

I HAD NOWHERE NEAR the emotional tools required to process our breakup. I'd been drinking and drugging so long, my coping skills had ceased developing in high school. My sole go-to strategy had backfired spectacularly. The drinking that once allowed me to connect had severed the only connection that mattered. I had no idea how to move on.

Had I the strength to put us in the past, there was no *me* left over to step forward. I'd lost touch with the fragile nugget of myself I'd managed to form years earlier, post-meth and pre-Joe. In a two-year window I'd summoned the strength and hope it took to stay off drugs and restart school, all on my own. Seven years later, I was a black hole where nothing could thrive or grow. The future was an abyss, the present, a vacuum sucking me in.

Despair came naturally to me. Like alcoholism and depression, suicide was in my family tree. Estrangement and withdrawal were familiar territory, and my temporary mutism at the Dune's implosion was not a first-time thing. At seven it had happened while surrounded by family on Christmas Day, none of who noticed anything strange. The livelier they became, the less my vocal cords would engage. When I couldn't feel their joy, I wished to disappear. Instead, my voice did it for me. With a house full of relatives, I couldn't reach out to my mom right then—better to suffer in silence than risk her rejection.

Our strained relationship, on its own, hadn't sparked the suicidal urge, but our failure to bond over the years hadn't helped matters. I'd lived my life exposed to the elements, admittedly often on purpose. I needed to feel tough, to know I could endure. Short on courage and long on bravado, I'd dive into a mosh pit or a strip club audition, but not four years of college or weeks alone in rehab. In grade school, I'd quit track the day of our first meet. I'd quit swim team *after* winning my first (surprisingly easy) ribbon. I feared failure and success equally. I made a splash now and then, but being a work in progress was unacceptable to me. I saw winners and losers, black and white, do or die. I'd never really done life well, but the alternative was worth a try.

I considered taking a razor to my wrist, but the suddenness of the act was off-putting. Part of me held out—one juror of an inner twelve—doggedly reviewing the evidence before the execution date rolled around. I was severely depressed. My self-esteem was shot. I thought I was worthless, yet I wasn't *convinced.* I'd experienced much good, after all: divine visions, psychic epiphanies, and sublime reality. I'd been touched by luck and unearned privilege. Beyond that, I believed in something—an energetic force or higher being—and crossing the line between "its" will and my own was something to avoid. I eschewed religious concepts, mortal sin, and eternal hell, but I was not blasé about spirituality. I may've been yanked from the cosmic energy source, but what if my outlet was still there? Where I could plug in and juice up, should it come my way again? The question haunted me, and until I got an answer, straight-up suicide was off the table.

Drinking myself to death was a way of inching backward out the door. *Guess I'll be leaving now. Grabbing my coat and waving goodbye...I'm almost outside. Anyone? Anyone?* I wouldn't stick around where I wasn't wanted, but I had to be sure first, you know?

#✽#

IF NOTHING INTERFERED, I would slip away with a clear conscience in two years' time.

It was the summer of 1995 and I was twenty-seven years old. I'd been drinking excessively since age fifteen, almost daily for a decade. Those years looked like a garden tea party compared to what lay in store for me.

My mission was twofold: earn enough money to cover my bills and imbibe enough booze to shut down my system. My plan, if you could call it that, was loosely written. I opened another credit card, with a higher limit than the first four combined, and for a while I made the minimum payments, occasionally on time. If my finances seemed precarious, my physical health was on par, but I cleaned up well enough to get by. Club lighting worked in my favor, and Vegas customers were drinkers, oblivious to my flaws and generous with drink orders.

At home, cheap wine had to do. On most days off, I went through four bottles of Sutter Home—*goodbye, Far Niente; so long, Lafite Rothschild. It was a pleasure knowing you.* At work, if I was lucky, I'd only have to buy my first shot—one double tequila, though that number ratcheted upward quickly. One double became two, then very soon three, until I was drinking six tequilas in a row, at noon on every workday. Bartenders lined them up when I entered the club. I'd pause on my way to the dressing room—*bam, bam, bam*—then saunter off to a smattering of applause. What the bartenders didn't know was that I needed all six to calm the tremble in my hands enough to apply makeup. Nor were they aware that those weren't my first drinks of the day. I drank a bottle of wine at home every morning to get my ass to work in the first place.

I had eight to ten drinks between 9:00 a.m. and noon, every day. Eight to ten to get started, another eight or ten to maintain.

***

IN OCTOBER, I MET a kindred spirit. Bill was a binge-drinking Vietnam vet, ex-fighter pilot, and Nellis Air Force Base instructor; sexy, reckless, wounded (no shocker there), terminally upbeat, and horny enough to keep up with me. He rode a high-handlebar Harley, dressed like Lorenzo Lamas (he pulled it off, I swear), and looked so much like Mel Gibson he'd twice been asked for his autograph. We met at the club and spent the next six months tearing up his bed, my bed, and every corner pub between. It ended the day Bill expressed real concern about my drinking. He said, "Are you trying to kill yourself?" as if the idea should scare me. I showed him the door, thinking, *It's like you don't even know me.*

Death was a constant, comforting fantasy, but I had a ways to go yet. Bill's absence left a hole in my life I wasn't prepared to deal with. If I was going to allow a man in, I reasoned, he must be strong, yet devoted. Someone to help prop me up without throwing me off course.

Enter Chuck. My third-in-a-row Vietnam vet, one whose civilian hardships had been on par with his wartime experience. Chuck had a chip on his shoulder and a quick temper (that was not once directed at me). He was my champion and protector, a deadhead stoner, and an ex-dope fiend (speed freak) who loved his Golden Retrievers as much as he disliked most human beings. He had a strong jaw, soft eyes, and lots of rough edges. Part teddy bear, part grizzly, he was intense and interesting, sweet and funny. Boyish like Joe and vulnerable like Maj, he wore his heart on his sleeve and it endeared him to me. For some crazy reason, he treated me like a queen.

Chuck was a driver—as in taxis and trucks. We'd bonded in his cab one night over acid trip stories and classic rock. A friendship arose, and once Bill was gone, I promoted Chuck to boyfriend status. It felt strange applying the term to a man I didn't love, but standards of the past were luxuries I could no longer afford. In exchange for his help avoiding hospitals and jail, I offered my female companionship—a last best bargaining chip.

Only through dumb luck had I skirted a second drunk driving arrest. One rainy night, turning hard and fast onto West Tropicana, I spun out in the Mustang, flying across six lanes, one median, and a curb, before landing in a parking lot, shaken but unhurt. With Chuck behind the wheel, all of Vegas was safer, and at home, he was shouting distance from the shower. Most mornings my body shook so badly, I'd grip the showerhead with one hand and use the other to wash my body. Having Chuck there made my morning routine less death defying. He did everything but hold my hair back when I vomited. That was my penance alone to bear. Besides, Chuck would've had to quit his job to find time for it.

By late 1996, the vomiting was extreme. It happened daily, often repeatedly, and sometimes without warning. In the morning it was a given, reliable as sunrise—were the sun a hot, bitter stream of bright green bile, that is (with two more green suns coming up behind it). I'd crawl from my futon on the floor to the bathroom, eight feet away, pull myself up by the door frame, then push off toward the sink. If I got it right, I'd land with a hand on the counter and one on the faucet. Dropping to my elbows, I'd blast the water as my body heaved and released.

It was an excruciating, sputtery stream. Unlike puke, bile has no chunks—it's slick, slimy, and such a ludicrous shade of green that despite mind-numbing pain I'd often feel sad that no one would see the humor. The pain wasn't funny, though—my throat was like Velcro ripping open, over and over and over. I'd gag and shake and gag and gag. Running water helped. The mirror did not, but I looked up anyway, into the eyes of the woman I was trying to kill. The snail I would dissolve cocktail by cocktail.

When it was over I'd collapse, careful not to bump my head. I'd need alcohol very soon after that, or I could become more violently ill. If I was too weak to drive or (just as often) had misplaced my car, I risked seizures and extreme withdrawal. In an emergency, Chuck went to the store for me, if he was not at work already. The nights I slept alone at my place were riskier, but I got by…most of the time.

❋❋❋

CHUCK SPENT THANKSGIVING AT his mother's. I spent a quiet night at home…until the moment a burglar was tackled on my patio. I jumped off the couch and peered through the blinds when one of the cops—the one not wrestling a masked man to the ground—shouted at me, "Get down! He's got a gun!"

I hit the floor, terrified and pissed. On that day, of all days, I'd had less to drink than any other that year. I had no explanation for my restraint, nor why my tremors had remained fairly mild. But thanks to the drama outside, I was suddenly shaking so hard I could barely turn the doorknob to let the cops inside. They told me an observant neighbor had seen the burglar sneak onto my patio, and their patrol car had been right around the corner. A serial rapist had been on the loose in Vegas for two years at that time, targeting single women in ground-floor apartments. The burglar turned out not to be him—just a regular criminal, it seemed—but my illusion of safety was shattered. Despite the fact that one neighbor and two police officers had, quite possibly, saved my life, I couldn't see it that way. That's not how my brain was wired.

I'd quit hanging out with meth dealers, crack addicts, and abusers. I lived in a safe neighborhood. But I still felt exposed and vulnerable. A relaxing evening at home was *a life-threatening situation*. I felt like a sitting duck with no one to protect me. It was the last straw.

❋❋❋

IT WAS TIME TO get serious. Time to disengage. I couldn't afford to mourn sunsets, campfires, kittens, balloon rides, relationships, or any of that shit. A stray cat had been coming by my apartment every day, waiting at the glass patio door for me to let him in and nap with me. One day he stopped coming and I took it as a sign. (In lieu of angelic voices, I put my faith in the whims of a fickle feline.) The fewer tethers binding me, the better off I'd be. When the time came, there could be no backward scramble, no last-minute clinging to life. I was systematically poisoning myself. At some point, the damage would be irreversible. I had to consider quality of life. Pancreatitis? Cirrhosis? Fuck that. I'd take toxicity, alcohol poisoning, or a good old-fashioned stroke—something quick and deadly. The sicker I got, the more committed I became.

It could not be called enjoyable, yet there was a morbid fascination to it. Facial bloat, jaundiced complexion, yellow eyes, excessive bruising, and signs of malnutrition and anemia all but screamed, *I make shit happen.* Maybe not hit records or blockbuster film scripts, but systematic defilement was its own twisted achievement. Snuffing out life was the new empowerment.

I discovered that my blood no longer coagulated when a nosebleed almost sent me to the hospital. Vegas was so dry that light nosebleeds were common. One day, a trickle progressed to a full-on stream that lasted twenty-four hours before abating. A similar situation arose when I suffered a vaginal laceration—same lack of coagulation, yet quite a bit more blood. My injury was the result of drunken enthusiasm and one unfortunate miscalculation, when Chuck's hips moved east and mine went west, and well... another fucking perforation. The pain was brief but intense (for both of us), and though Chuck was soon fine, I was bleeding. Not heavily at first, but the rate at which it increased could arguably be called alarming. I refused to go to the ER, having yet to pay off three previous visits—one kidney infection, two bouts of alcohol poisoning. I wasn't in the mood for another lecture. ("Keep this up and it'll kill you," the doctor had snarled. *That's the point*, I'd thought to myself, *you fucking dick*.) But after going through every towel in Chuck's house, I finally gave in. Wrapping the last bath towel around my crotch like a diaper, secured with a bathrobe strap, I pulled my baggiest sweatpants over it and went the ER like that. When I couldn't describe the situation to the head nurse's liking, she followed me into the bathroom, took one look, and ran back out, barking, "This one's next!" Her final question before they wheeled me off was posed very gently. "How many were there, hon?"

"What do you mean?"

"You were raped, right? What did they use, a bottle? Hairbrush?"

"Good God!" I gasped, envisioning poor Chuck, in the waiting room, getting arrested. "That's not what happened, I swear it!"

When the doctor tried to examine me, I screamed as loud as I ever had and damn near kicked him in the head. While we waited for the nurse to return with pain meds, I asked the doctor how rare this situation was. "Do other women get torn inside, just from having sex?"

"It's uncommon," he said, "but not unheard of. Some people have thinner skin than others." He paused, then, "You have some of the thinnest skin I've ever seen, actually."

It was the last thing I heard before the Demerol hit.

❖❖❖

WHEN CHRISTINE CAME TO visit, I gave (what I thought was) an Oscar-worthy performance of hiding the truth of my condition. We shopped, dined, and laughed as much as we always had. Back in LA, she called my parents in tears, begging them to help. My parents made their own calls, including one to Joe, who agreed to be part of an intervention should they have one. My parents' priest talked them out of it. He said our relationship was such that they had no leverage to force me into rehab.

He wasn't wrong about that. What my parents didn't know was that I wanted to go. What prevented me? Twenty thousand in credit card debt, mounting medical bills, and monthly rent. My parents couldn't cover any of that and there was no one else to ask. Why burden them with the scope of it? Wired into my brain as a kid—right or wrong, it is simply a fact—was the belief that things like bodily injury, incontinence, bad haircuts, and behaviors outside the framework of a typical Norman Rockwell portrait deserved condemnation and punishment. I'd been dragged down the sidewalk by my wrist as a kid for my insufficient (toddler-level) bladder strength. Twenty-five years later, no way would I reveal a mess of this magnitude to my parents. Besides, thanks to Christine they had some idea. That they did nothing validated my silence.

In their own way, my parents were respecting my boundaries. They had no experience with addiction, nor could they scale the walls I'd built. They put their faith in God and hoped for the best. I put my faith in the bottle and hoped for the worst. Each of us were doing what we thought was right. And Joe was busy with his own life.

In desperation, I sold everything I had left, letting go of a $10,000 golden island fox fur for fifteen cents on the dollar. I got half that for the Mustang, barely making a dent in my debt. Adding insult to injury, the buyers asked how it was I knew the car's previous owner. (I'd mentioned Joe's name in the ad hoping to attract more offers.) Their disbelief was palpable, as if an icon like him would associate with the yellow, bloated urchin before them.

I stopped mentioning Joe's name altogether after a similar incident at work. A coworker happened to have a friend who had a friend who knew him. When she fact-checked my claim, word came back that I was a harmless, obsessed fan. "She was never my girlfriend," Joe said.

It knocked me to my knees. His betrayal negated everything I had left—a handful of memories I now couldn't share or speak about freely. Joe refused to be associated with me. I was gross and he was an Eagle. That was life, black and white...another tether released.

❈❈❈

THEN I GOT FIRED. The speech my manager gave me was eerily similar to the one from Sugar's ten years earlier (when I'd relapsed briefly on speed, days after being hired): *We like you a lot. Come back when you get your shit together.*

I moved to Cheetahs, a mid-range club where my dwindling income took another hit. A string of short-term roommates offset my expenses. When one of them robbed my medicine cabinet of a low dose Xanax prescription, it set me back a bit. It would take months to stockpile that amount again.

Homelessness became a lurking threat, which was never part of the plan. Chuck already had boarders; there was no room left at his inn. Nor could I live with my parents (couldn't or wouldn't—it wasn't happening). I had a panic attack realizing my income might give out before my body did. I made despondent calls to Austin, scaring the hell out of old friends. I even called my parents (to talk, not move in), but my slurred, repetitive speech didn't go over well. Dad withdrew for self-protection in light of my impending death. It came across as disinterest, but I didn't blame him. My mother was more pointed with a smart, sane request—*please don't call*

when you're drinking—but since I was never *not* drinking, what
I heard was *please don't call us.*

In some ways, losing touch was a relief. Our time to bond had
come and gone and we had not done it well. I could finally stop
pining for a relationship that didn't exist and my parents could
finally relax...as if awaiting a call from the morgue was some kind
of vacation for them.

We had always seen things so differently.

I was a hypersensitive child, easily hurt and attuned to stress.
Born with a nervous system that went to eleven, there was
nothing I could do about it then. I felt every emotion in the room,
especially my mom's fear, anger, and depression, and I didn't
know any better than to blame myself. I was not resilient. I faked
it, like any savvy kid.

I wasn't what my parents signed up for. I was complicated—
more than they understood or had the resources to deal with.
At five, I pondered the nature of God, appalled to hear He saw
everything and would follow me around forever. I didn't have the
words then, but it felt horribly intrusive. Anyway, it wasn't God's
approval I craved but my mother's. My childhood memories are
filled with that singular desire. To do or be whatever she needed
to make her love me. Which she did, I am certain, despite that
I couldn't feel it. At three, I was awash in panic that my connect-
the-dots drawing made no discernible image. I had yet to learn my
numbers, but my older sister already knew which digit came after
which. Distraught, I was convinced she'd get all Mom's love, and
there would be none left over for me. It was different with Dad,
but he was spread thin. I didn't know my numbers, but I knew
who ruled the house we lived in.

My folks had more kids than they had time for and didn't think
there was anything wrong with that. I did and grew resentful. As a
survival mechanism, I shut down inside, unaware that in detaching

from pain, I would lose touch with joy and therein plant the seeds of my alcoholism.

My first drink changed everything, reconnecting me with my birthright: confidence, connection, contentment—all three in a single shot. I had a drinking problem at fifteen for a reason—without it I was an emotional wreck, my turmoil interpreted as arrogance. The day my mother slapped me and I hit her back, I walked away completely disconnected. Hers was the first tether to snap and that one never came back.

The strongest tether was my youngest sister, a freshman in college in Austin. Instead of being there for her, I was dying in a desert three states over. In February of 1997 I went to visit, adding to her burdens with my blatant deterioration. I had a violent vomiting attack in a downtown bar on her birthday. She didn't shame or scorn me, but the look on her face said everything. I'd horrified my most cherished person. Her tether didn't snap, but I knew that when it did, I'd wrap *that* one around my neck.

Back in Vegas, I fell apart in a quickening of sorts, incapable of even collecting my mail. The mailman quit delivering it—thoughtfully, when you think about it (months later I discovered he'd told the post office I was dead, so "thoughtful" may not be entirely accurate). To some I seemed brain-damaged (the question had been debated) and certain behaviors supported the argument...like the time I stepped in front of a moving car for no apparent reason. On a residential street, the driver wasn't coming at me all that fast, slowing, in fact, as she approached a stop sign half a block up. All I recall is being impatient to cross, then getting hit straight on. The poor woman was far more upset than I was, helping me to my feet, insisting she drive me to the hospital. I slapped her hands away and told her to leave me alone. Instead of remorseful for making her hit me, I was furious she hadn't finished me off.

❊❊❊

THE DEBASEMENT OF THOSE final months is difficult to detail. Some I don't recall, some I wish I didn't, and the rest would be redundant. I didn't expect to live through it, especially with my sanity intact— no one expected that—because around that time something happened in my brain, something broke. Something snapped.

I experienced episodes each morning, like night terrors that crept up on me as I woke. As soon as I'd come to, I'd succumb to impending doom, visions I knew to be wholly untrue that felt one hundred percent real. Awake and lucid, overcome with fear and dread, I would be convinced I was alone in a battlefield foxhole, seconds away from slaughter. I'd howl into my pillow, eyes rolled back, begging for help that never came, then pray to die quickly, for God to *please, please, kill me.* Within an hour, the horror would fade. It felt like a lifetime every goddamn day.

One morning I woke up in Chuck's bed, where I frequently slept. His presence cushioned my morning terrors, as did Mutt, his cat, curled around my head. That day, I emerged from sleep in a physically traumatic state. Extreme pain in every cell, like nothing I'd ever felt—muscles, flesh, bones, brain, and each individual hair in howling, tortured agony. As with the foxhole visions, I thought, *I will never be able to describe this.* I didn't know that pain like that existed.

Unlike me, Chuck had a habit of jumping out of bed, into the shower, and off to work. This time, he stopped up short. "Something's wrong. What is it?" I couldn't answer because my vocal chords were frozen. Then my motor skills went, and that's how I spent the day—mute and paralyzed, in excruciating pain. Chuck couldn't miss work or he'd be fired. I refused a ride to the hospital through grunts and eye movements. He left not knowing if I'd be alive when he returned.

I vomited thirteen times over the next three hours, pure toxic
bile into a trash bin near the bed. The effort was harrowing, over
and over again, so intense I thought I'd die from it. If not that, then
toxicity, delirium tremens, or God only knew. Something awful
was raging inside me, a battle to the death, and I felt strangely
neutral about it. First, there was a feeling of accomplishment.
I'd formed a plan and seen it through, taken control of the
situation, and killed myself *like I'd meant to*. Well, almost.

Waiting to see what would happen, I had a lot of time to think.
My first question was, *Why am I not more excited?* My mind chewed
long and hard on that. Eventually, it dawned on me that suicide,
methodical or otherwise, wasn't how I was meant to leave this
planet. That wasn't how life was played. Quitting midstream was
cheating. It was weak and negated every forward move I'd made.
I'd known it all along. I'd simply refused to face it.

The clincher came midafternoon, while I pondered
reincarnation. If life was a place to learn, grow, and overcome
challenges, I'd be reborn with the exact same problems, except
I'd have to go through high school again. I began reevaluating
everything (having nothing better to do, unable still to speak or
move): all my reasons for checking out (incalculable) and as many
as I could fathom not to (the high school thing, mostly). The
entire time, I hovered in limbo waiting for a sign. Where were
my angels? Those guiding, soothing voices telling me what to do?
Marry him; clean the house; don't worry; play twenty-six!

*I'm at death's door, dammit. Don't leave the biggest decision of my
life up to me!*

Who, then? After twenty-nine years of deferring, avoiding,
and refusing to take a stand, cowering in fear and inaction,
I'd paved the road to this dead end. Only *I* could turn it around.
My life was, literally, up to me. Choosing not to decide was still
a choice (if Rush could be believed) and one that hadn't worked
too well for me. I'd hit the wall, and on it was the question: *Life or*

death, honey...pick one. I knew what I had to do, and though I did it grudgingly, I vowed that if I were alive tomorrow, I'd get help quitting drinking.

I'd been checking my pulse regularly. An hour after my silent vow, for the first time all day, it dropped under two hundred beats per minute. That's when I knew I was going to live.

Dream On

EASIER SAID THAN DONE. Two days later and fifteen pounds lighter, I shuffled into the corner store for cigarettes and kept going till I hit the wine refrigerator. My legs were weak and trembly, my sense of balance off. Staying upright was a crapshoot; I'd made it that far on autopilot. The shelves were fully stocked, their tidy, spring-loaded rows filled with the antidote to my life. I tried not to collapse on the Frito display. Instead, I collapsed inward. Torn between desperation to kill the pain and knowledge of where it would lead, I had a mini meltdown. It made me do the strangest thing.

I pivoted. Barreling for the door, literally stumbling to my car, I fell inside, slammed the door, and burst into sobs. My body weighed a thousand pounds; my heart was an empty hole. My head exploded on a loop, over and over and over. I had never felt so wretched. So cannibalized and laid bare.

I was four blocks from Chuck's house, a doable distance. At the halfway mark was a pub, where my hands yanked the wheel a hard right. I whipped into the lot, slammed the brakes, and threw the gearshift in park. Hysterical again, sobbing and thrashing, I pounded the steering wheel, roof, and dashboard. When my arms gave out and my fists seared with pain, I dropped them to my lap, then wailed to the heavens. *Do something! Help me! My way isn't working!* A calm came over me, instantly. I pulled out and drove to Chuck's.

I called him at work. *"I need a drink,"* I choked out. "It's too hard. I can't bear it and I don't know what to do."

"Try to think of something else," he crooned.

"There is nothing else," I screamed. *"There is nothing else!"*

I slammed the phone down and fell to the floor, unable to prop myself up any longer. I buckled under the weight of defying my deepest (albeit utterly fucked-up) instincts. What I knew right then was one thing: I would *stay put* if it killed me. If it meant clinging to filthy strands of dog-hair-covered carpet for the rest of that day, I would not budge. I would not move, I would not leave that goddamn house. I turned my back on the familiar and stepped into the abyss.

That night I called a dancer friend, a girl I'd once partied with. She'd sobered up in AA two years earlier and had been "saving me a seat" since. Nadia was a petite, sultry, dark-haired beauty of Russian descent, with a dry sense of humor and a Rock of Gibraltar countenance. Out of town when I called, she directed me to a meeting to attend on my own. I barely spoke to anyone there. What they said made no sense. It was gibberish and I despised them for it. What did "humility" have to do with anything? *I'm dying here, people!*

I went back every other day or so. I had nowhere else to go.

They were a wildly eclectic group of strangers who cared nothing about who I was or what I could do for them. I was scum—the ultimate loser, by any definition—and those freaks, fifteen in all, embraced me without question. They didn't push me to do, or be, anything specific. They seemed to think *I* was the confused one and said other things suggesting I deserved a better life than the one I'd created. I didn't have the heart to set them straight. Their attitude was *Hang tight, dear. It'll all make sense soon. We'll show you how to fix the broken stuff (and besides, we've probably seen worse)*.

I wasn't sure I wanted to be part of their odd little tribe (after all, they wanted me as a member), but knowing it was there brought me comfort. In time, I became a regular.

With eight days sober, I returned to work against everyone's advice. "You work in a bar," Nadia reminded me. "Maybe wait a few months, or a year...or forever."

I was so physically fragile that one last binge could conceivably kill me. But while I hadn't the luxury of slipping up, neither would I have food and shelter without income. I was locked into the Vegas strip club scene, basically sitting on a gold mine. With eight years' experience under my belt, there was no learning curve for me. I had skills and I had hustle. I was frail, but perky and slender. I had youth, wit, brains, sex appeal, and a full-length locker at one of the top clubs in the country. True to their word, the Horse rehired me— my own Hell Freezes Over Tour. Like the Eagles had been for Joe, stripping was my salvation in practical terms. I'd be a fool not to ride that magnificent beast in the direction it was going. Besides, it was the only area of my life in which I had any competence.

I'd hit my proverbial "bottom" and it was a low one. Any lower would be six feet under. Four days past my last drink, I had found the strength to walk a grocery store aisle (at which point Chuck had to carry me back down it, to the car). Four days after that, I entered the club with a singular goal: finish the shift without drinking or dying of exhaustion. I vowed to stay eight hours if that meant alone in a corner for seven and a half. Either I'd function in that environment or the temptation would be too great, in which case I'd respect my limitations (for a change) and quit stripping that very day.

I didn't have to quit. Though I tired easily and was shy at times, it was nothing I couldn't overcome. More importantly, temptation to drink never overtook me, as if blocked by a shroud of protection. My desire to drink never rose above that—it was a simple, manageable desire, not a craving.

Driving home was a different story. For the next few months, every hour outside the club took more effort than eight hours in. Vegas was riddled with pubs, one on every other block. I sped past them, using mental blinders and a made-up mantra: *One day at a time, one street at a time, one step at a time...I'll make it home safe, I'll make it home sober.*

❋❋❋

EVERY WEEK IT GOT easier. Every day I felt more alive. Claustrophobia and vertigo loosened their grip; morning terrors ceased entirely. I quit vomiting and bleeding out. All my bruises disappeared (twenty-six from my legs alone—I'd counted the day before getting sober). Yellow skin turned healthy pink, the whites of my eyes white again. Puffiness in my face lingered; then one day, cheekbones emerged. I saw myself in the mirror—or someone who resembled her. To others, I was an entirely new woman.

My apartment manager barely knew what to say when I paid my rent on time. "Kristi?" He double-checked the signature on my money order, then caught up to me at the door. "Wow, what happened to you?" I had no idea what he meant. "Don't take this the wrong way, but you look incredible."

"Oh," I laughed, feeling myself blush. "*That*. I quit drinking."

"Well, it shows, honey," he said, beaming. It was the first time he'd ever smiled at me.

I got that a lot over the first few weeks. Most came as a surprise, but one I reached out for personally. I'd placed the call twenty-four hours after my last drink. Still in Chuck's bed and unable to sit up, I'd had him dial and hold the receiver. I reported my status to my mother—alive with one day sober. She replied with something cautiously supportive. I'd called the next day, and then regularly, eager to share with her, above all, the one thing I'd done right in so long. I didn't weigh the risk. There are times in life a girl needs her mom. And she was there for me—whatever mistakes and traumas littered our history, she was exactly the mother I needed in early sobriety.

Dad's reaction was just as stunning. He dropped everything to fly to Vegas (literally, I think he sprouted wings, he was *that* excited). He came to my AA meetings and took me shopping for kitchen and bath items—a scaled-down housewares spree that lasted an hour. It could not have been more fun—not with fine china and a million dollars.

For the most part, learning to function again was beyond nerve-racking. Once in a while I got stupidly giddy—totally next level. At two or three weeks sober, I had a pair of old shoes resoled, then called my dad to boast.

"Uh...good for you, honey," he said, a bit nonplussed.

"You don't understand, Dad. I dropped them off, then days later *returned to pick them up!*" I sounded bonkers, to be that darn proud of myself. Dad was just happy I was excited and not suicidal. I was just excited to have a dad who took my calls.

I'd once been incapable of collecting the mail. Now I did it every day (after spending weeks convincing the post office I was not, in fact, deceased as their records indicated). When the first bundle arrived, I called my credit card companies, explaining that I'd been ill for months but was back to work full-time and would catch up immediately. They were very nice about it. They sounded tickled I'd called at all. The hospital gave me a deal for paying in one lump sum. My love of detail and organization kicked in. Paying down debt gave me a buzz.

One day, at 7-Eleven to buy money orders, I heard gasps from the two young clerks. "Whoa," said one. "You're alive."

I gave her a strange look. "Have you been talking to my mailman?"

"What? No...it's just, we used to see you here all the time, and then you disappeared."

Her coworker explained. "You'd looked so bad, we figured you must've died."

It hit me for the first time how close I'd come.

❀❀❀

WITHOUT MEDICATION, THE ODDS of surviving a detox like mine were about two to one. Odds of relapse were the same or worse, but I was tenacious about sobriety. Reluctant, yet resolute, I'd made a decision and committed to it, exercising the free will I'd long claimed to cherish yet seldom used.

With six weeks under my belt, I called Joe to share the news. I kept the conversation light. We both did, our voices high-pitched with positivity and laced with tenderness for all that went unsaid.

"I'm happy for you, Kristi. I knew you could do it, just didn't know if you would."

"I wish I'd done it sooner—"

"Don't think like that. It takes what it takes...that's all that matters."

"Mm-hmm, I guess." It was time to hang up. I heard subtle cues in his inflection shifts. I knew him so well, I could read his thoughts on the current of his breath. It hit me that this might be the last time we talked, and I fought the urge to cry. "Joe, before you go, I need to tell you something." I paused. "I just..."

"It's okay. Don't worry about it."

Apparently, I was an open book, too, but I persisted, knowing it might be my only chance. I'd barely started my twelve-step work and didn't know the amends process yet. I only knew I owed him one. One too big to articulate.

"I'm sorry," I said, just as he had to me, a fibrous pit of regret dropped at his feet. "For all of it, I'm so sorry."

"I know you are. We're good. That's all you have to say."

It seemed a perfect segue from that chapter of my life, to hang up, walk away, and love him from a distance, however long it took for that love to fade. But damn if he didn't have a gig in Vegas scheduled (solo, sans the Eagles). Instead of bothering Joe, I called Smokey, who agreed to arrange tickets and a quick visit backstage.

Chuck and I stood near the stage, four or five fans deep. Though I never caught Joe's eye, I noticed a pretty woman off to the side, the same spot I'd occupied, and Lisa before me. It was Denise, of course, and I looked away, feeling as if I'd been caught snooping.

I wanted to be happy for Joe's happiness. I also wanted him to see me sober, to leave him with a better image than the blubbering alcoholic I'd been at our breakup two years earlier. Instead, I ended up in tears again, informed by a security guard that the band had driven off as soon as the show ended. No one stayed to say goodbye. No one wanted to see me. I went home and cried and was depressed for days but didn't drink, get high, or contemplate suicide. I accepted that I couldn't change him or the situation—only myself and my reaction to it.

❖❖❖

MY PROBLEMS WERE BIGGER than substances. My addictions were symptoms of a deeper illness that took root long before my first tequila shot. I lacked self-esteem, coping skills, and guiding principles to help me create a life of purpose. When Nadia taught me the program—twelve steps, nothing more, nothing less— she gave me tools with which to manage my life and, to whatever degree I could, direct it.

By the time I found recovery, I had no problem admitting I was powerless over alcohol. *What could be more obvious?* It was a relief to turn it over to a higher power. What shape that power took, I would figure out later. The real work began with an honest look at my fear, resentment, and misbehavior. Decoding that jumbled mess opened the door for forgiveness and compassion, for myself as well as others.

My twelve steps took one year to complete. Some were harder than others, and some of the simplest proved to be the most challenging. For example, around the time I finally got real clarity on my character flaws, I became unwilling to let them go. I called Nadia in tears. She was sympathetic, up to a point. "These two steps may be the easiest thing you'll do in recovery, a few minutes of reading and reflection, basically. You *might* be making this harder than it has to be...I'm just saying."

I went off on her. "You can't expect me to give up greed and self-seeking! *How do you think I've gotten by for thirty years?*" But for the most part, I surrendered to the process, exchanging old ways of denial and manipulation—also sloth, envy, and the other seven deadlies, except lust (sorry, Nadia, but to thine own self be true, right?)—for courage, honesty, discipline, accountability, and service to others. Proud of myself, I thought it was a good time to take a breather. Nadia didn't.

"Christmas at your folks' is the perfect time to make amends to your family."

"Really? Because it sounds like the perfect way to ruin the holiday for everybody."

I did it anyway, and, to a man, they were gracious and understanding. In the process, I learned the difference between humiliation and humility. Cleaning my side of the street became as addictive as cocaine. I started meditating and working out. I did estimable things and tried to make something of myself. Having a purpose in life—for me, that was key. I also thought it wouldn't hurt to find a tribe. None of it happened overnight.

In the beginning, I obsessed on the tiniest things. I made to-do lists every night, down to the minute:

7:00 a.m.: wake-up/get out of bed

7:15 a.m.: make hot tea

7:30 a.m.: shower, brush teeth

God forbid I break a nail or have an AA friend request a ride. If I got to the bank at 9:45 a.m. instead of the 9:35 a.m. written in my memo pad, I just might have had an anxiety attack. I hoarded money and clipped coupons obsessively, while earning a better living than I'd ever dreamed. I developed an eating disorder in all its cunning complexity. Depression came roaring back with debilitating insomnia and extreme fatigue—each taking years to loosen their grip on me. A thorough checkup showed no less than five organs under-functioning. My endocrine system was on its last legs. My digestion shut down almost entirely (complications from which resulted in two surgeries, years later). My lumbar spine was severely degenerated and my libido DOA (though thankfully, one of them came roaring back eventually). Living with a perforated septum required minor daily considerations, and when it unexpectedly contributed to the slow collapse of my nose years later, it took two complicated surgeries (and $50,000) to rebuild. Healing the physical stuff—what I could of it—took time, money, and patience. The mental and emotional damage was a longer road to trudge.

Had I known that day, as I lay in Chuck's bed, debating life or death, how long life would take to feel more like a gift than a sentence, how long before I would greet each day with more eagerness than trepidation, I'm not sure I would've made the choice I did. I suppose it's a good thing I'm not psychic. But, like Joe said, it takes what it takes. And with so many tethers snapped... well, some of it took decades. Thankfully, some of it didn't.

❋❋❋

I HAD SIX MONTHS sober on my thirtieth birthday. I spent it with Christine, at the beach in LA, and at the Sportsmen's Lodge. Being so close to Blairwood, I couldn't resist calling Joe. I convinced him to meet me at the Bistro Garden, where we'd celebrated our engagement. I was excited to hang out like normal people, friends who hadn't left their "brains behind" in a limo or a sex dungeon; for him to see me at my best. I also wanted him to take one look and fall in love again—of course I did. But I knew which outcome I'd get.

I wore a dark green velvet A-line dress with three-quarter sleeves and subtle ruching across the chest. It was flattering and elegant—Grace Kelly with a kick. My jewelry, too, was new and sparkling—a tennis bracelet and choker, birthday gifts from a roguish Vegas doctor. We had met at the club, at his friend's bachelor party, and discovered shared interests in art, music, outdoor sports, and Eastern spiritual traditions. He liked betting big at Caesars's crap tables, and I liked dressing up and cheering him on. I wasn't the doctor's girlfriend and we diverged on social issues and politics, but I could be myself in his company and he treated me with respect. It was a fascinating concept: to have connection and autonomy simultaneously. It all felt very new to me.

Dinner with Joe flew by. He skipped appetizers and dessert. I was bubbly and engaging. He acted distracted and tired. I had no idea what was going on in his life. A new kid and a busy career, though he didn't disclose much. I carried the conversation, talking about my AA group, my job, and my favorite new books. Joe feigned interest, but I knew him too well. I maintained a cheery demeanor and kept my hurt feelings to myself.

I cared about my life—I didn't need Joe to anymore. It was small and contained but it was mine and I liked it. Meetings inspired me and I excelled at work. My social circle was tiny— AA friends and Chuck—but I went hiking and swimming, and a trainer at the gym had asked me to be his partner in a fitness competition. I looked *that* healthy and fit. I went to Lake Mead more times that summer than I'd gone to the beach over five years in LA. I got a new apartment and decorated it myself—the whole thing, not just a hallway. I spent Wednesday nights in a dive bar, drinking cranberry juice and dancing to a blues band. I read two or three books a week and was amassing quite a CD collection. I hadn't thrown myself into writing, but I jotted down story ideas. I may have traded it all to spoon naked with Joe for an hour, but to his credit, he didn't offer.

The joyous dinner I'd hoped for was awkward and rushed. Outside, Joe hugged me, then looked me in the eyes and smiled— *really* looked and *really* smiled. He didn't hold my gaze long, but long enough. And I didn't look away, for once. It was the Joe I knew and would always love, even if I never saw him again. He drove off and I was fine. Later, at the hotel, I curled up and cried. The next morning, I packed my things and flew home to my life.

Epilogue
Walk Away

I DID SEE JOE again, a few years after our Bistro Garden dinner. It was in Austin, where I'd returned to live, and he had a gig. We met backstage before the show for the length of a long hug and short chat—a closure thing, at my request. It was easy and sweet and just what I needed. Afterward, he hit the stage and I grabbed a spot on the outdoor venue's grass. During one of the first songs, Joe caught my eye. He held my gaze, singing a line from the chorus that told me what I should do next. I agreed, and I did just that.

I got up, turned my pretty head, and walked away.

I didn't expect to hear from him again, but the next two visits were at his request, short weekends together in cities near Austin where he'd stopped on tour. We met as friends to reconnect and reminisce, our easy laughter like a salve smoothing over the few remaining raw bits. Lingering wounds aside, our connection was strong, soulful, and tender.

The last time I saw him we were both doing well, more settled and content than ever. He was getting a divorce (though no one knew about it yet). I'd had a few small pieces published (and was telling everyone I met). We compared daily routines, vitamin supplements, and workout regimens. He talked about Buddhism and meditation. I showed him my blog and taught him how MySpace worked. That night, after dinner, we went to my room to watch TV. He lay on the covers, and I slid beside him without a thought. My heart pressed to his ribs, my head nestled in the soft space between his shoulder and chest. His arm wrapped around my back, holding me to him.

Before we parted company, Joe suggested we try dating again, gradually, like regular folks, with toe-in-the-water dinner dates...maybe a weekend in Hawaii. It never happened and perhaps that's for the best (in this lifetime, though there's always the next). But at that moment, for that one night, I was happy in his arms. For a brief, contented moment, we had an authentic intimate connection, independent of expectation, judgment, and disappointment...of everything that came before or after it.

The End

Acknowledgments

GETTING THIS MANUSCRIPT UP to speed was a long-ass four-year process, yet it would've been fourteen or forty without so much encouragement and guidance. Whatever talents or tenacity I brought to it alone, were not enough to get me where I thankfully ended up.

My undying gratitude belongs to every friend who saw me through the (many) darker years, despite my paucity of presence for them in return. For supporting, sound-boarding, anxiety-calming, off-the-ledge talking, and adamantly insisting on my future success until I actually managed to manifest it: Graham H., Mandy D., Mike and Betty Newman, Melvis Lara, Tiffany Sipos, Christine Ocean, and Howard Lenett.

For reading, advising, illuminating, and validating my journey, Nancy "Like Yoda-Only-Hotter" Eldridge, Tina Dubin, Joe Nicols, Sean Harribance, Marc Eliot, and Daryl Kinney.

3 6 4   KRISTIN CASEY

For a lifetime of wind-beneath-my-wings kinda things, and the unique innate ability to keep me feeling connected and sane, my first and last tether and greatest sister ever, Sarah H.

To every twelve-step sponsor and Las Vegas Twisted Sister, who committed to paying it forward instead of taking what they needed and walking away unencumbered. Special thanks to Jessica and Toni, my personal tool kit instructors.

To Dr.'s Litner and Solieman, for their triumphant repairs and reconstruction where others had tried and failed, giving me long overdue closure—literally!—on a twenty-five-year-old internalized wound.

To Claire Harris and everyone at Foundry Lit and Media, especially Peter McGuigan, my Top Ten dream agent (who let me query 140 others before telling me he was interested, then proceeded to make me feel legit enough to say for the first time ever, "I'm a writer" without cringing for the overreach). Thanks also, Peter, for your well of patience and calming, reassuring nature, while you found a home for my manuscript with the best publishing team I could hope for.

To the best publishing team this writer ever hoped for, Tyson Cornell, Julia Callahan, Gregory Henry, Hailie Johnson, Guy Intoci, Jake Levens, and everyone at Rare Bird. I've spent fifty years trying to get my authentic voice heard, and you let me do it in print, word for word. Special thanks to my editor, Alice Marsh-Elmer, without whose wisdom, vision, skill, and guidance this book would not be what it is. To have it miss the mark even a little would've weighed on me the rest of my life. For ensuring that didn't happen, my gratitude is immeasurable (with incalculable misplaced commas).

Printed in the USA
CPSIA information can be obtained
at www.ICGtesting.com
JSHW031224150224
PP13339500002B/1

9 781644 281307